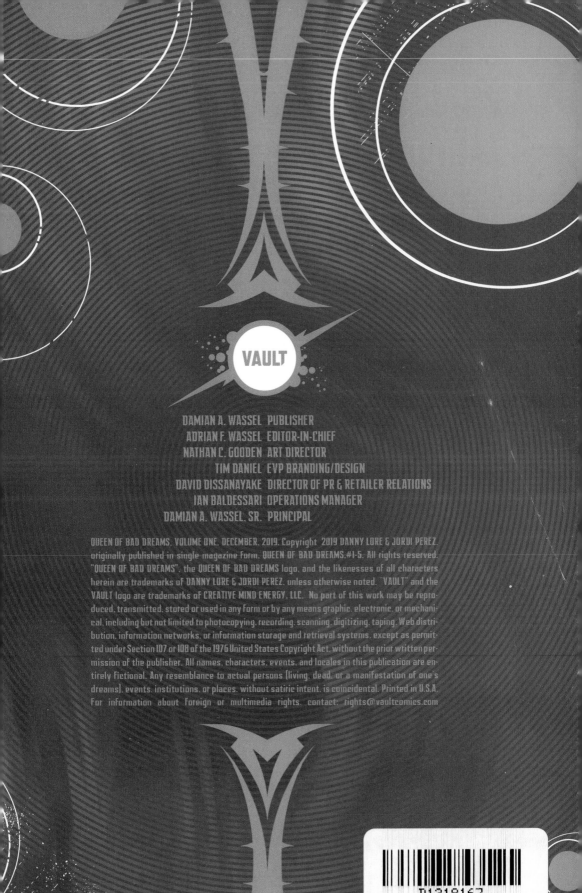

VAULT

DAMIAN A. WASSEL PUBLISHER
ADRIAN F. WASSEL EDITOR-IN-CHIEF
NATHAN C. GOODEN ART DIRECTOR
TIM DANIEL EVP BRANDING/DESIGN
DAVID DISSANAYAKE DIRECTOR OF PR & RETAILER RELATIONS
IAN BALDESSARI OPERATIONS MANAGER
DAMIAN A. WASSEL, SR. PRINCIPAL

D1218167

DANNY LORE
WRITER
JORDI PÉREZ
ARTIST
DEARBHLA KELLY
COLORIST
KIM McLEAN
LETTERER

ADDITIONAL LETTERS BY
ANDWORLD

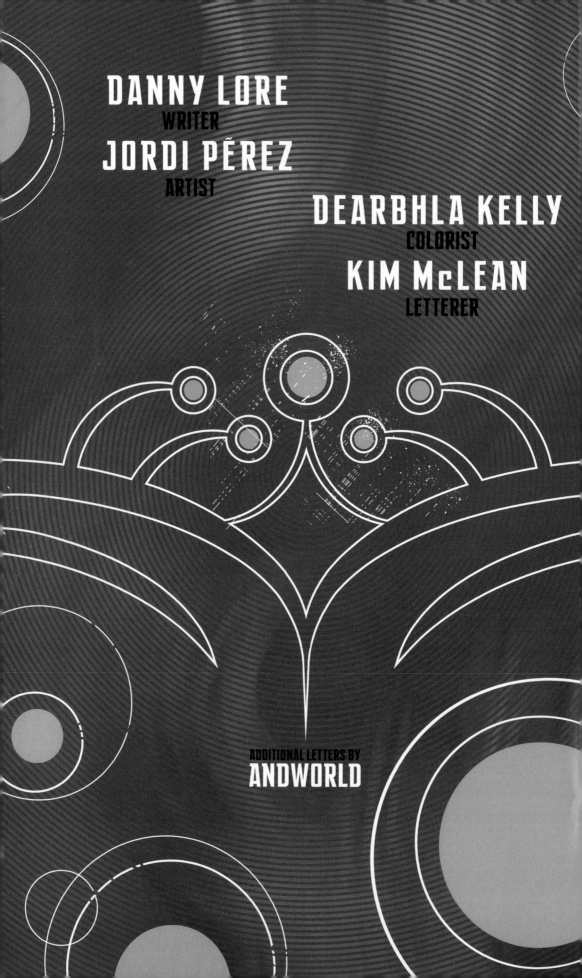

VAULT COMICS
PRESENTS

QUEEN
of
BAD DREAMS

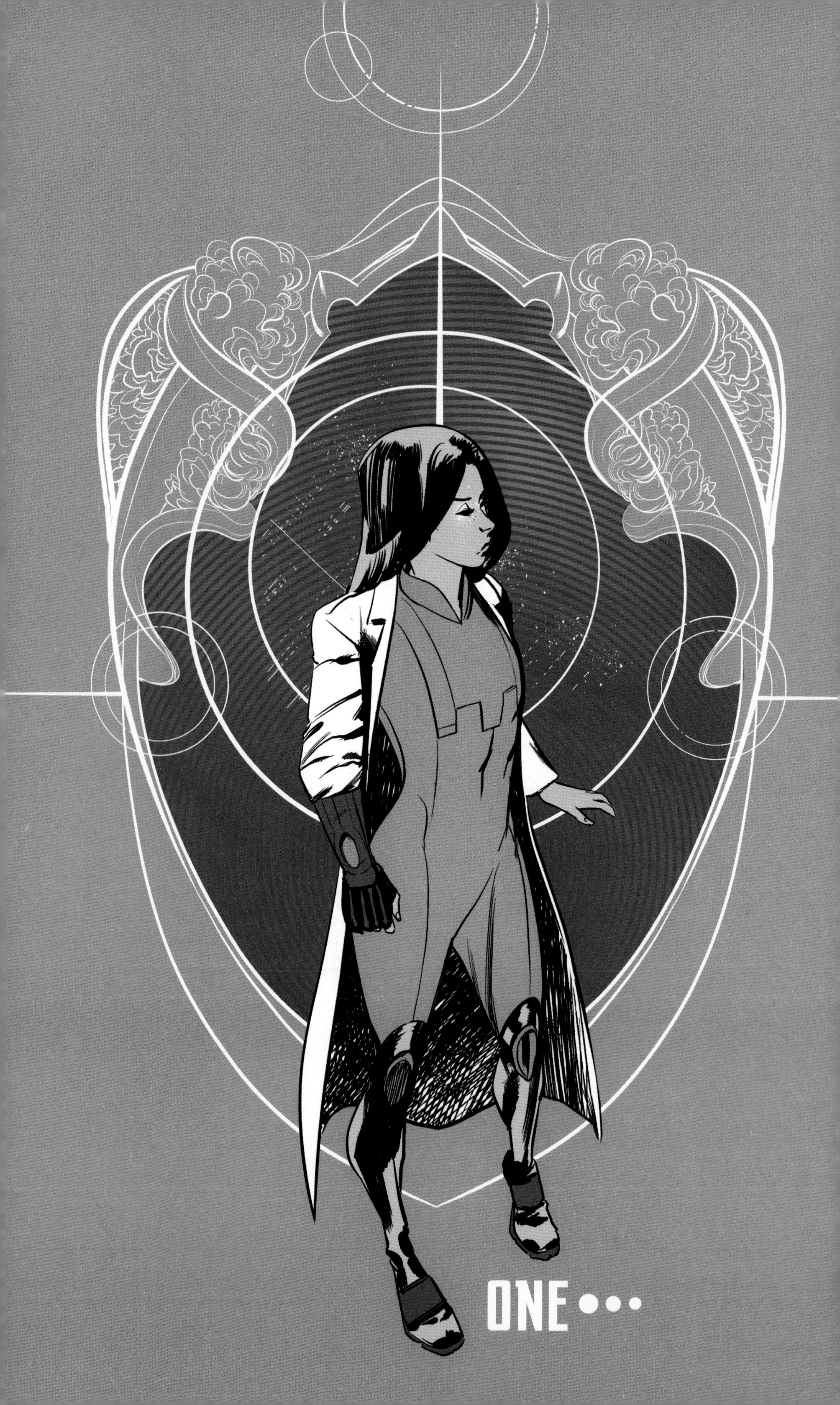

ONE •••

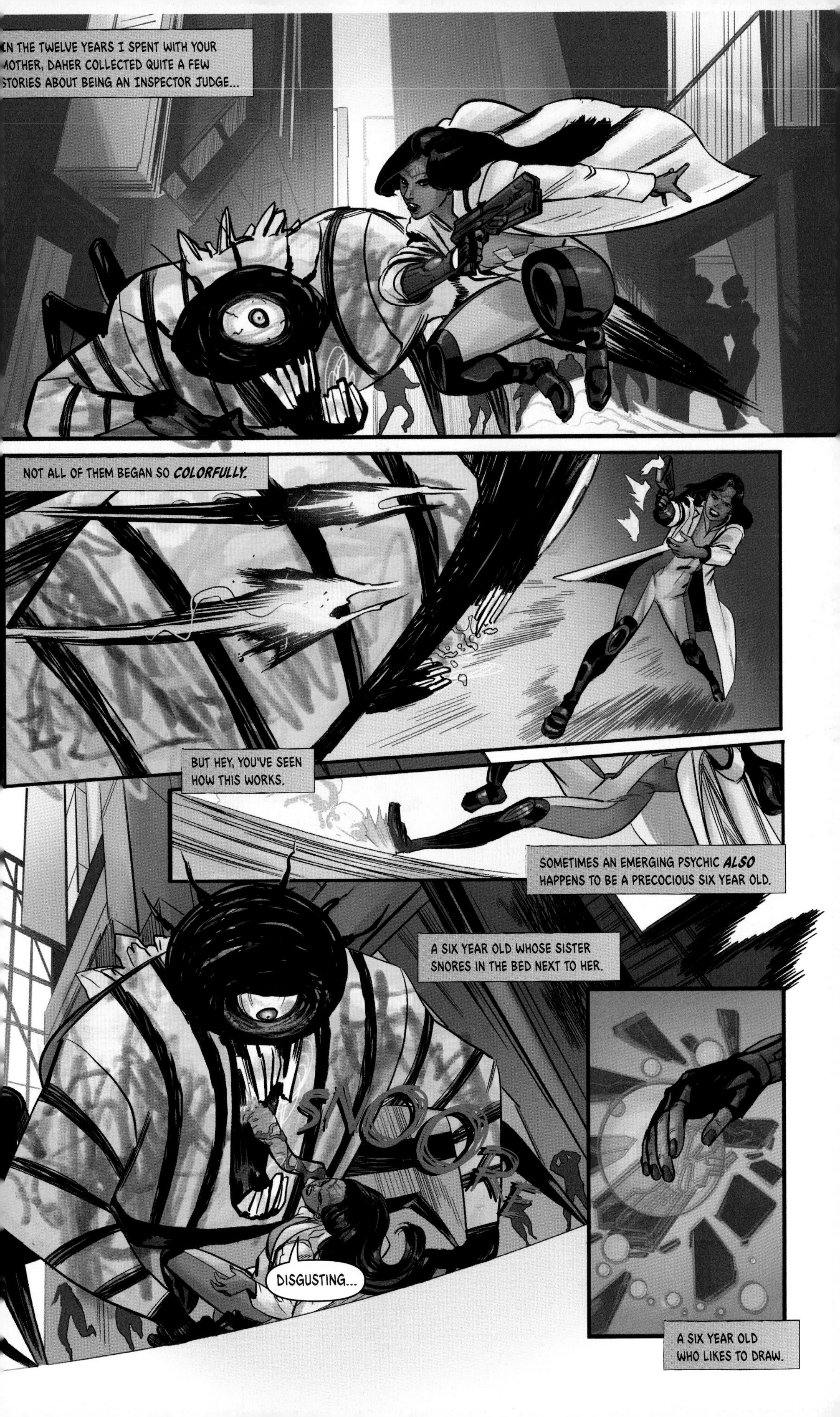
IN THE TWELVE YEARS I SPENT WITH YOUR MOTHER, DAHER COLLECTED QUITE A FEW STORIES ABOUT BEING AN INSPECTOR JUDGE...
NOT ALL OF THEM BEGAN SO *COLORFULLY.*
BUT HEY, YOU'VE SEEN HOW THIS WORKS.
SOMETIMES AN EMERGING PSYCHIC *ALSO* HAPPENS TO BE A PRECOCIOUS SIX YEAR OLD.
A SIX YEAR OLD WHOSE SISTER SNORES IN THE BED NEXT TO HER.
SNOORE
DISGUSTING...
A SIX YEAR OLD WHO LIKES TO DRAW.

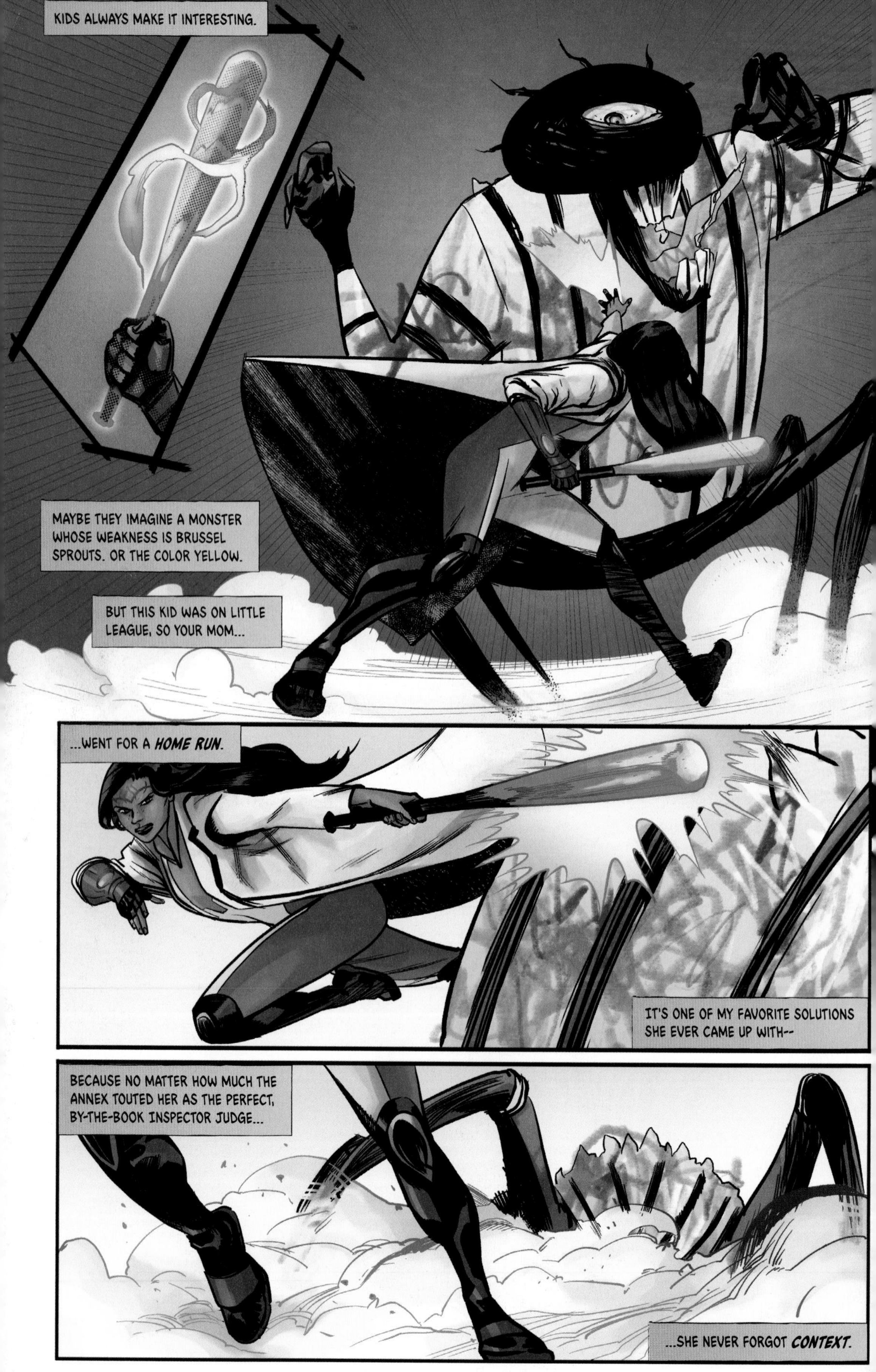
KIDS ALWAYS MAKE IT INTERESTING.
MAYBE THEY IMAGINE A MONSTER WHOSE WEAKNESS IS BRUSSEL SPROUTS. OR THE COLOR YELLOW.
BUT THIS KID WAS ON LITTLE LEAGUE, SO YOUR MOM...
...WENT FOR A ***HOME RUN***.
IT'S ONE OF MY FAVORITE SOLUTIONS SHE EVER CAME UP WITH--
BECAUSE NO MATTER HOW MUCH THE ANNEX TOUTED HER AS THE PERFECT, BY-THE-BOOK INSPECTOR JUDGE...
...SHE NEVER FORGOT ***CONTEXT***.

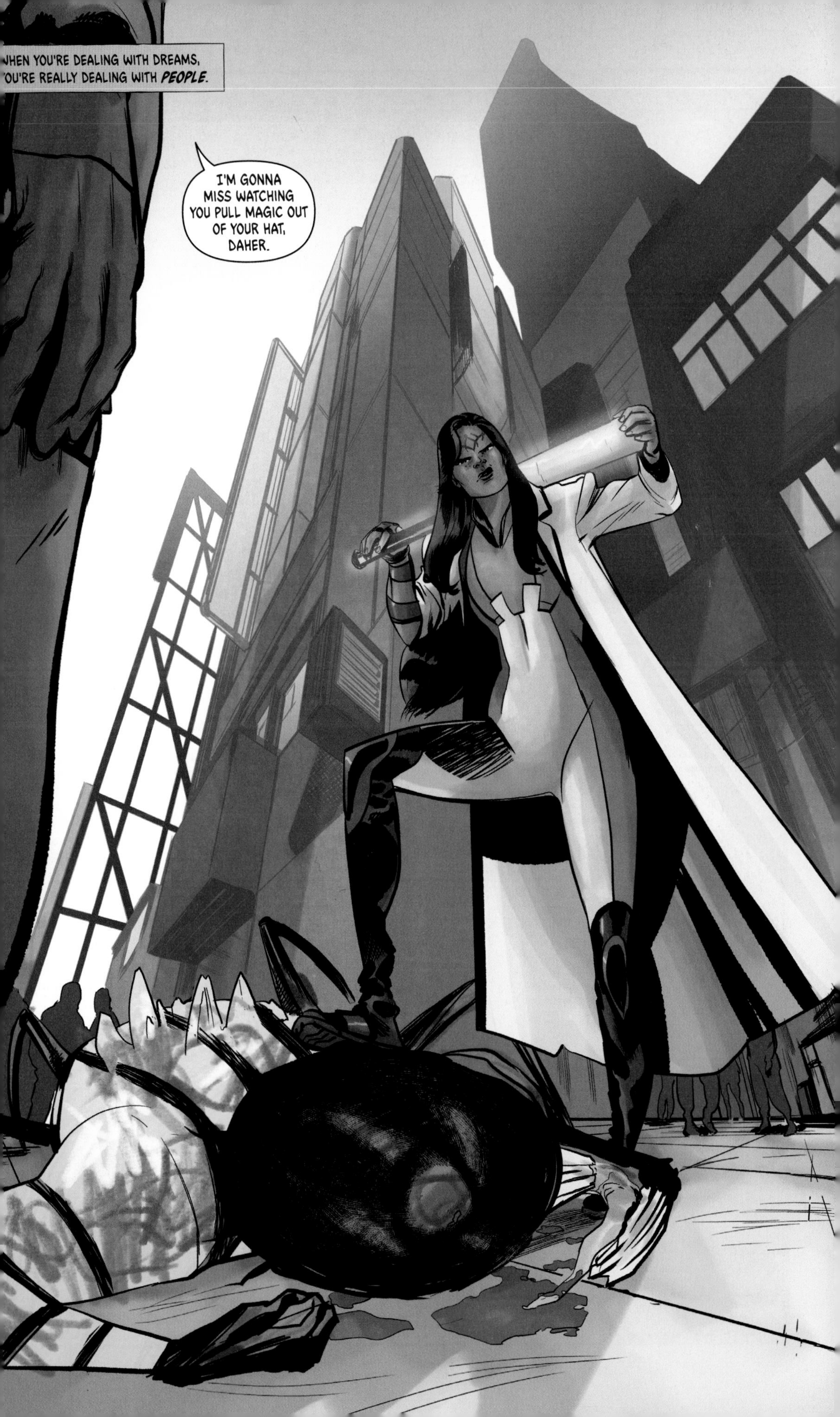
WHEN YOU'RE DEALING WITH DREAMS, YOU'RE REALLY DEALING WITH *PEOPLE*.
I'M GONNA MISS WATCHING YOU PULL MAGIC OUT OF YOUR HAT, DAHER.

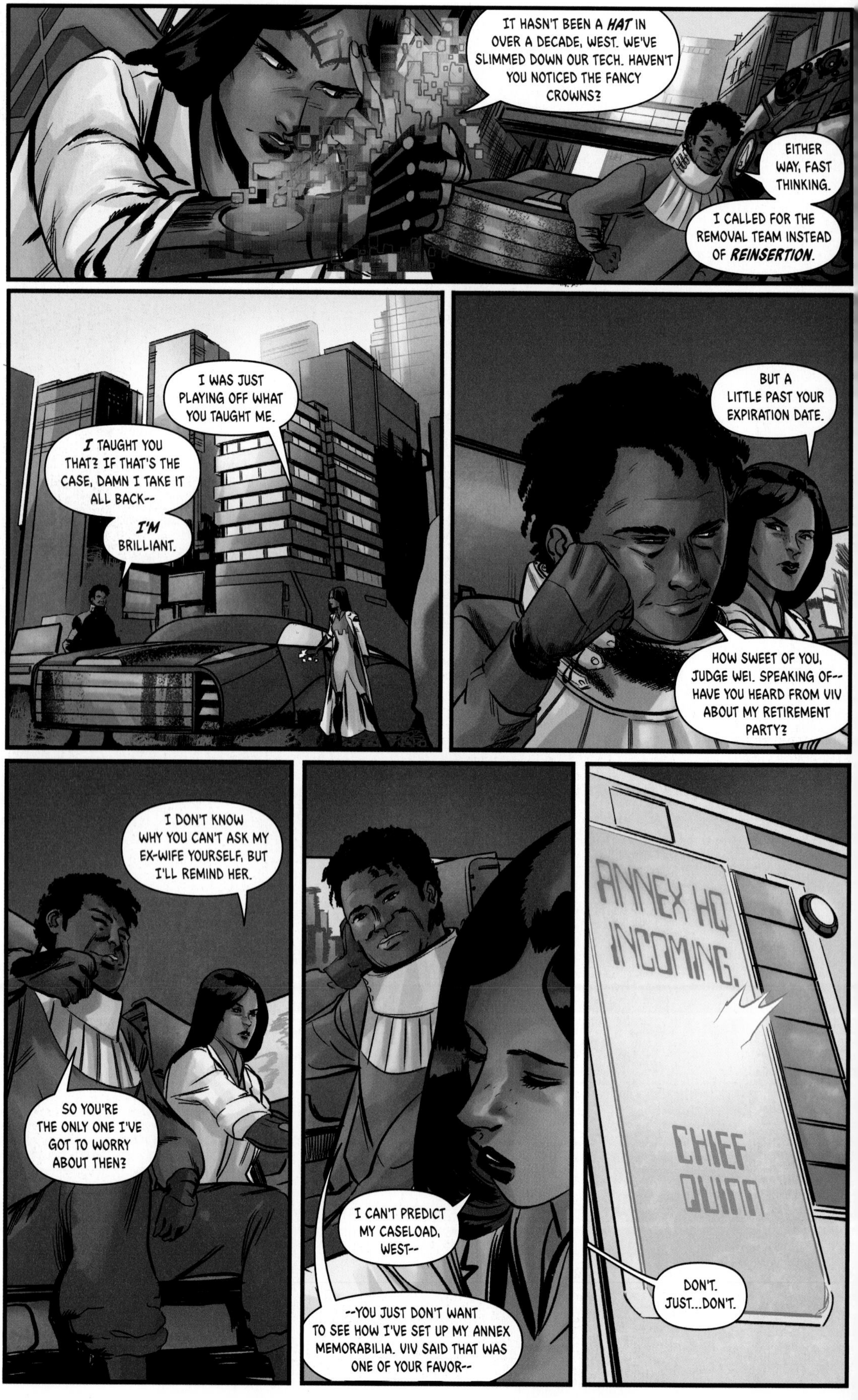
IT HASN'T BEEN A *HAT* IN OVER A DECADE, WEST. WE'VE SLIMMED DOWN OUR TECH. HAVEN'T YOU NOTICED THE FANCY CROWNS?
EITHER WAY, FAST THINKING.
I CALLED FOR THE REMOVAL TEAM INSTEAD OF *REINSERTION*.
I WAS JUST PLAYING OFF WHAT YOU TAUGHT ME.
I TAUGHT YOU THAT? IF THAT'S THE CASE, DAMN I TAKE IT ALL BACK--
I'M BRILLIANT.
BUT A LITTLE PAST YOUR EXPIRATION DATE.
HOW SWEET OF YOU, JUDGE WEI. SPEAKING OF--HAVE YOU HEARD FROM VIV ABOUT MY RETIREMENT PARTY?
I DON'T KNOW WHY YOU CAN'T ASK MY EX-WIFE YOURSELF, BUT I'LL REMIND HER.
SO YOU'RE THE ONLY ONE I'VE GOT TO WORRY ABOUT THEN?
I CAN'T PREDICT MY CASELOAD, WEST--
--YOU JUST DON'T WANT TO SEE HOW I'VE SET UP MY ANNEX MEMORABILIA. VIV SAID THAT WAS ONE OF YOUR FAVOR--
ANNEX HQ INCOMING.
CHIEF QUINN
DON'T. JUST...DON'T.

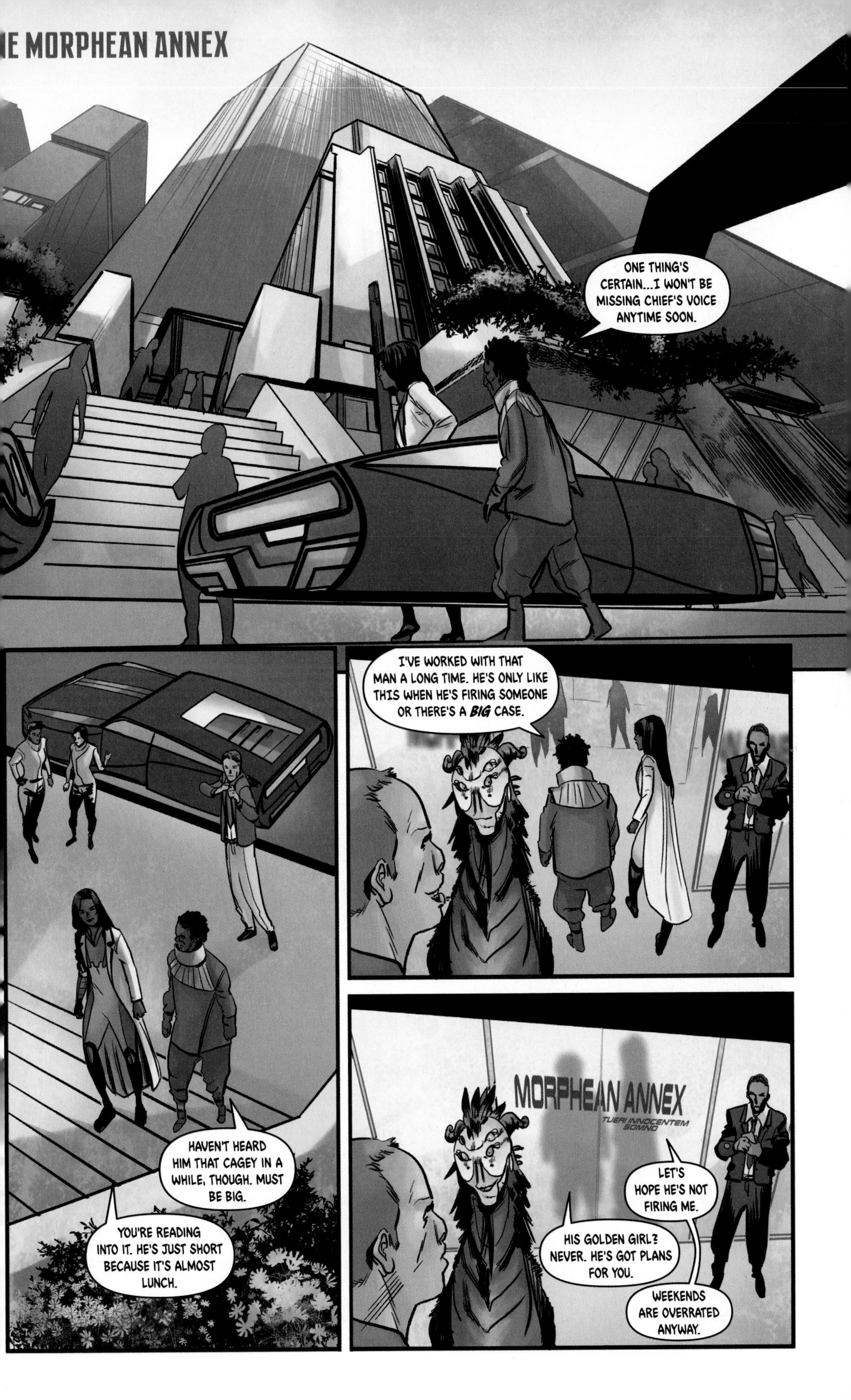
E MORPHEAN ANNEX
ONE THING'S CERTAIN...I WON'T BE MISSING CHIEF'S VOICE ANYTIME SOON.
HAVEN'T HEARD HIM THAT CAGEY IN A WHILE, THOUGH. MUST BE BIG.
YOU'RE READING INTO IT. HE'S JUST SHORT BECAUSE IT'S ALMOST LUNCH.
I'VE WORKED WITH THAT MAN A LONG TIME. HE'S ONLY LIKE THIS WHEN HE'S FIRING SOMEONE OR THERE'S A BIG CASE.
MORPHEAN ANNEX
TUERI INNOCENTEM SOMNO
LET'S HOPE HE'S NOT FIRING ME.
HIS GOLDEN GIRL? NEVER. HE'S GOT PLANS FOR YOU.
WEEKENDS ARE OVERRATED ANYWAY.

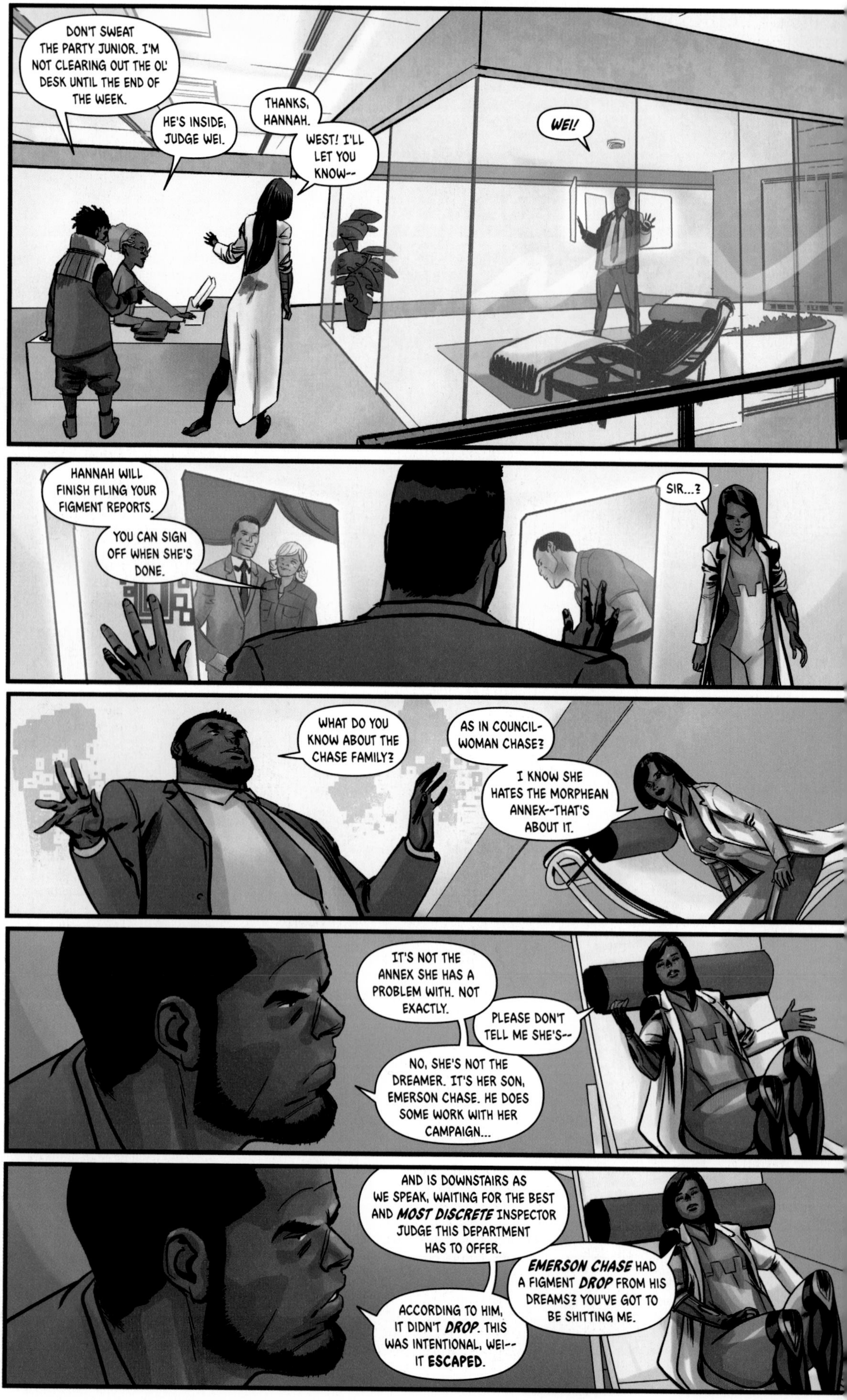
DON'T SWEAT THE PARTY JUNIOR. I'M NOT CLEARING OUT THE OL' DESK UNTIL THE END OF THE WEEK.
HE'S INSIDE, JUDGE WEI.
THANKS, HANNAH.
WEST! I'LL LET YOU KNOW--
WEI!
HANNAH WILL FINISH FILING YOUR FIGMENT REPORTS.
YOU CAN SIGN OFF WHEN SHE'S DONE.
SIR...?
WHAT DO YOU KNOW ABOUT THE CHASE FAMILY?
AS IN COUNCIL-WOMAN CHASE?
I KNOW SHE HATES THE MORPHEAN ANNEX--THAT'S ABOUT IT.
IT'S NOT THE ANNEX SHE HAS A PROBLEM WITH. NOT EXACTLY.
PLEASE DON'T TELL ME SHE'S--
NO, SHE'S NOT THE DREAMER. IT'S HER SON, EMERSON CHASE. HE DOES SOME WORK WITH HER CAMPAIGN...
AND IS DOWNSTAIRS AS WE SPEAK, WAITING FOR THE BEST AND MOST DISCRETE INSPECTOR JUDGE THIS DEPARTMENT HAS TO OFFER.
EMERSON CHASE HAD A FIGMENT DROP FROM HIS DREAMS? YOU'VE GOT TO BE SHITTING ME.
ACCORDING TO HIM, IT DIDN'T DROP. THIS WAS INTENTIONAL, WEI--IT ESCAPED.

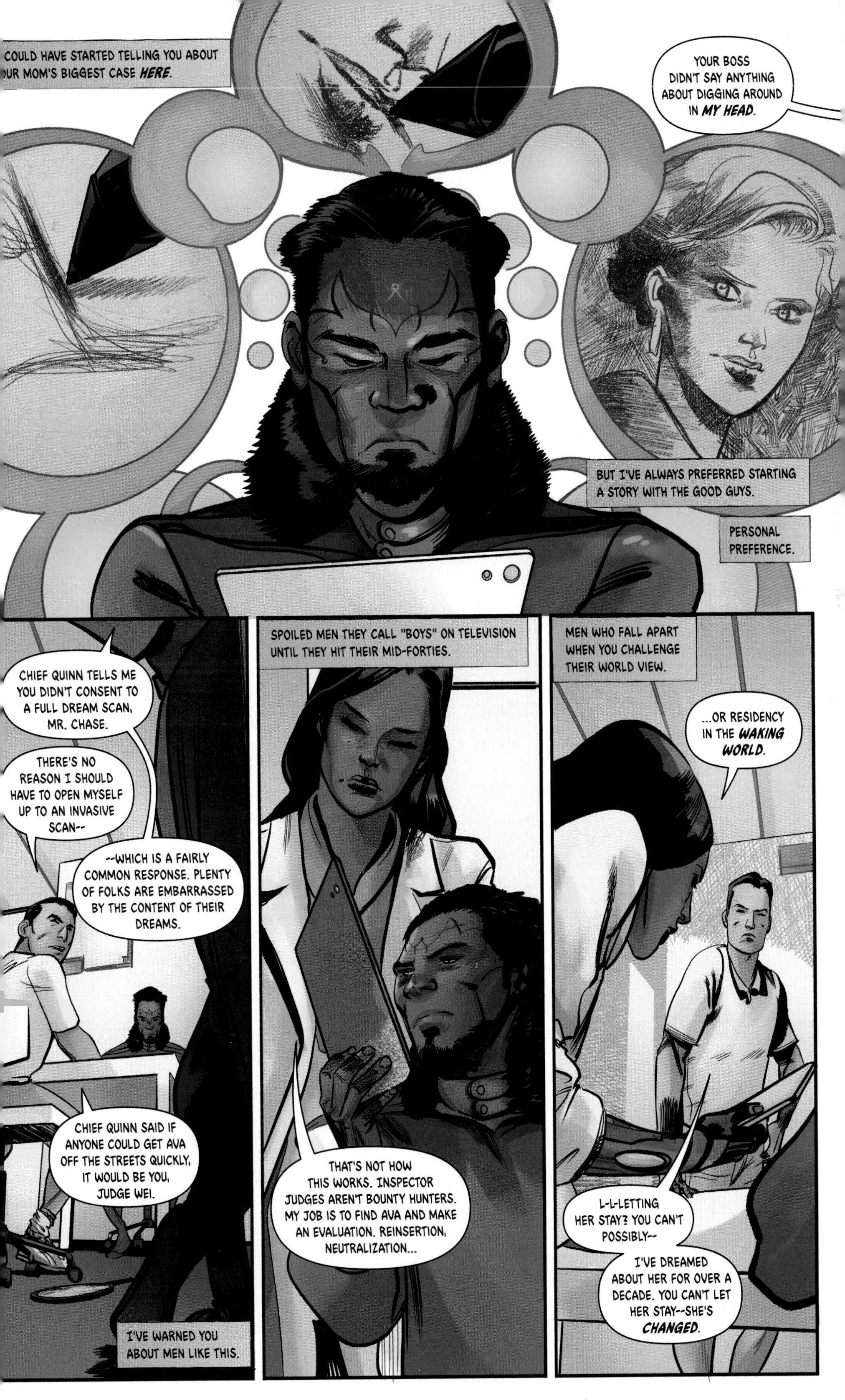
COULD HAVE STARTED TELLING YOU ABOUT
UR MOM'S BIGGEST CASE *HERE*.
YOUR BOSS DIDN'T SAY ANYTHING ABOUT DIGGING AROUND IN *MY HEAD*.
BUT I'VE ALWAYS PREFERRED STARTING A STORY WITH THE GOOD GUYS.
PERSONAL PREFERENCE.
CHIEF QUINN TELLS ME YOU DIDN'T CONSENT TO A FULL DREAM SCAN, MR. CHASE.
THERE'S NO REASON I SHOULD HAVE TO OPEN MYSELF UP TO AN INVASIVE SCAN--
--WHICH IS A FAIRLY COMMON RESPONSE. PLENTY OF FOLKS ARE EMBARRASSED BY THE CONTENT OF THEIR DREAMS.
CHIEF QUINN SAID IF ANYONE COULD GET AVA OFF THE STREETS QUICKLY, IT WOULD BE YOU, JUDGE WEI.
I'VE WARNED YOU ABOUT MEN LIKE THIS.
SPOILED MEN THEY CALL "BOYS" ON TELEVISION UNTIL THEY HIT THEIR MID-FORTIES.
THAT'S NOT HOW THIS WORKS. INSPECTOR JUDGES AREN'T BOUNTY HUNTERS. MY JOB IS TO FIND AVA AND MAKE AN EVALUATION. REINSERTION, NEUTRALIZATION...
MEN WHO FALL APART WHEN YOU CHALLENGE THEIR WORLD VIEW.
...OR RESIDENCY IN THE *WAKING WORLD*.
L-L-LETTING HER STAY? YOU CAN'T POSSIBLY--
I'VE DREAMED ABOUT HER FOR OVER A DECADE. YOU CAN'T LET HER STAY--SHE'S *CHANGED*.

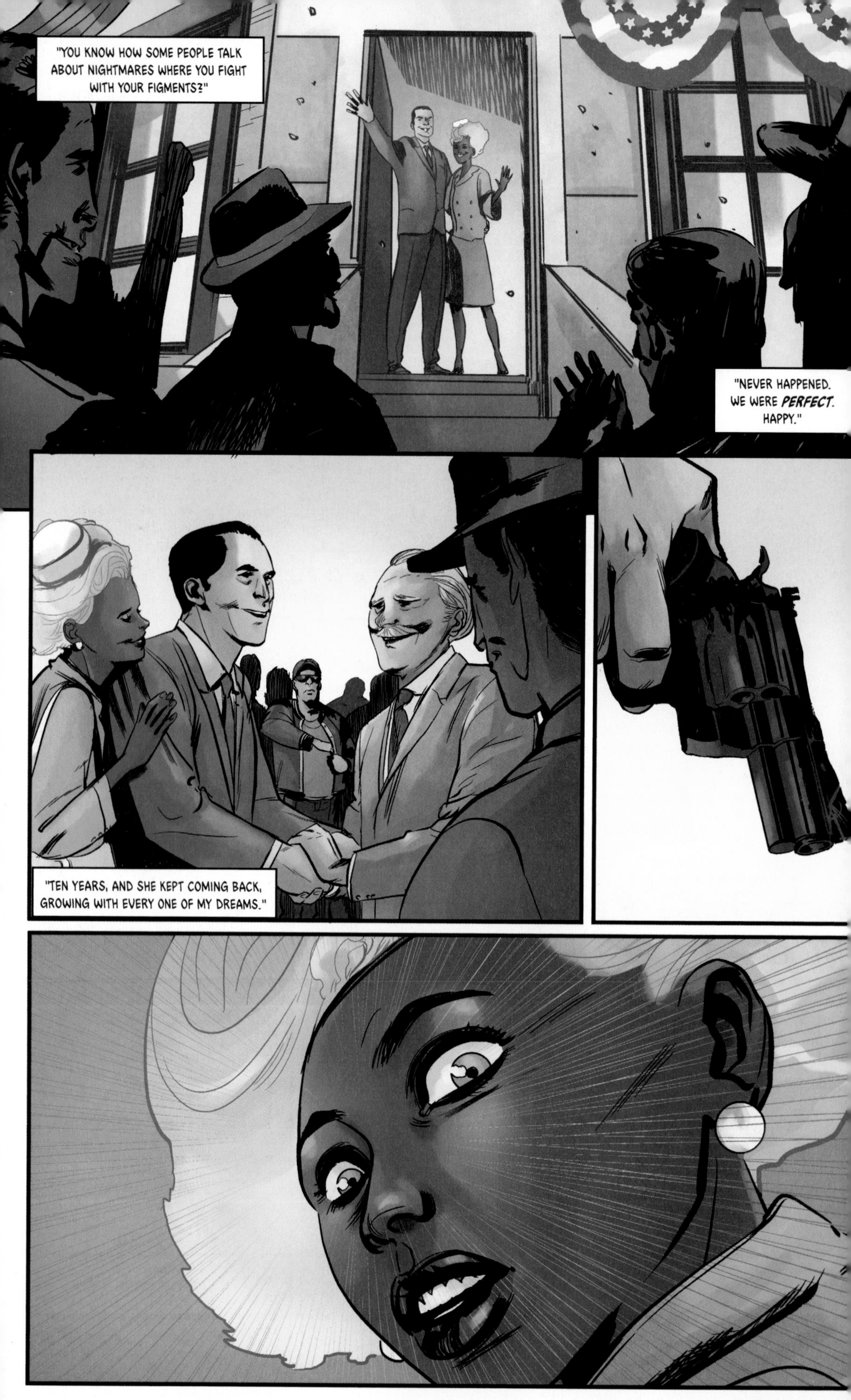
"YOU KNOW HOW SOME PEOPLE TALK ABOUT NIGHTMARES WHERE YOU FIGHT WITH YOUR FIGMENTS?"
"NEVER HAPPENED. WE WERE *PERFECT*. HAPPY."
"TEN YEARS, AND SHE KEPT COMING BACK, GROWING WITH EVERY ONE OF MY DREAMS."

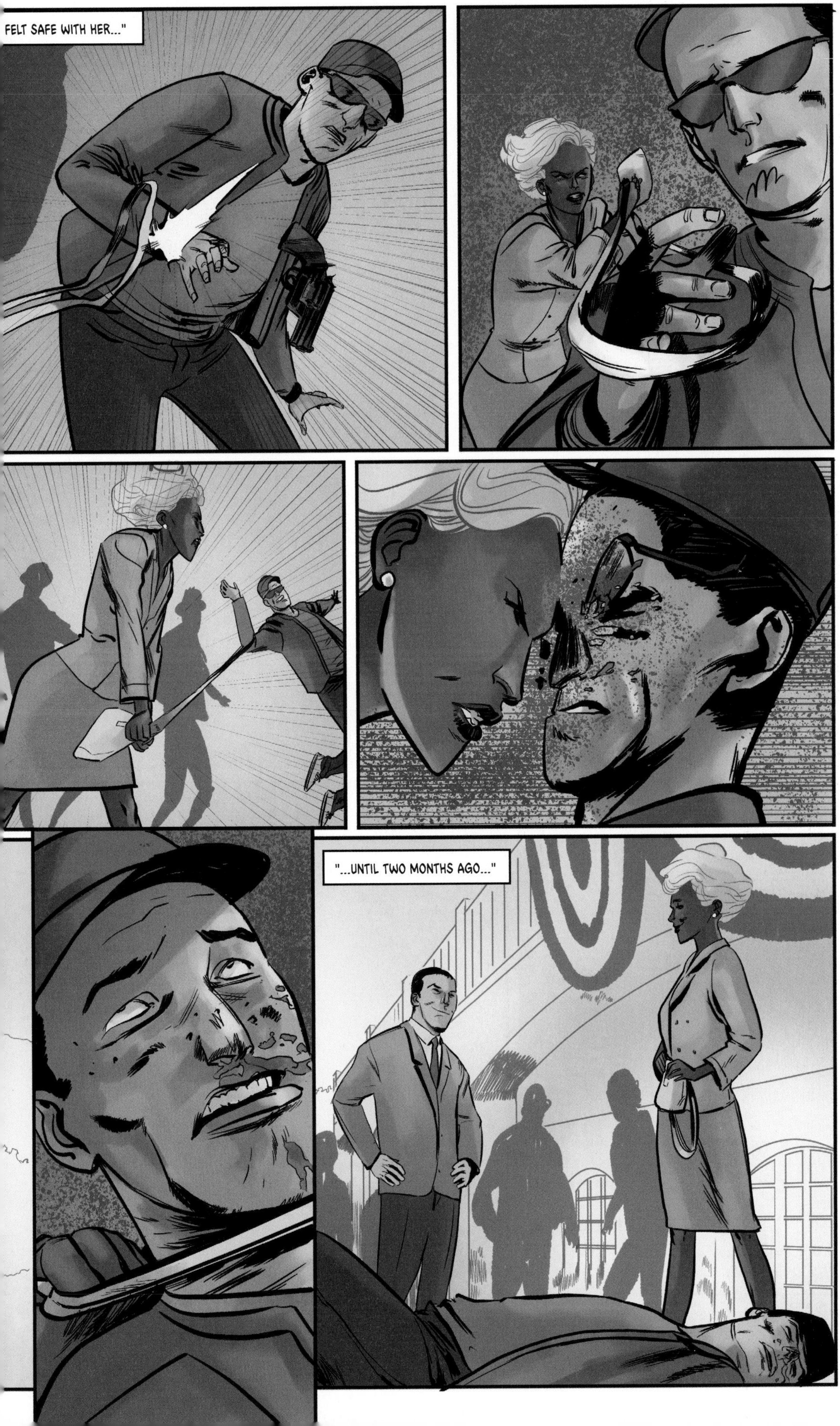
FELT SAFE WITH HER..."
"...UNTIL TWO MONTHS AGO..."

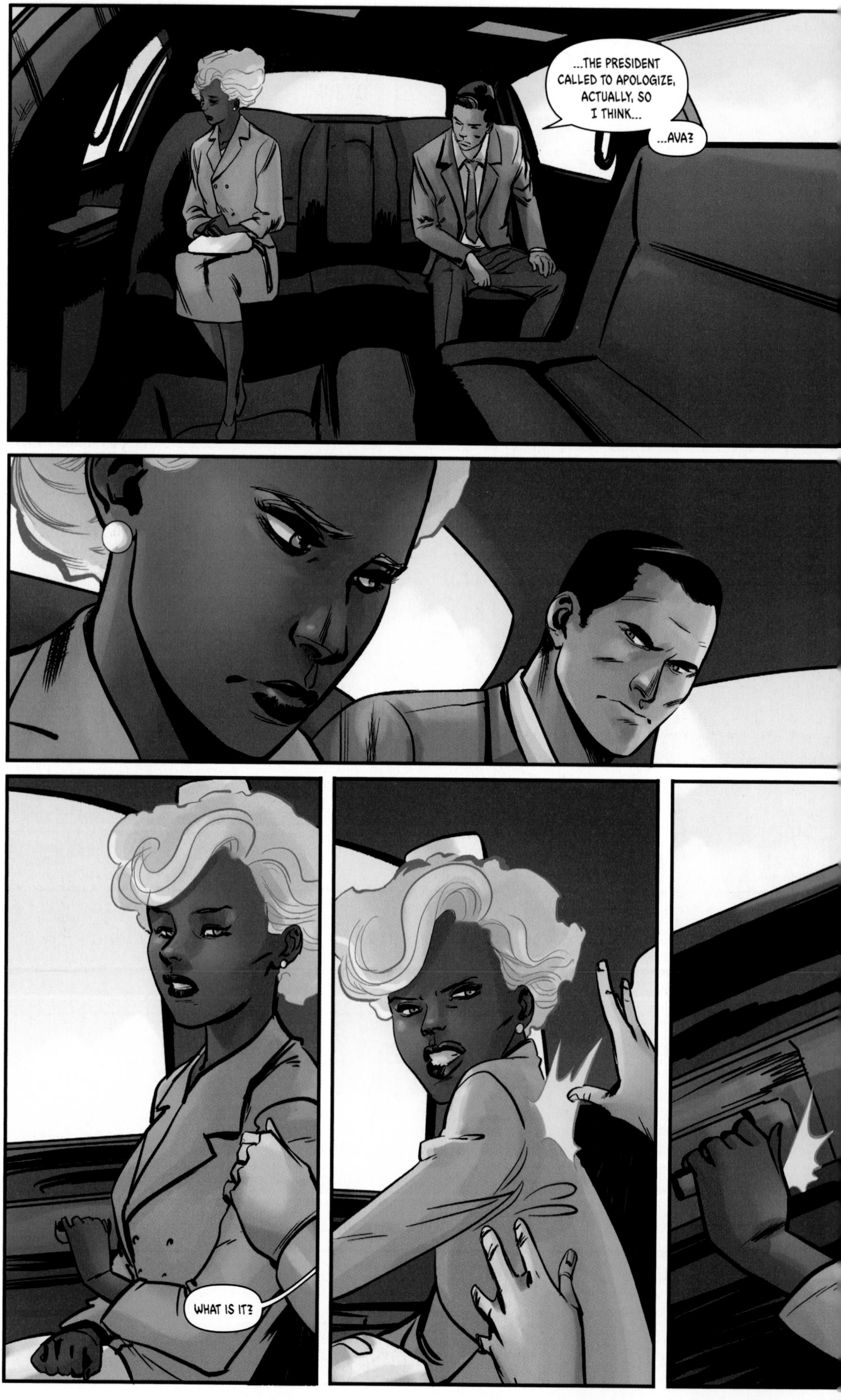
...THE PRESIDENT CALLED TO APOLOGIZE, ACTUALLY, SO I THINK...
...AVA?
WHAT IS IT?

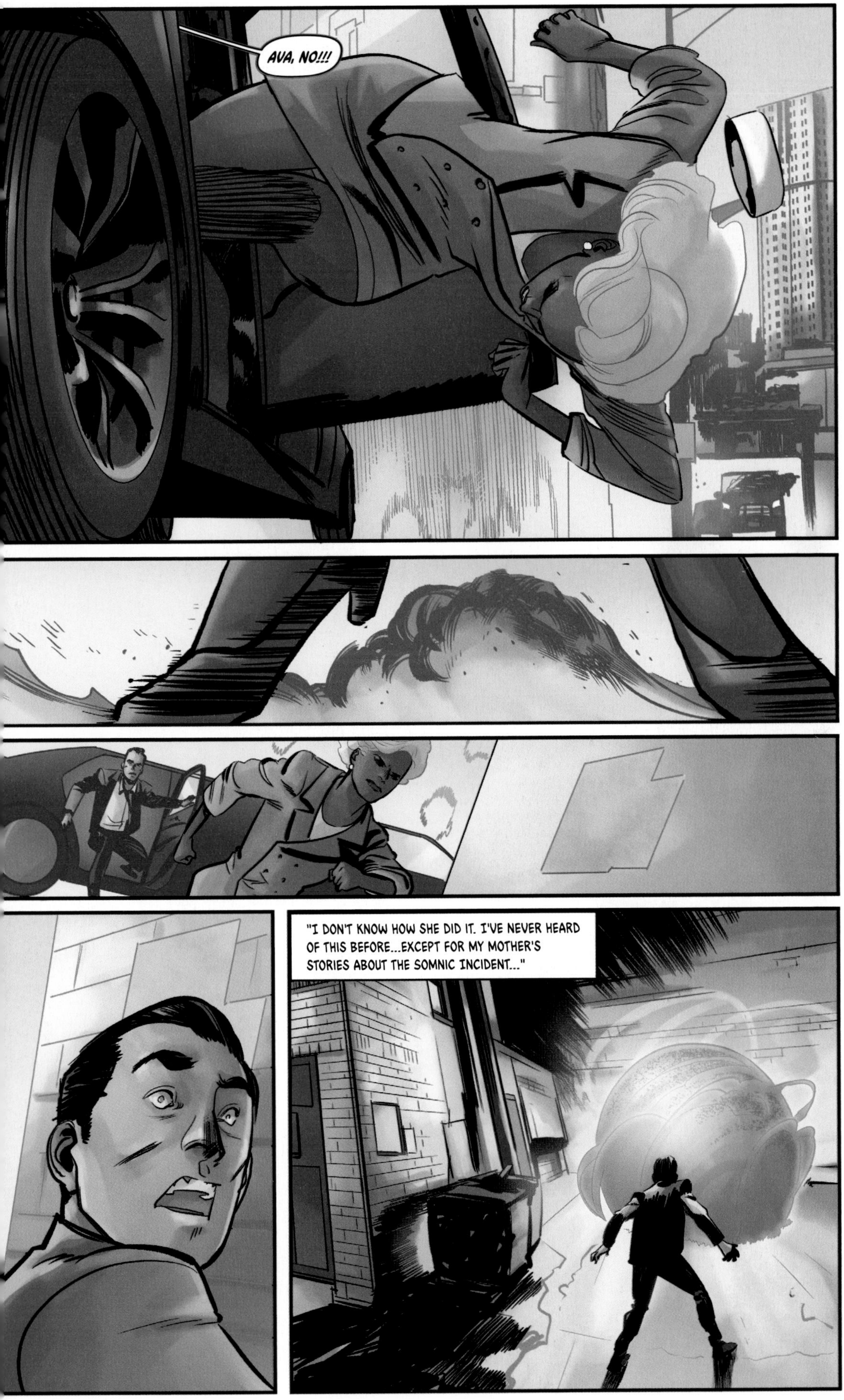
AVA, NO!!!
"I DON'T KNOW HOW SHE DID IT. I'VE NEVER HEARD OF THIS BEFORE...EXCEPT FOR MY MOTHER'S STORIES ABOUT THE SOMNIC INCIDENT..."

YOU REALLY THINK THIS IS SIMILAR TO THE SOMNIC INCIDENT?

A YOUNG PSYCHIC WITHOUT PROPER TRAINING LOST CONTROL OF THEIR DREAMS IN THE EARLY DAYS OF THE MORPHEAN ANNEX.

A LOT OF DANGEROUS FIGMENTS WERE LET LOOSE ON THE CITY, AND A LOT OF GOOD PEOPLE *DIED*.

OBVIOUSLY! I KNOW HOW IT STARTED. WITH THE PERSONALITY CHANGES, THE *ESCAPE*--

THE *SOMNIC INCIDENT* WAS A ONCE IN A LIFETIME TRAGEDY, MR. CHASE.

THAT'S NOT THIS SITUATION. AVA IS *ONE* FIGMENT, WHO MAY HAVE SIMPLY *DROPPED*-- FALLEN OUT OF YOUR DREAMS, THAT IS.

DO YOU KNOW WHO I--

OF COURSE I DO. WHICH IS WHY I TAKE YOUR CLAIMS *VERY* SERIOUSLY.

FINE THEN. WHAT'S YOUR NEXT STEP, IN THIS INVESTIGATION?

THERE ARE A FEW PLACES WE ALWAYS START, IN A CASE WHERE THE FIGMENT IS LIKELY CAPABLE OF INDEPENDENT THOUGHT.

AND YOU WILL KEEP ME APPRISED OF THE SITUATION?

MR. CHASE, I ASSURE YOU...

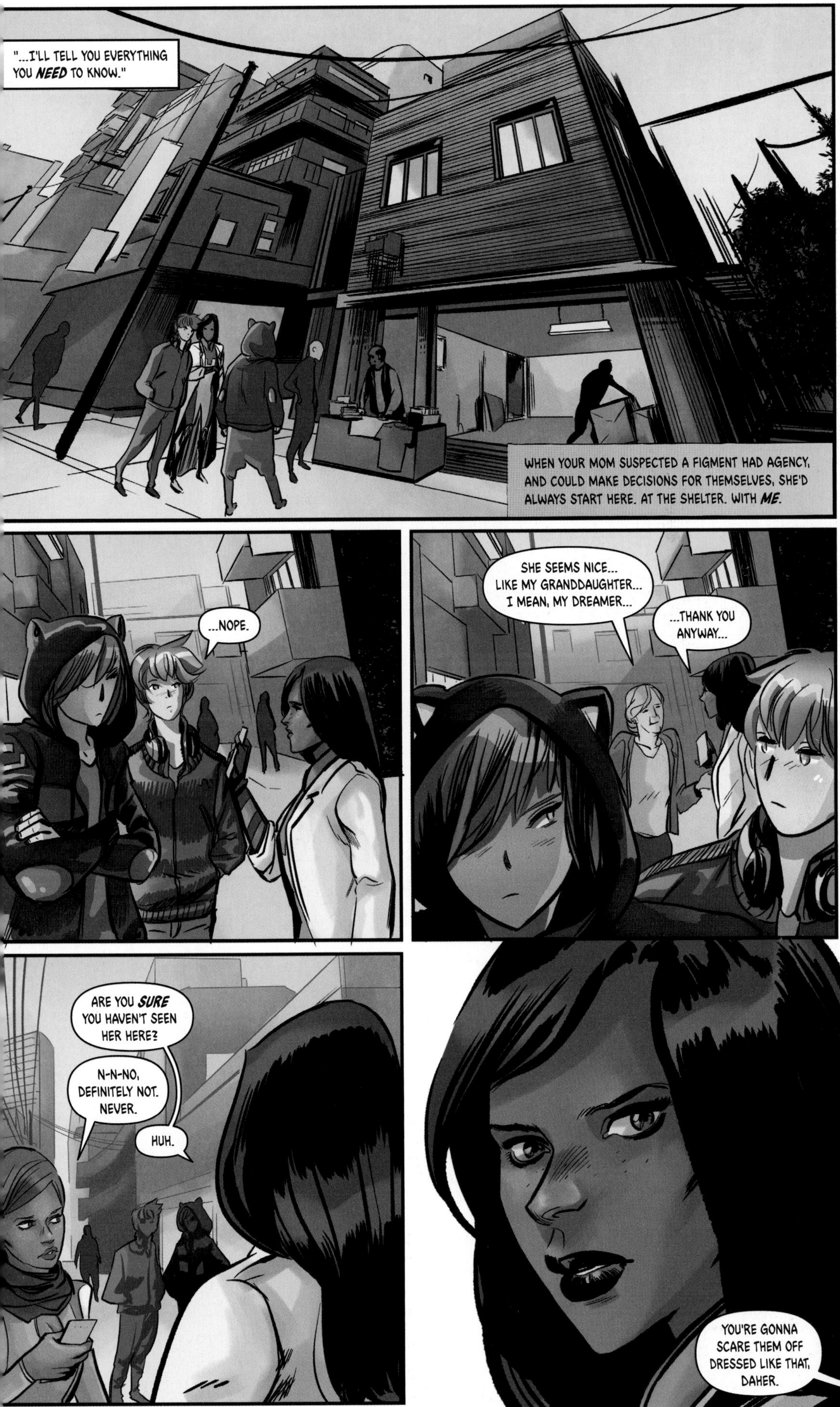
"...I'LL TELL YOU EVERYTHING YOU NEED TO KNOW."
WHEN YOUR MOM SUSPECTED A FIGMENT HAD AGENCY, AND COULD MAKE DECISIONS FOR THEMSELVES, SHE'D ALWAYS START HERE. AT THE SHELTER. WITH ME.
...NOPE.
SHE SEEMS NICE... LIKE MY GRANDDAUGHTER... I MEAN, MY DREAMER...
...THANK YOU ANYWAY...
ARE YOU SURE YOU HAVEN'T SEEN HER HERE?
N-N-NO, DEFINITELY NOT. NEVER.
HUH.
YOU'RE GONNA SCARE THEM OFF DRESSED LIKE THAT, DAHER.

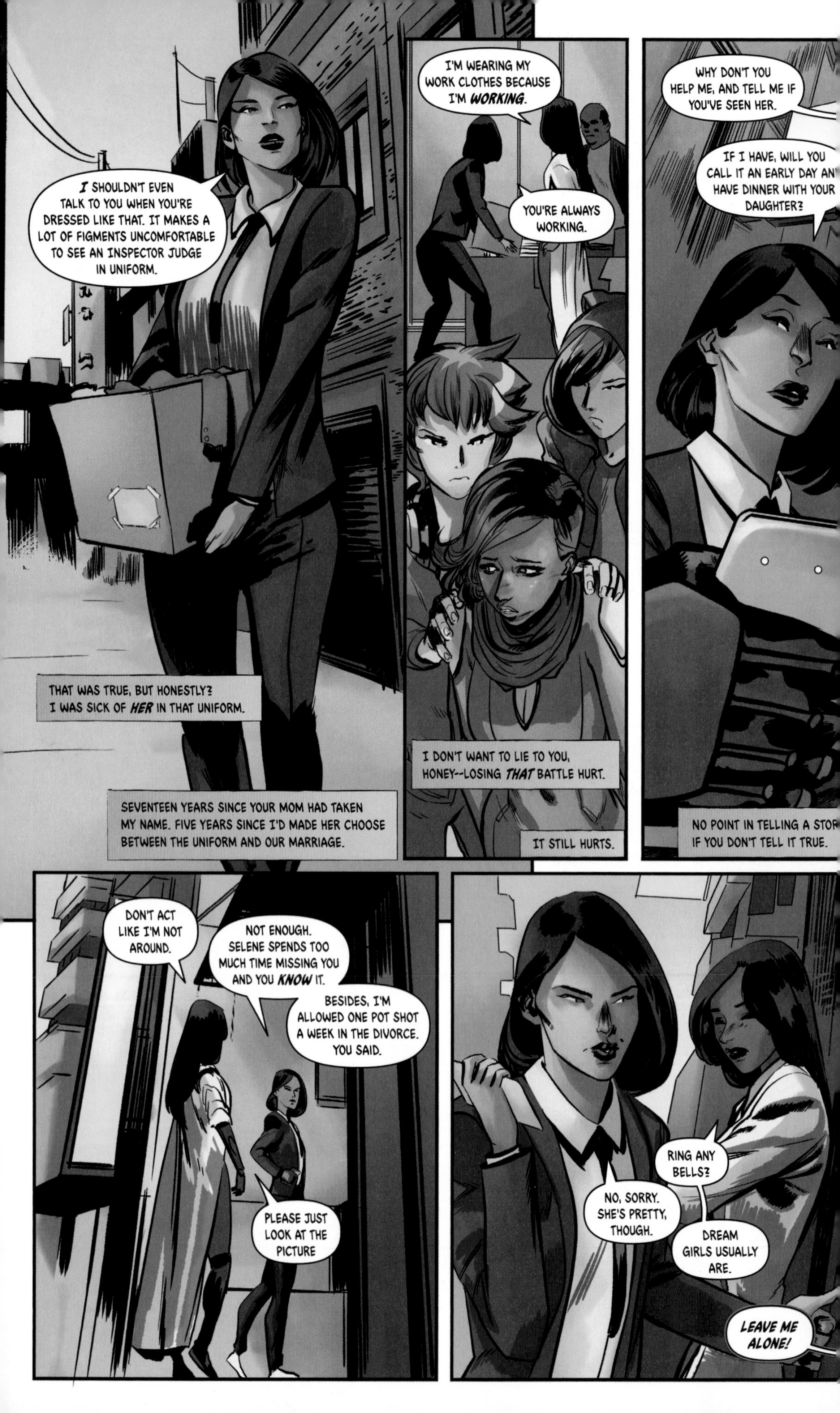
I SHOULDN'T EVEN TALK TO YOU WHEN YOU'RE DRESSED LIKE THAT. IT MAKES A LOT OF FIGMENTS UNCOMFORTABLE TO SEE AN INSPECTOR JUDGE IN UNIFORM.
THAT WAS TRUE, BUT HONESTLY? I WAS SICK OF HER IN THAT UNIFORM.
SEVENTEEN YEARS SINCE YOUR MOM HAD TAKEN MY NAME. FIVE YEARS SINCE I'D MADE HER CHOOSE BETWEEN THE UNIFORM AND OUR MARRIAGE.
I'M WEARING MY WORK CLOTHES BECAUSE I'M WORKING.
YOU'RE ALWAYS WORKING.
I DON'T WANT TO LIE TO YOU, HONEY--LOSING THAT BATTLE HURT.
IT STILL HURTS.
WHY DON'T YOU HELP ME, AND TELL ME IF YOU'VE SEEN HER.
IF I HAVE, WILL YOU CALL IT AN EARLY DAY AN
HAVE DINNER WITH YOUR DAUGHTER?
NO POINT IN TELLING A STOR
IF YOU DON'T TELL IT TRUE.
DON'T ACT LIKE I'M NOT AROUND.
NOT ENOUGH. SELENE SPENDS TOO MUCH TIME MISSING YOU AND YOU KNOW IT.
BESIDES, I'M ALLOWED ONE POT SHOT A WEEK IN THE DIVORCE. YOU SAID.
PLEASE JUST LOOK AT THE PICTURE
RING ANY BELLS?
NO, SORRY. SHE'S PRETTY, THOUGH.
DREAM GIRLS USUALLY ARE.
LEAVE ME ALONE!

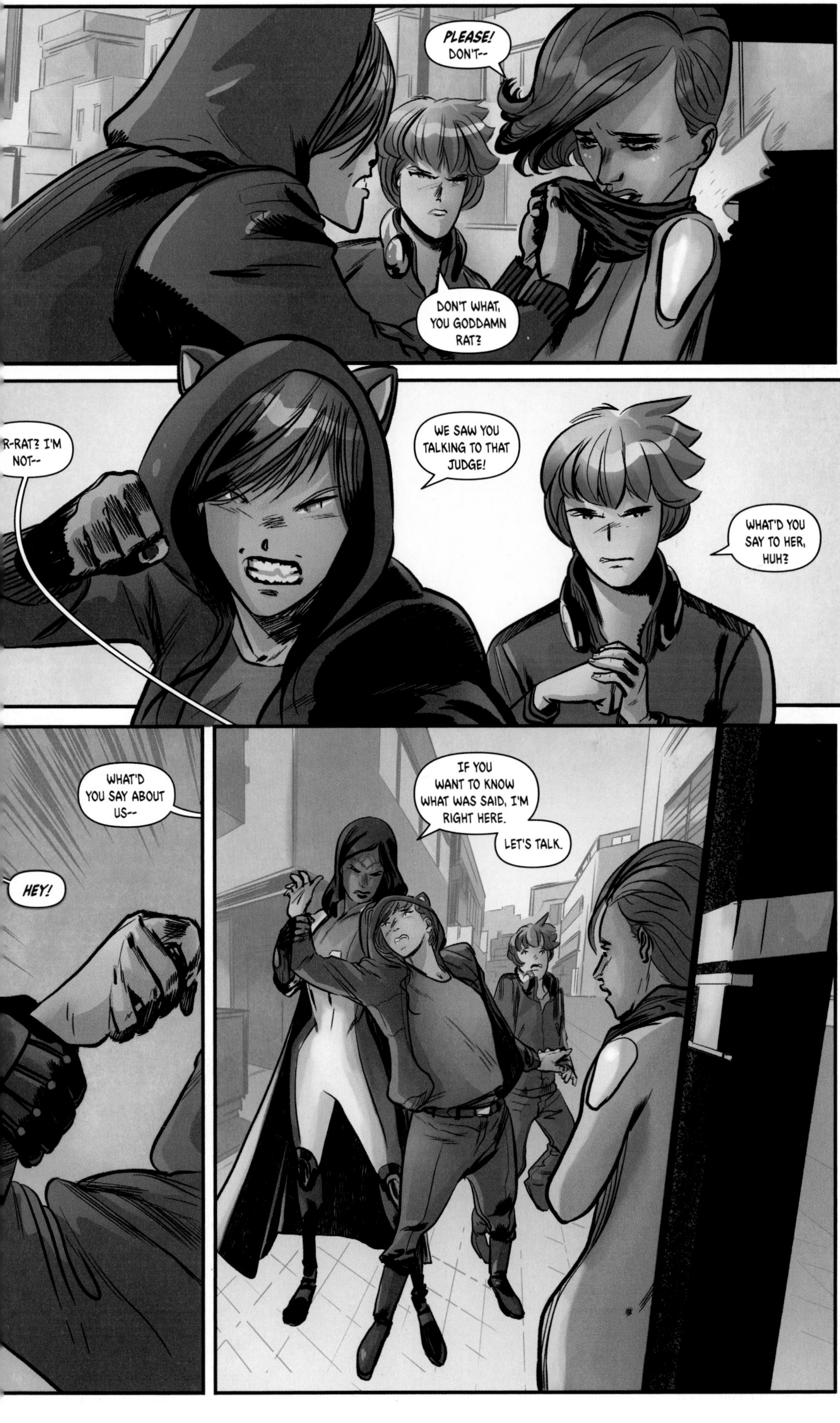
PLEASE! DON'T--
DON'T WHAT, YOU GODDAMN RAT?
R-RAT? I'M NOT--
WE SAW YOU TALKING TO THAT JUDGE!
WHAT'D YOU SAY TO HER, HUH?
WHAT'D YOU SAY ABOUT US--
HEY!
IF YOU WANT TO KNOW WHAT WAS SAID, I'M RIGHT HERE.
LET'S TALK.

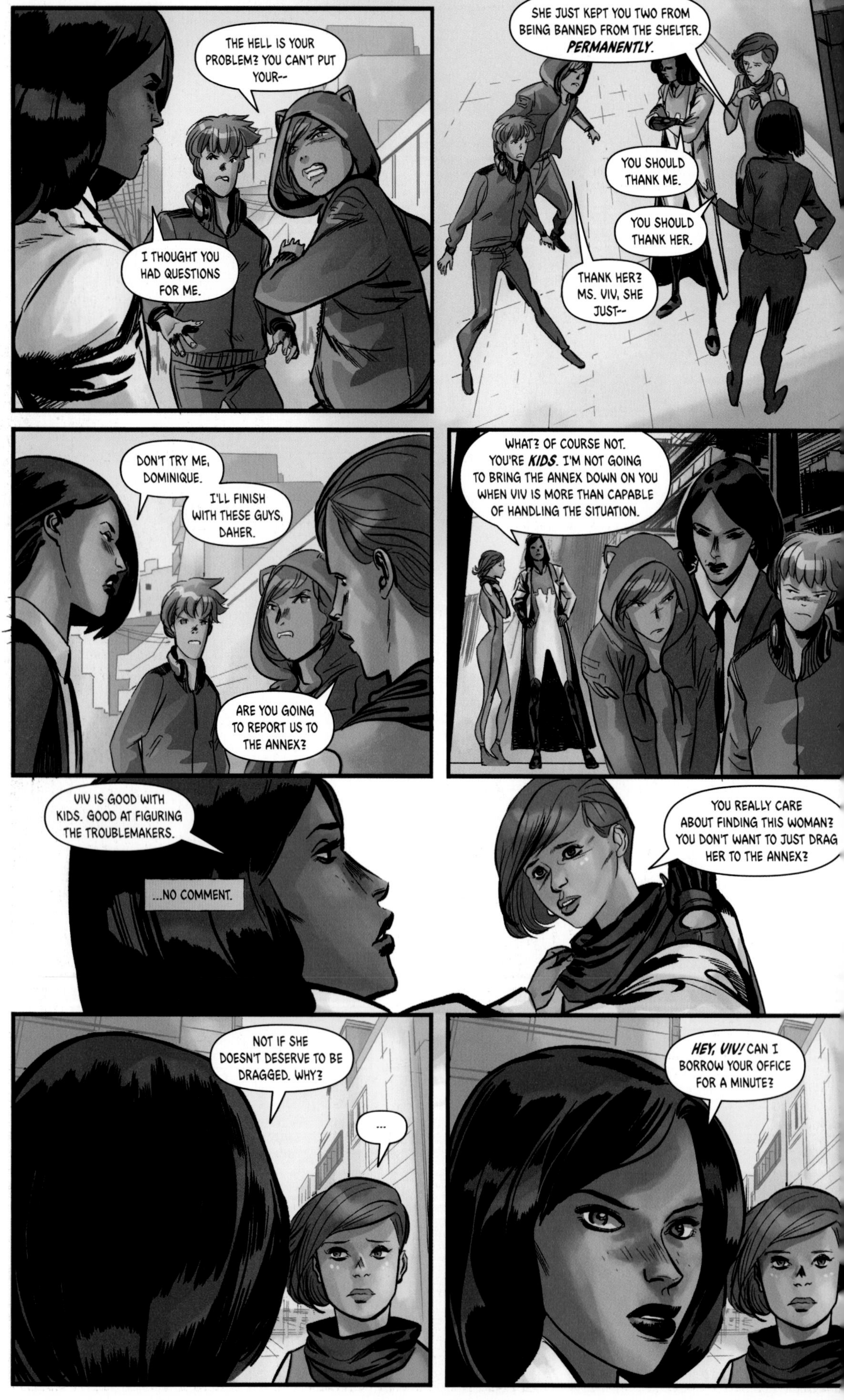
THE HELL IS YOUR PROBLEM? YOU CAN'T PUT YOUR--
I THOUGHT YOU HAD QUESTIONS FOR ME.
SHE JUST KEPT YOU TWO FROM BEING BANNED FROM THE SHELTER. *PERMANENTLY*.
YOU SHOULD THANK ME.
YOU SHOULD THANK HER.
THANK HER? MS. VIV, SHE JUST--
DON'T TRY ME, DOMINIQUE.
I'LL FINISH WITH THESE GUYS, DAHER.
ARE YOU GOING TO REPORT US TO THE ANNEX?
WHAT? OF COURSE NOT. YOU'RE *KIDS*. I'M NOT GOING TO BRING THE ANNEX DOWN ON YOU WHEN VIV IS MORE THAN CAPABLE OF HANDLING THE SITUATION.
VIV IS GOOD WITH KIDS. GOOD AT FIGURING THE TROUBLEMAKERS.
...NO COMMENT.
YOU REALLY CARE ABOUT FINDING THIS WOMAN? YOU DON'T WANT TO JUST DRAG HER TO THE ANNEX?
NOT IF SHE DOESN'T DESERVE TO BE DRAGGED. WHY?
...
HEY, VIV! CAN I BORROW YOUR OFFICE FOR A MINUTE?

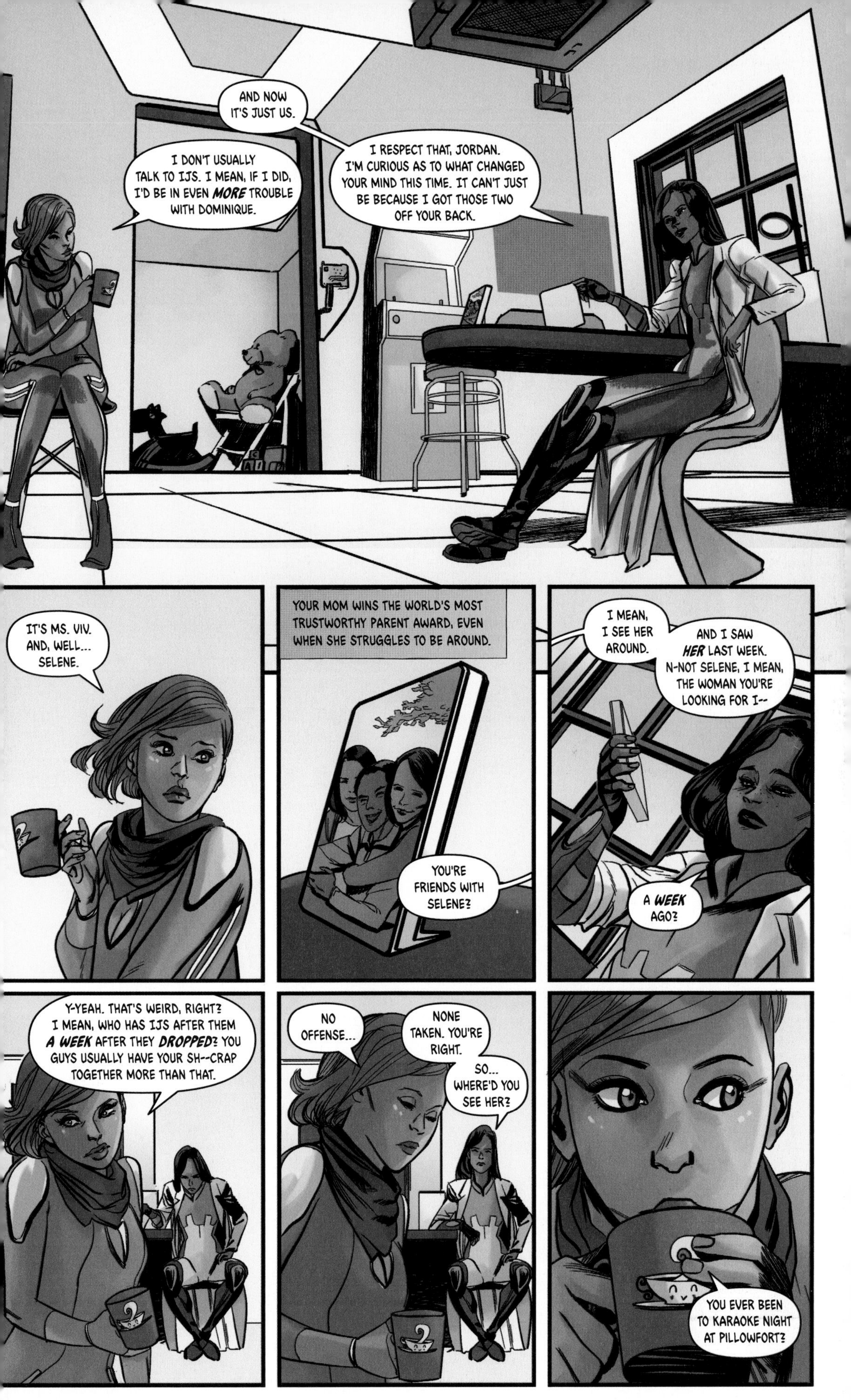
AND NOW IT'S JUST US.
I DON'T USUALLY TALK TO IJS. I MEAN, IF I DID, I'D BE IN EVEN MORE TROUBLE WITH DOMINIQUE.
I RESPECT THAT, JORDAN. I'M CURIOUS AS TO WHAT CHANGED YOUR MIND THIS TIME. IT CAN'T JUST BE BECAUSE I GOT THOSE TWO OFF YOUR BACK.
IT'S MS. VIV. AND, WELL... SELENE.
YOUR MOM WINS THE WORLD'S MOST TRUSTWORTHY PARENT AWARD, EVEN WHEN SHE STRUGGLES TO BE AROUND.
YOU'RE FRIENDS WITH SELENE?
I MEAN, I SEE HER AROUND.
AND I SAW HER LAST WEEK. N-NOT SELENE, I MEAN, THE WOMAN YOU'RE LOOKING FOR I--
A WEEK AGO?
Y-YEAH. THAT'S WEIRD, RIGHT? I MEAN, WHO HAS IJS AFTER THEM A WEEK AFTER THEY DROPPED? YOU GUYS USUALLY HAVE YOUR SH--CRAP TOGETHER MORE THAN THAT.
NO OFFENSE...
NONE TAKEN. YOU'RE RIGHT.
SO... WHERE'D YOU SEE HER?
YOU EVER BEEN TO KARAOKE NIGHT AT PILLOWFORT?

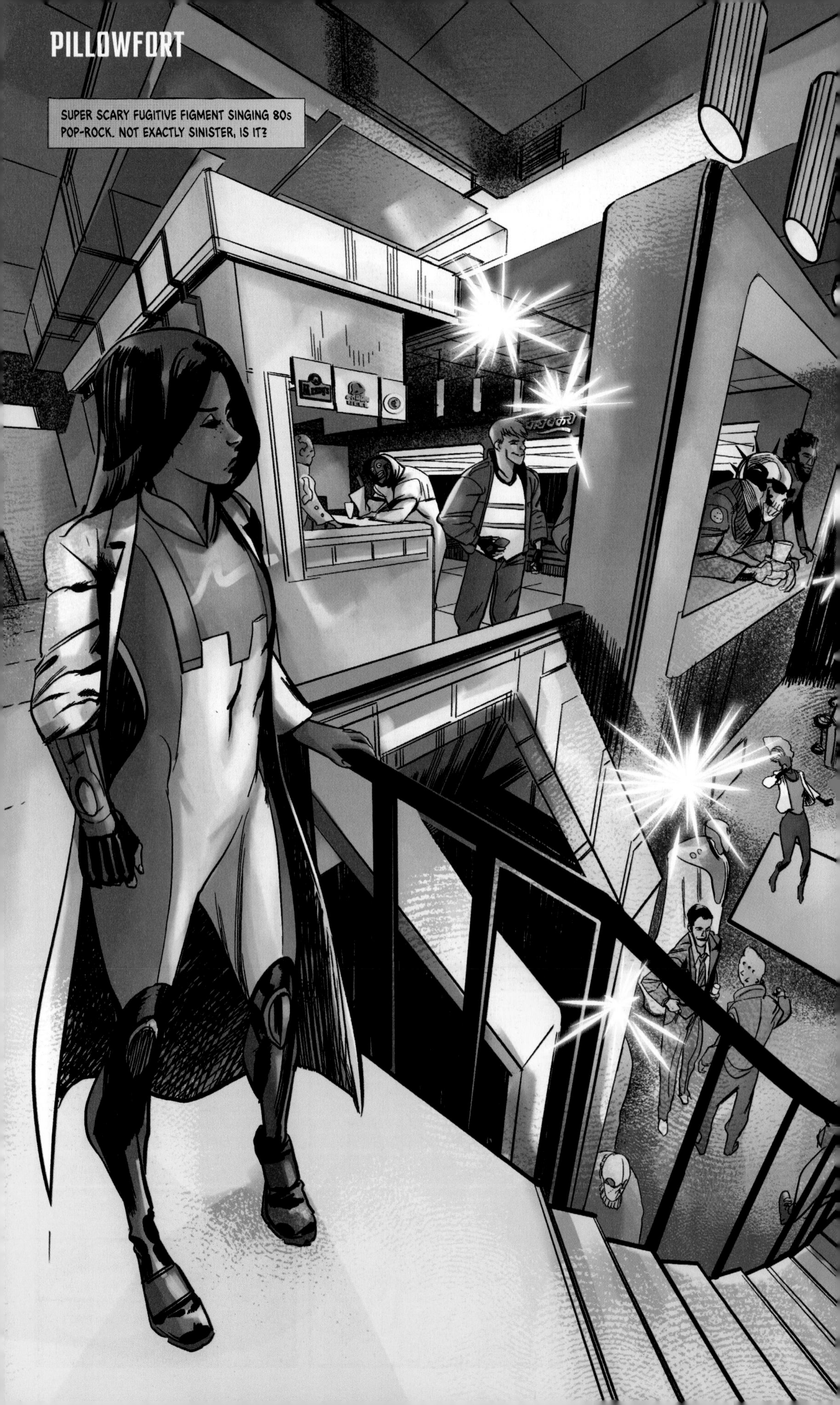
PILLOWFORT
SUPER SCARY FUGITIVE FIGMENT SINGING 80s POP-ROCK. NOT EXACTLY SINISTER, IS IT?

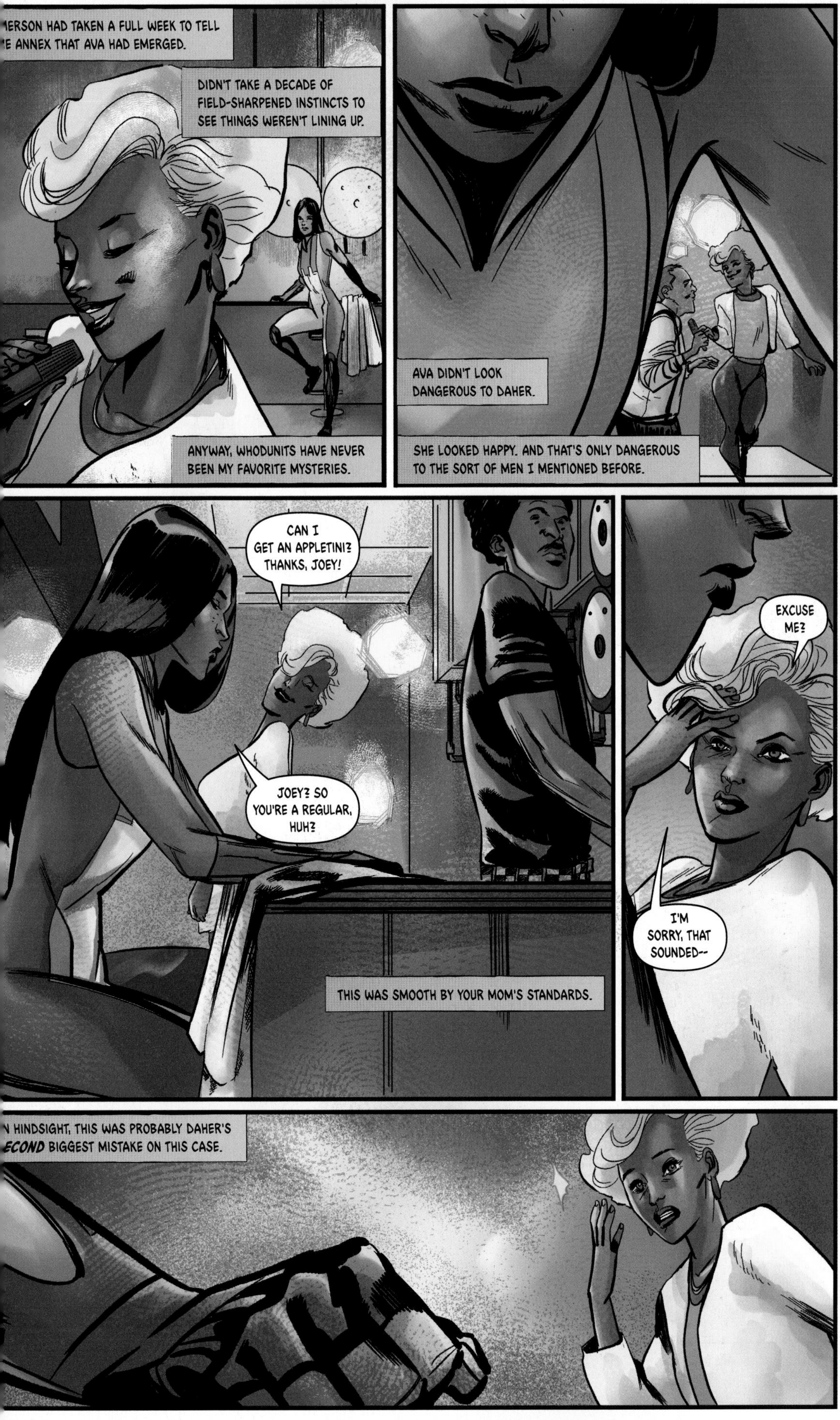

ERSON HAD TAKEN A FULL WEEK TO TELL
E ANNEX THAT AVA HAD EMERGED.
DIDN'T TAKE A DECADE OF FIELD-SHARPENED INSTINCTS TO SEE THINGS WEREN'T LINING UP.
ANYWAY, WHODUNITS HAVE NEVER BEEN MY FAVORITE MYSTERIES.
AVA DIDN'T LOOK DANGEROUS TO DAHER.
SHE LOOKED HAPPY. AND THAT'S ONLY DANGEROUS TO THE SORT OF MEN I MENTIONED BEFORE.
CAN I GET AN APPLETINI? THANKS, JOEY!
JOEY? SO YOU'RE A REGULAR, HUH?
THIS WAS SMOOTH BY YOUR MOM'S STANDARDS.
EXCUSE ME?
I'M SORRY, THAT SOUNDED--
N HINDSIGHT, THIS WAS PROBABLY DAHER'S
ECOND BIGGEST MISTAKE ON THIS CASE.

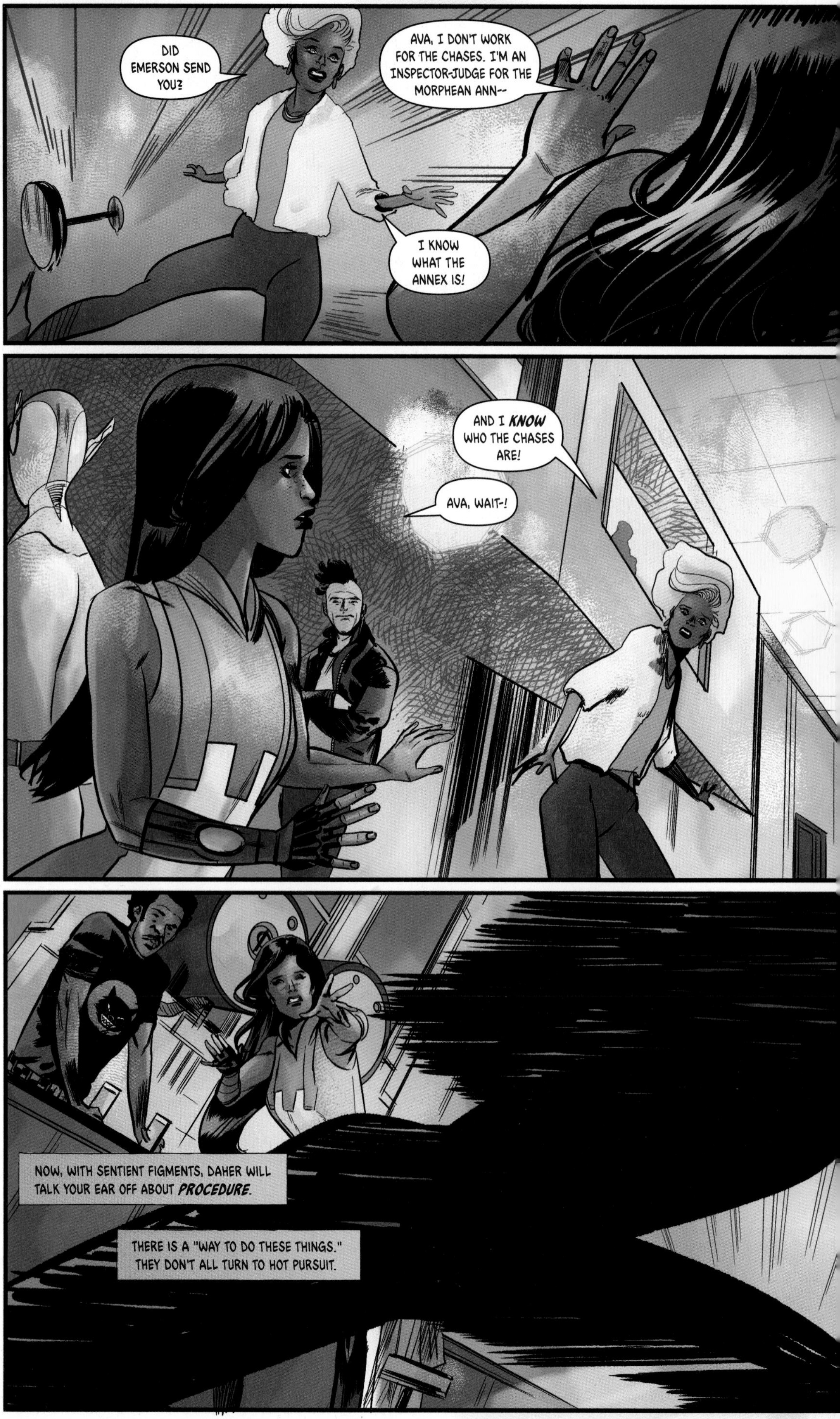
DID EMERSON SEND YOU?
AVA, I DON'T WORK FOR THE CHASES. I'M AN INSPECTOR-JUDGE FOR THE MORPHEAN ANN--
I KNOW WHAT THE ANNEX IS!
AND I KNOW WHO THE CHASES ARE!
AVA, WAIT-!
NOW, WITH SENTIENT FIGMENTS, DAHER WILL TALK YOUR EAR OFF ABOUT PROCEDURE.
THERE IS A "WAY TO DO THESE THINGS." THEY DON'T ALL TURN TO HOT PURSUIT.

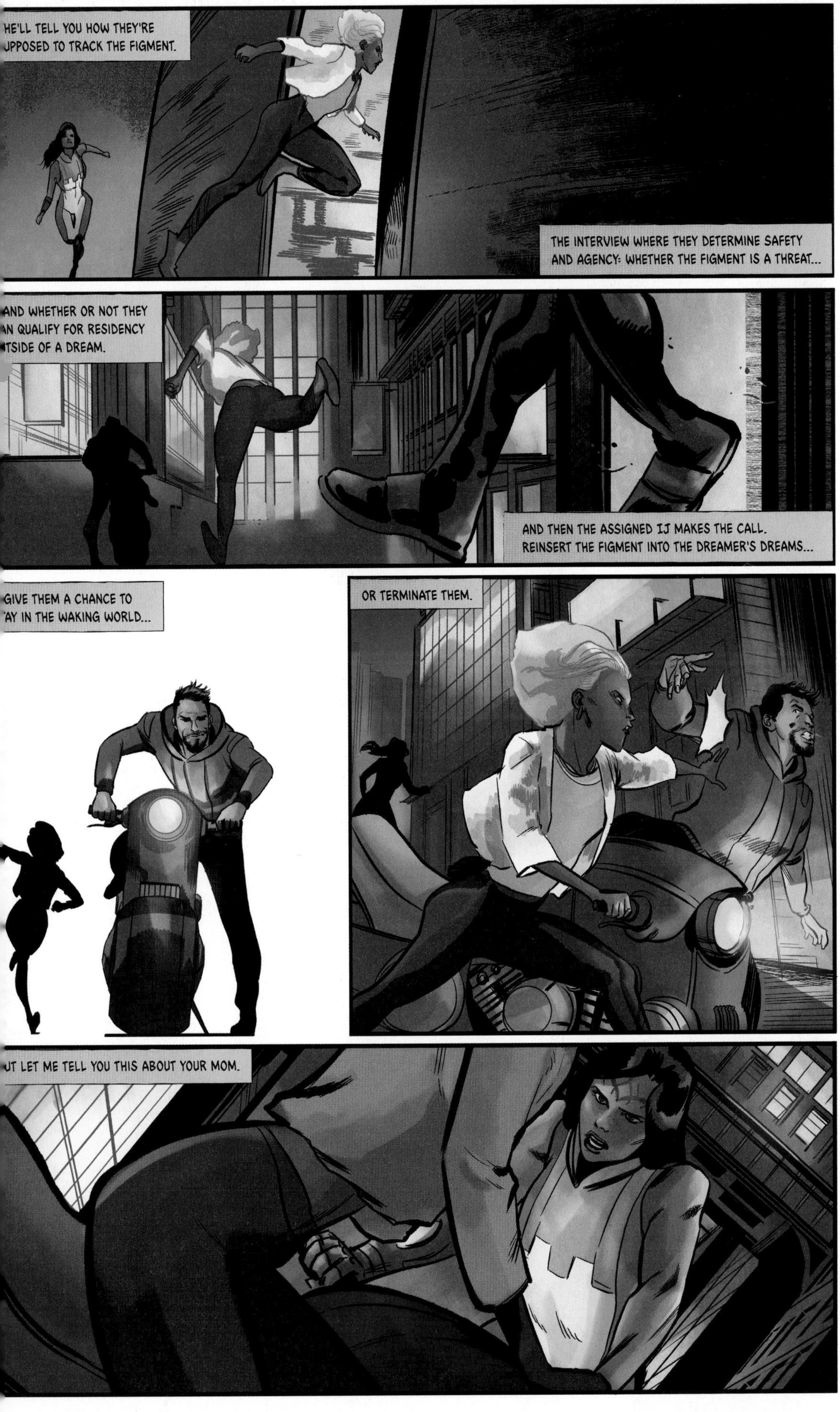
HE'LL TELL YOU HOW THEY'RE UPPOSED TO TRACK THE FIGMENT.
THE INTERVIEW WHERE THEY DETERMINE SAFETY AND AGENCY: WHETHER THE FIGMENT IS A THREAT...
AND WHETHER OR NOT THEY AN QUALIFY FOR RESIDENCY TSIDE OF A DREAM.
AND THEN THE ASSIGNED IJ MAKES THE CALL. REINSERT THE FIGMENT INTO THE DREAMER'S DREAMS...
GIVE THEM A CHANCE TO AY IN THE WAKING WORLD...
OR TERMINATE THEM.
UT LET ME TELL YOU THIS ABOUT YOUR MOM.

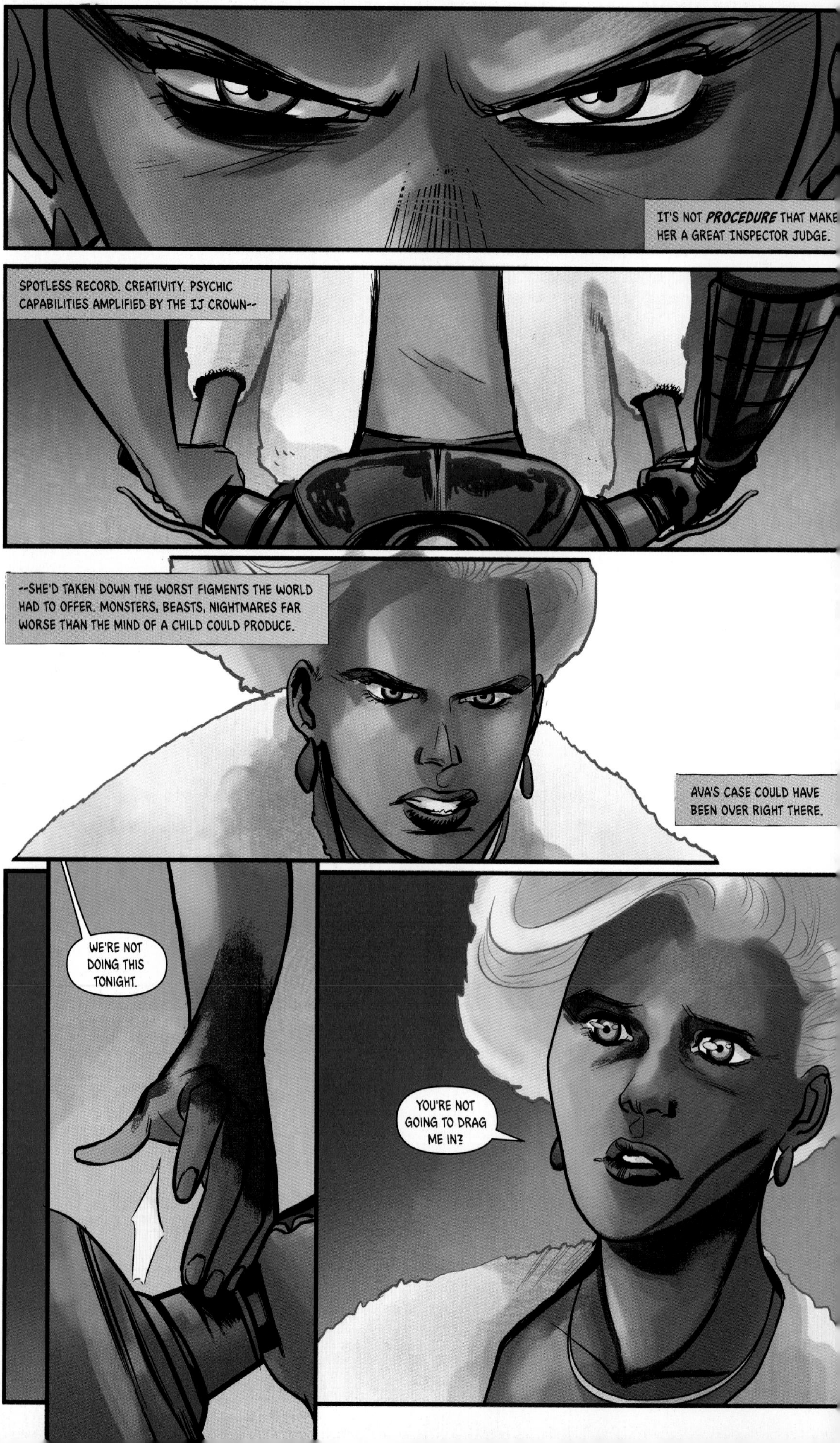
IT'S NOT *PROCEDURE* THAT MAKE HER A GREAT INSPECTOR JUDGE.
SPOTLESS RECORD. CREATIVITY. PSYCHIC CAPABILITIES AMPLIFIED BY THE IJ CROWN--
--SHE'D TAKEN DOWN THE WORST FIGMENTS THE WORLD HAD TO OFFER. MONSTERS, BEASTS, NIGHTMARES FAR WORSE THAN THE MIND OF A CHILD COULD PRODUCE.
AVA'S CASE COULD HAVE BEEN OVER RIGHT THERE.
WE'RE NOT DOING THIS TONIGHT.
YOU'RE NOT GOING TO DRAG ME IN?

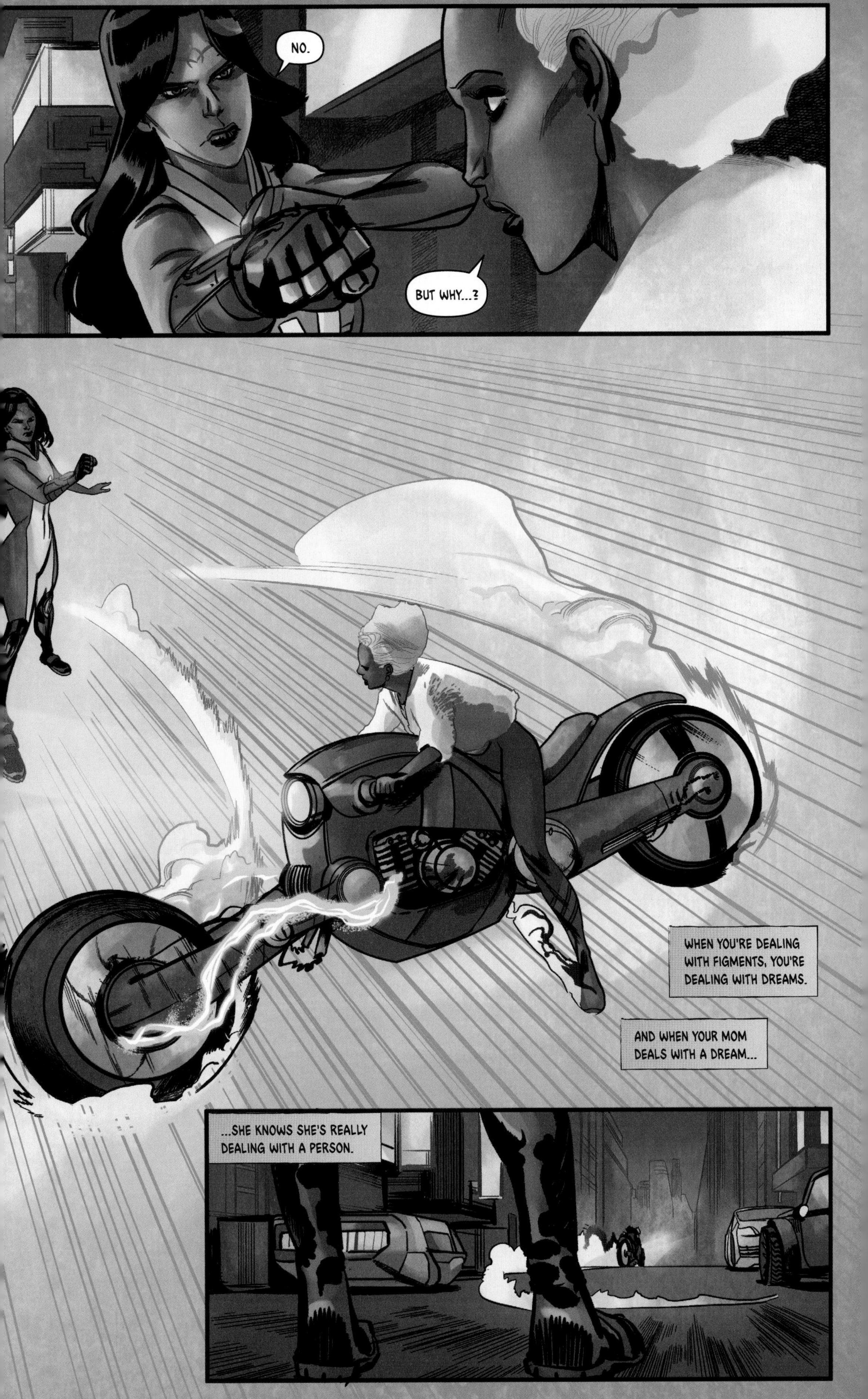
NO.
BUT WHY...?
WHEN YOU'RE DEALING WITH FIGMENTS, YOU'RE DEALING WITH DREAMS.
AND WHEN YOUR MOM DEALS WITH A DREAM...
...SHE KNOWS SHE'S REALLY DEALING WITH A PERSON.

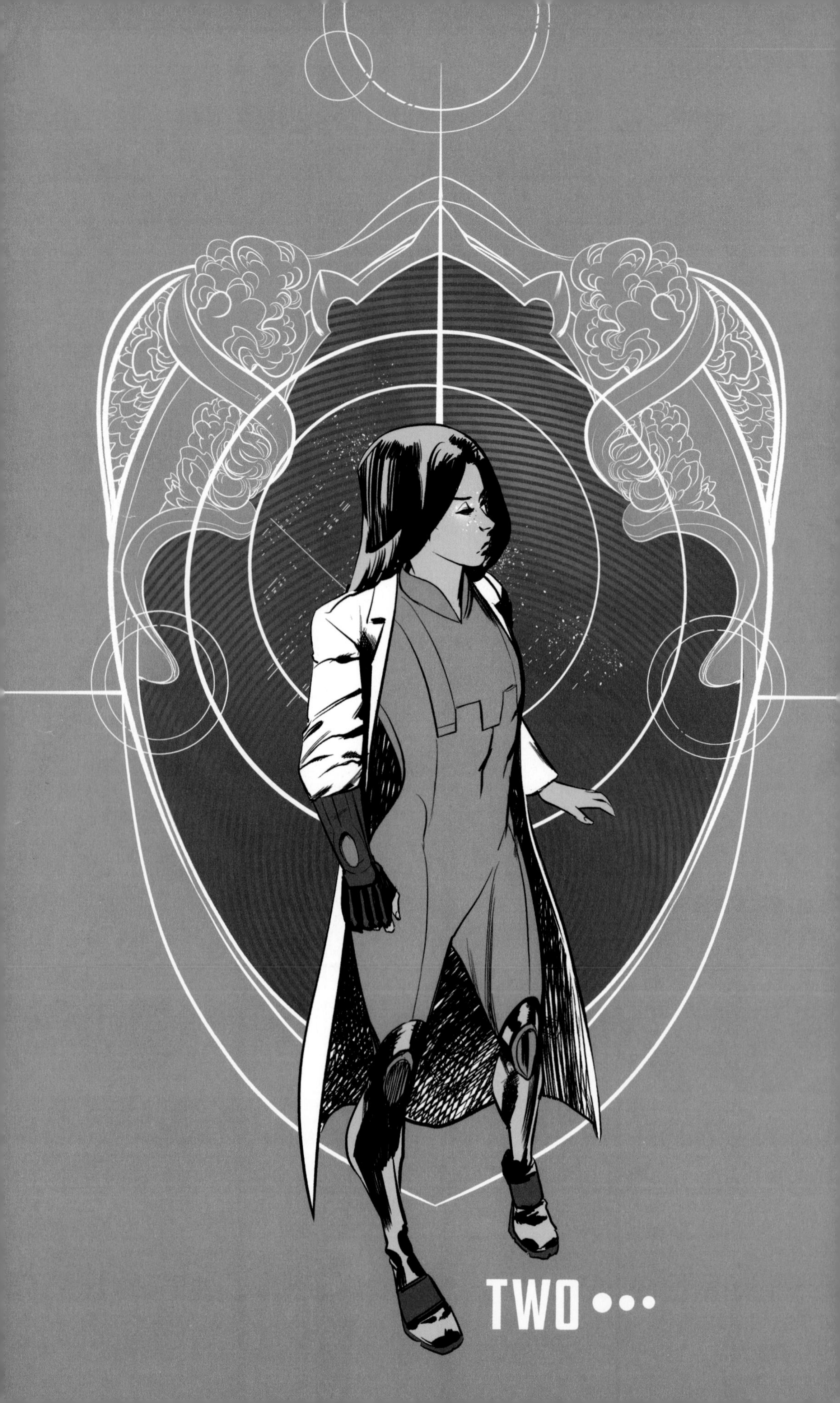

TWO

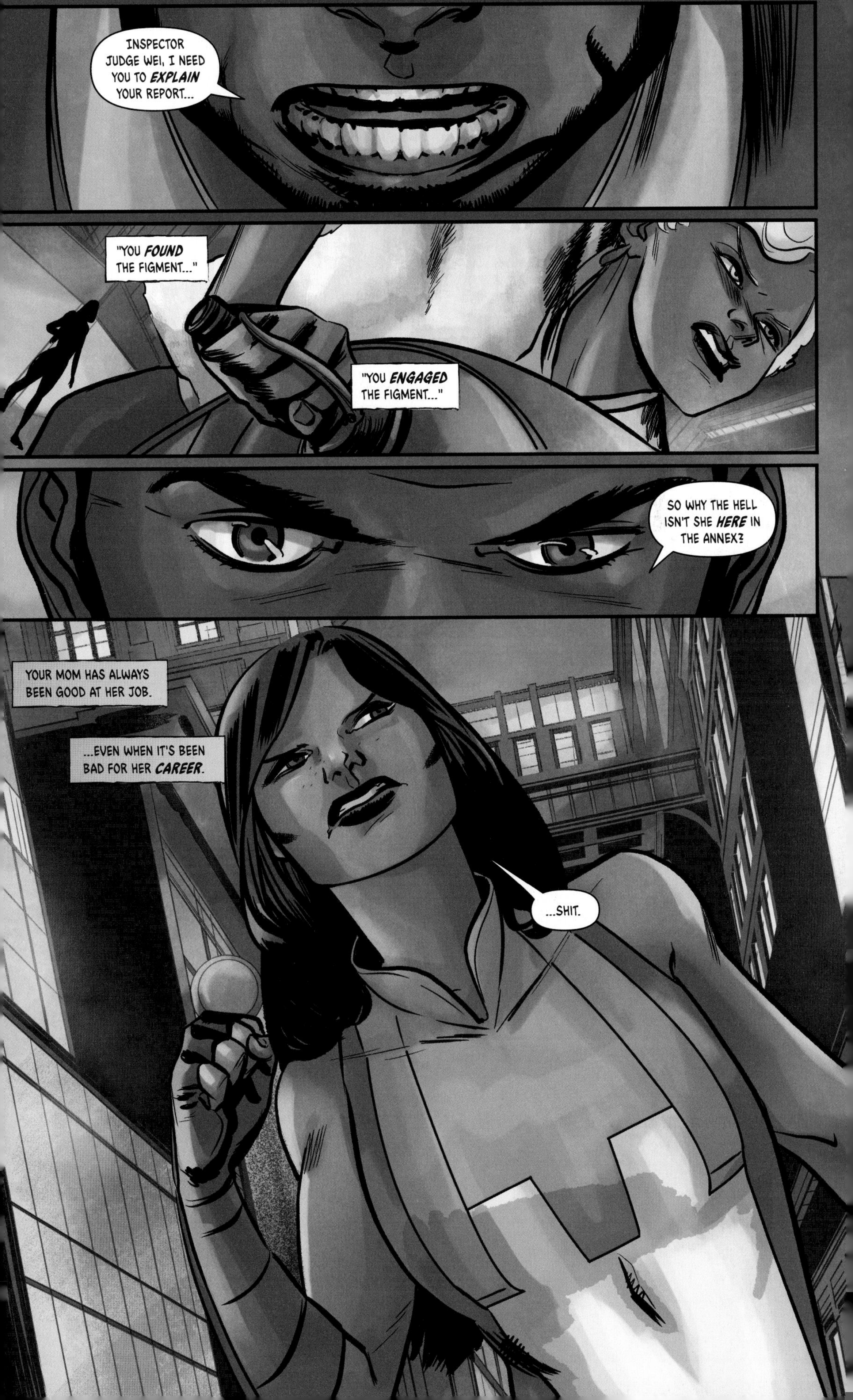
INSPECTOR JUDGE WEI, I NEED YOU TO EXPLAIN YOUR REPORT...
"YOU FOUND THE FIGMENT..."
"YOU ENGAGED THE FIGMENT..."
SO WHY THE HELL ISN'T SHE HERE IN THE ANNEX?
YOUR MOM HAS ALWAYS BEEN GOOD AT HER JOB.
...EVEN WHEN IT'S BEEN BAD FOR HER CAREER.
...SHIT.

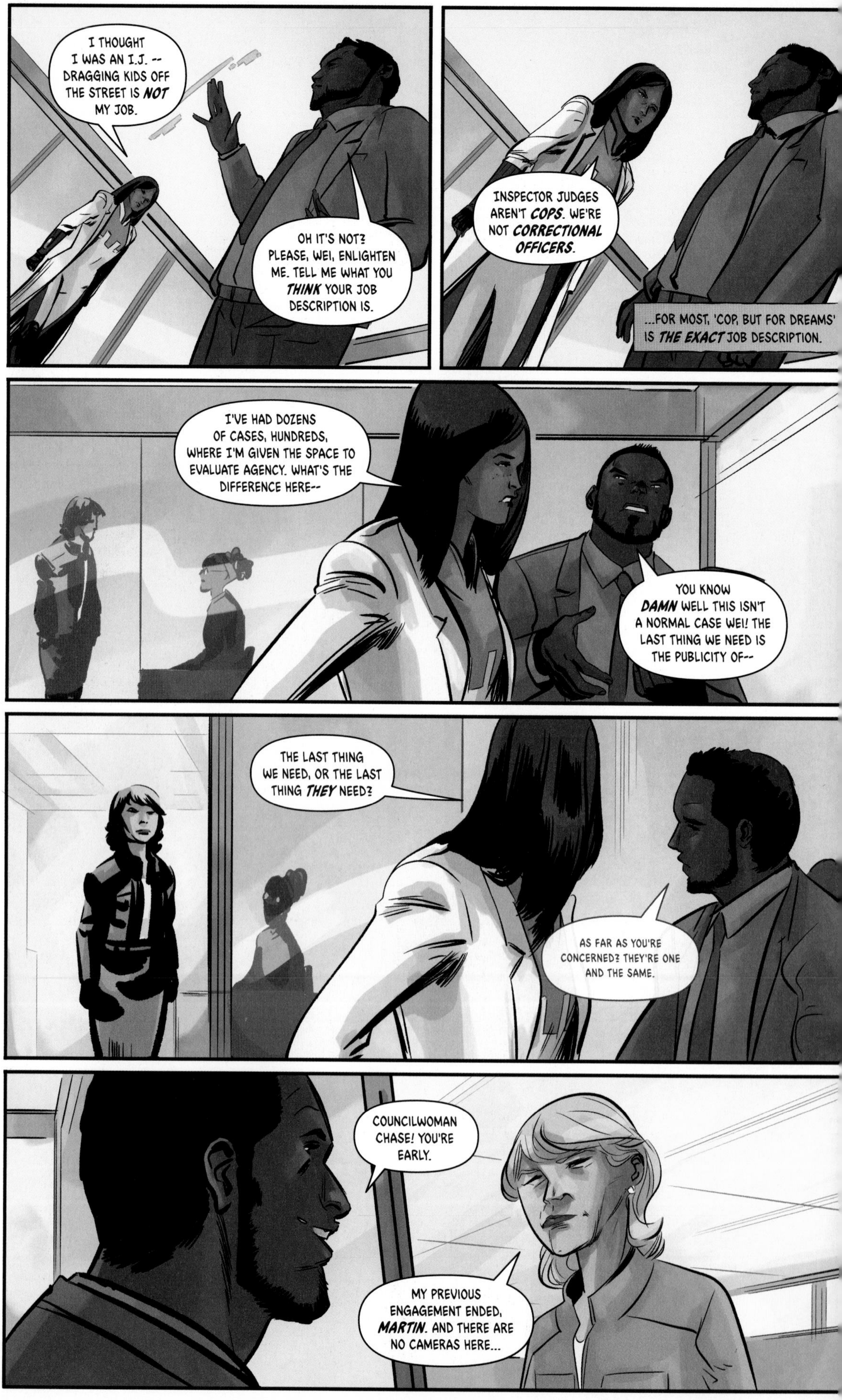
I THOUGHT I WAS AN I.J. -- DRAGGING KIDS OFF THE STREET IS NOT MY JOB.
OH IT'S NOT? PLEASE, WEI, ENLIGHTEN ME. TELL ME WHAT YOU THINK YOUR JOB DESCRIPTION IS.
INSPECTOR JUDGES AREN'T COPS. WE'RE NOT CORRECTIONAL OFFICERS.
...FOR MOST, 'COP, BUT FOR DREAMS' IS THE EXACT JOB DESCRIPTION.
I'VE HAD DOZENS OF CASES, HUNDREDS, WHERE I'M GIVEN THE SPACE TO EVALUATE AGENCY. WHAT'S THE DIFFERENCE HERE--
YOU KNOW DAMN WELL THIS ISN'T A NORMAL CASE WEI! THE LAST THING WE NEED IS THE PUBLICITY OF--
THE LAST THING WE NEED, OR THE LAST THING THEY NEED?
AS FAR AS YOU'RE CONCERNED? THEY'RE ONE AND THE SAME.
COUNCILWOMAN CHASE! YOU'RE EARLY.
MY PREVIOUS ENGAGEMENT ENDED, MARTIN. AND THERE ARE NO CAMERAS HERE...

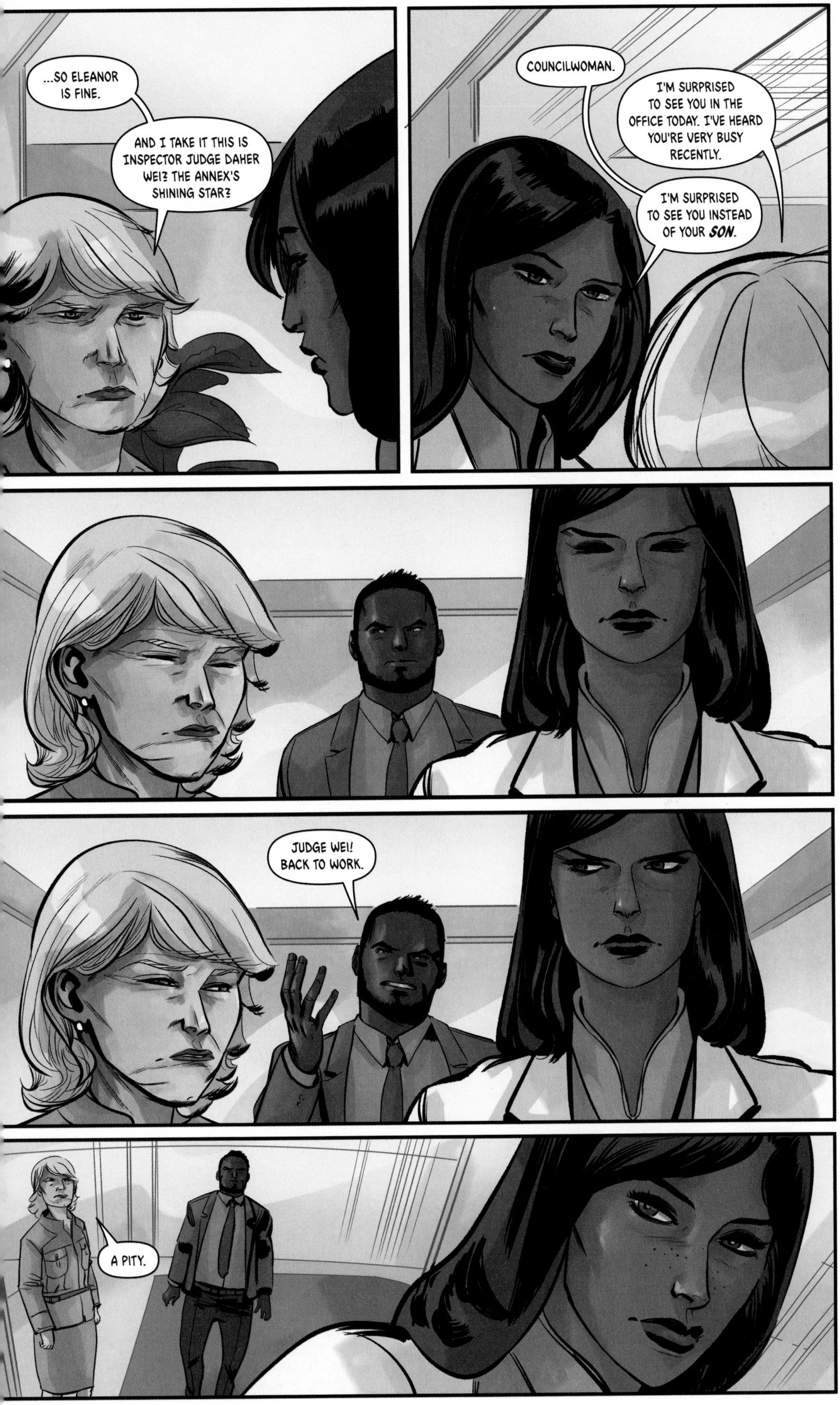
...SO ELEANOR IS FINE.
AND I TAKE IT THIS IS INSPECTOR JUDGE DAHER WEI? THE ANNEX'S SHINING STAR?
COUNCILWOMAN.
I'M SURPRISED TO SEE YOU IN THE OFFICE TODAY. I'VE HEARD YOU'RE VERY BUSY RECENTLY.
I'M SURPRISED TO SEE YOU INSTEAD OF YOUR ***SON***.
JUDGE WEI! BACK TO WORK.
A PITY.

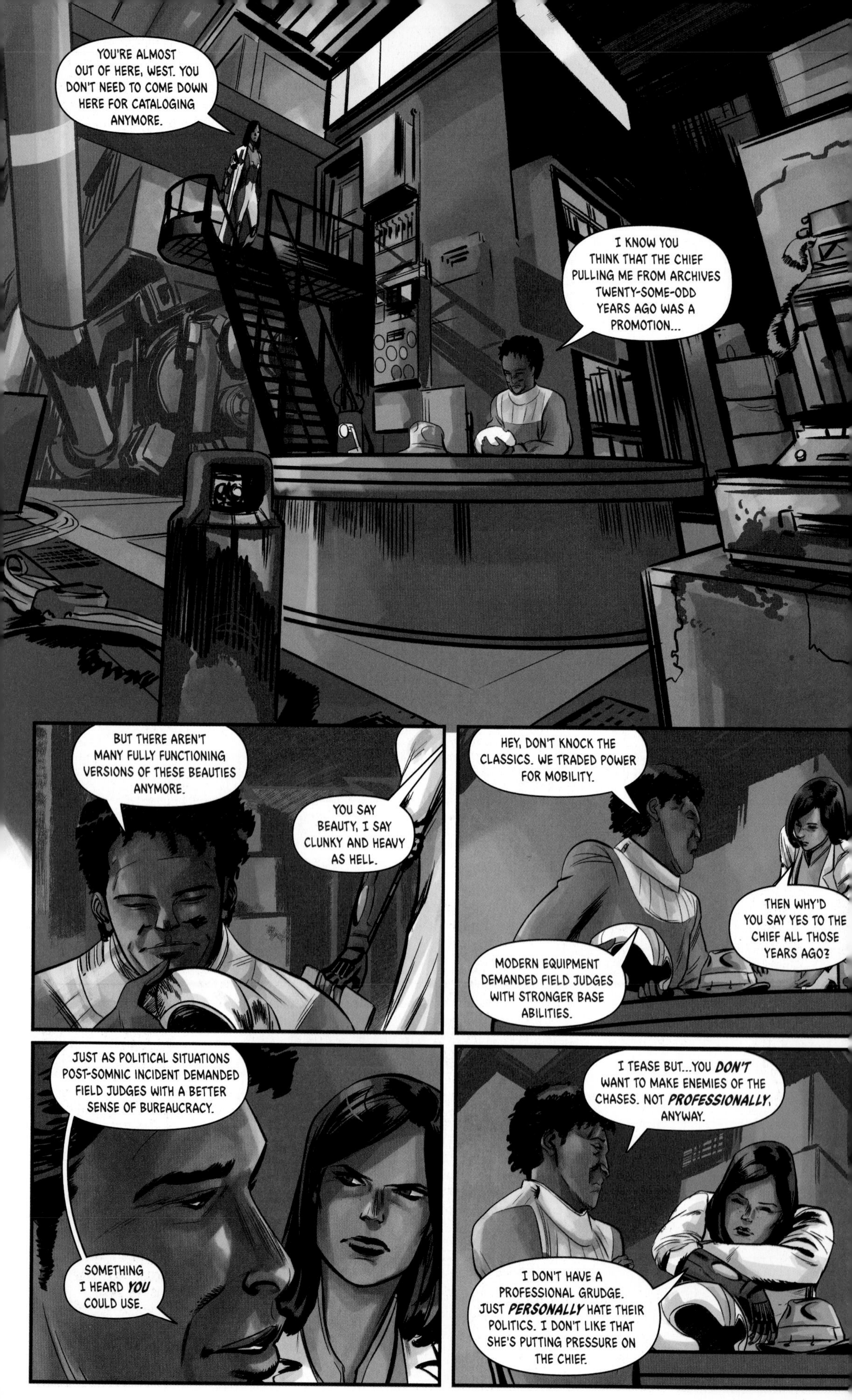
YOU'RE ALMOST OUT OF HERE, WEST. YOU DON'T NEED TO COME DOWN HERE FOR CATALOGING ANYMORE.
I KNOW YOU THINK THAT THE CHIEF PULLING ME FROM ARCHIVES TWENTY-SOME-ODD YEARS AGO WAS A PROMOTION...
BUT THERE AREN'T MANY FULLY FUNCTIONING VERSIONS OF THESE BEAUTIES ANYMORE.
YOU SAY BEAUTY, I SAY CLUNKY AND HEAVY AS HELL.
HEY, DON'T KNOCK THE CLASSICS. WE TRADED POWER FOR MOBILITY.
MODERN EQUIPMENT DEMANDED FIELD JUDGES WITH STRONGER BASE ABILITIES.
THEN WHY'D YOU SAY YES TO THE CHIEF ALL THOSE YEARS AGO?
JUST AS POLITICAL SITUATIONS POST-SOMNIC INCIDENT DEMANDED FIELD JUDGES WITH A BETTER SENSE OF BUREAUCRACY.
SOMETHING I HEARD *YOU* COULD USE.
I TEASE BUT...YOU *DON'T* WANT TO MAKE ENEMIES OF THE CHASES. NOT *PROFESSIONALLY*, ANYWAY.
I DON'T HAVE A PROFESSIONAL GRUDGE. JUST *PERSONALLY* HATE THEIR POLITICS. I DON'T LIKE THAT SHE'S PUTTING PRESSURE ON THE CHIEF.

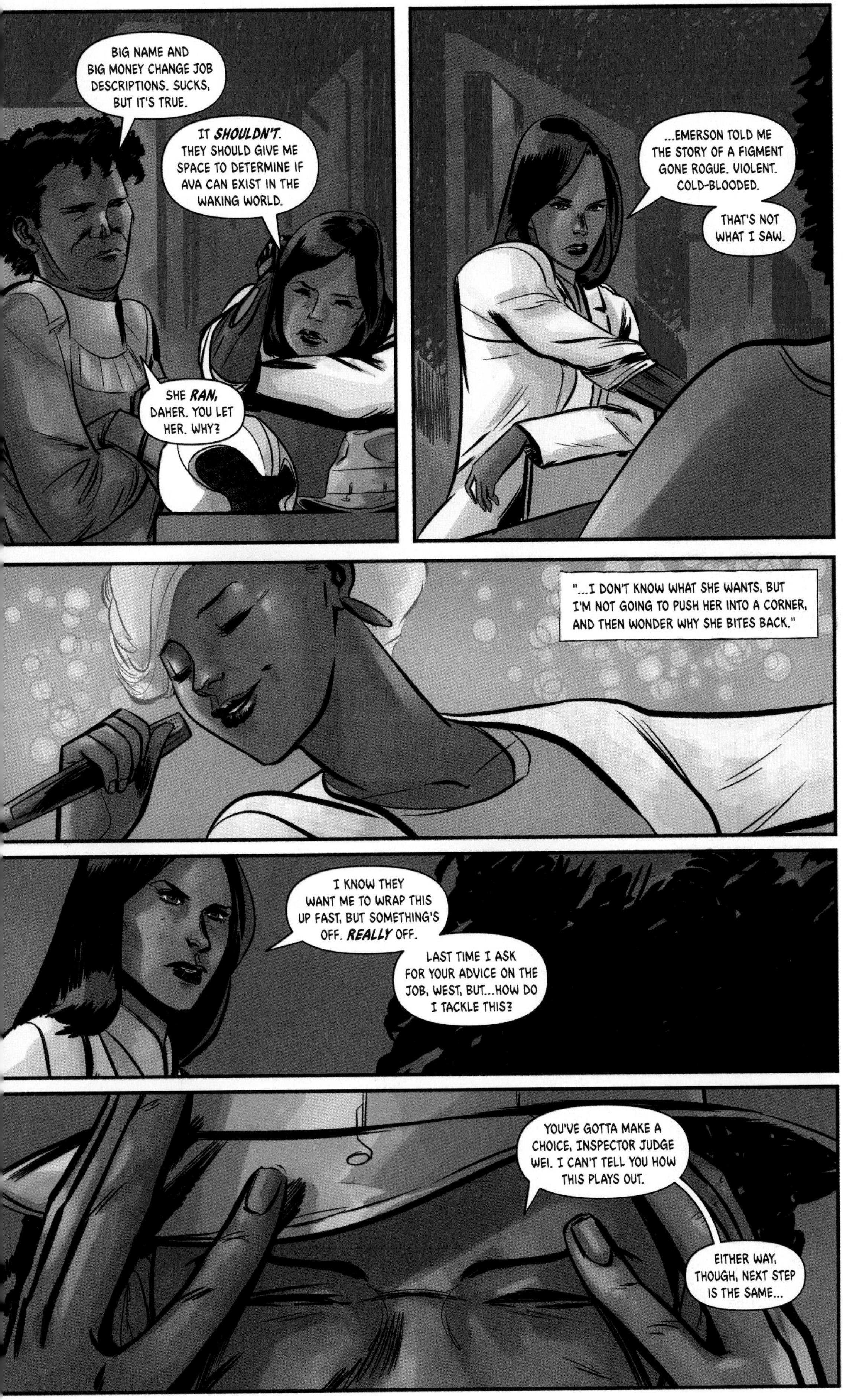
BIG NAME AND BIG MONEY CHANGE JOB DESCRIPTIONS. SUCKS, BUT IT'S TRUE.
IT SHOULDN'T. THEY SHOULD GIVE ME SPACE TO DETERMINE IF AVA CAN EXIST IN THE WAKING WORLD.
SHE RAN, DAHER. YOU LET HER. WHY?
...EMERSON TOLD ME THE STORY OF A FIGMENT GONE ROGUE. VIOLENT. COLD-BLOODED.
THAT'S NOT WHAT I SAW.
"...I DON'T KNOW WHAT SHE WANTS, BUT I'M NOT GOING TO PUSH HER INTO A CORNER, AND THEN WONDER WHY SHE BITES BACK."
I KNOW THEY WANT ME TO WRAP THIS UP FAST, BUT SOMETHING'S OFF. REALLY OFF.
LAST TIME I ASK FOR YOUR ADVICE ON THE JOB, WEST, BUT...HOW DO I TACKLE THIS?
YOU'VE GOTTA MAKE A CHOICE, INSPECTOR JUDGE WEI. I CAN'T TELL YOU HOW THIS PLAYS OUT.
EITHER WAY, THOUGH, NEXT STEP IS THE SAME...

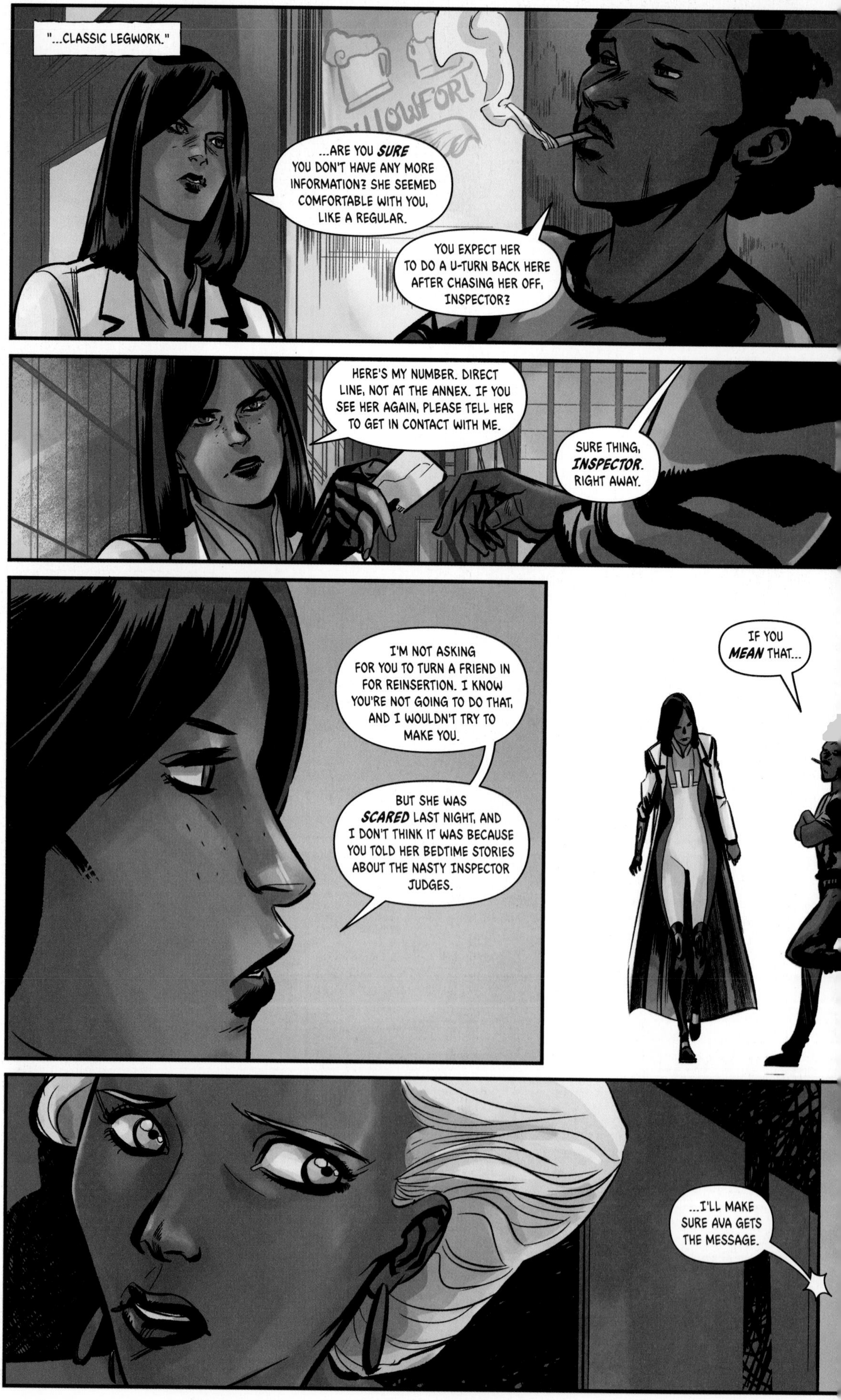
"...CLASSIC LEGWORK."
...ARE YOU SURE YOU DON'T HAVE ANY MORE INFORMATION? SHE SEEMED COMFORTABLE WITH YOU, LIKE A REGULAR.
YOU EXPECT HER TO DO A U-TURN BACK HERE AFTER CHASING HER OFF, INSPECTOR?
HERE'S MY NUMBER. DIRECT LINE, NOT AT THE ANNEX. IF YOU SEE HER AGAIN, PLEASE TELL HER TO GET IN CONTACT WITH ME.
SURE THING, INSPECTOR. RIGHT AWAY.
I'M NOT ASKING FOR YOU TO TURN A FRIEND IN FOR REINSERTION. I KNOW YOU'RE NOT GOING TO DO THAT, AND I WOULDN'T TRY TO MAKE YOU.
BUT SHE WAS SCARED LAST NIGHT, AND I DON'T THINK IT WAS BECAUSE YOU TOLD HER BEDTIME STORIES ABOUT THE NASTY INSPECTOR JUDGES.
IF YOU MEAN THAT...
...I'LL MAKE SURE AVA GETS THE MESSAGE.

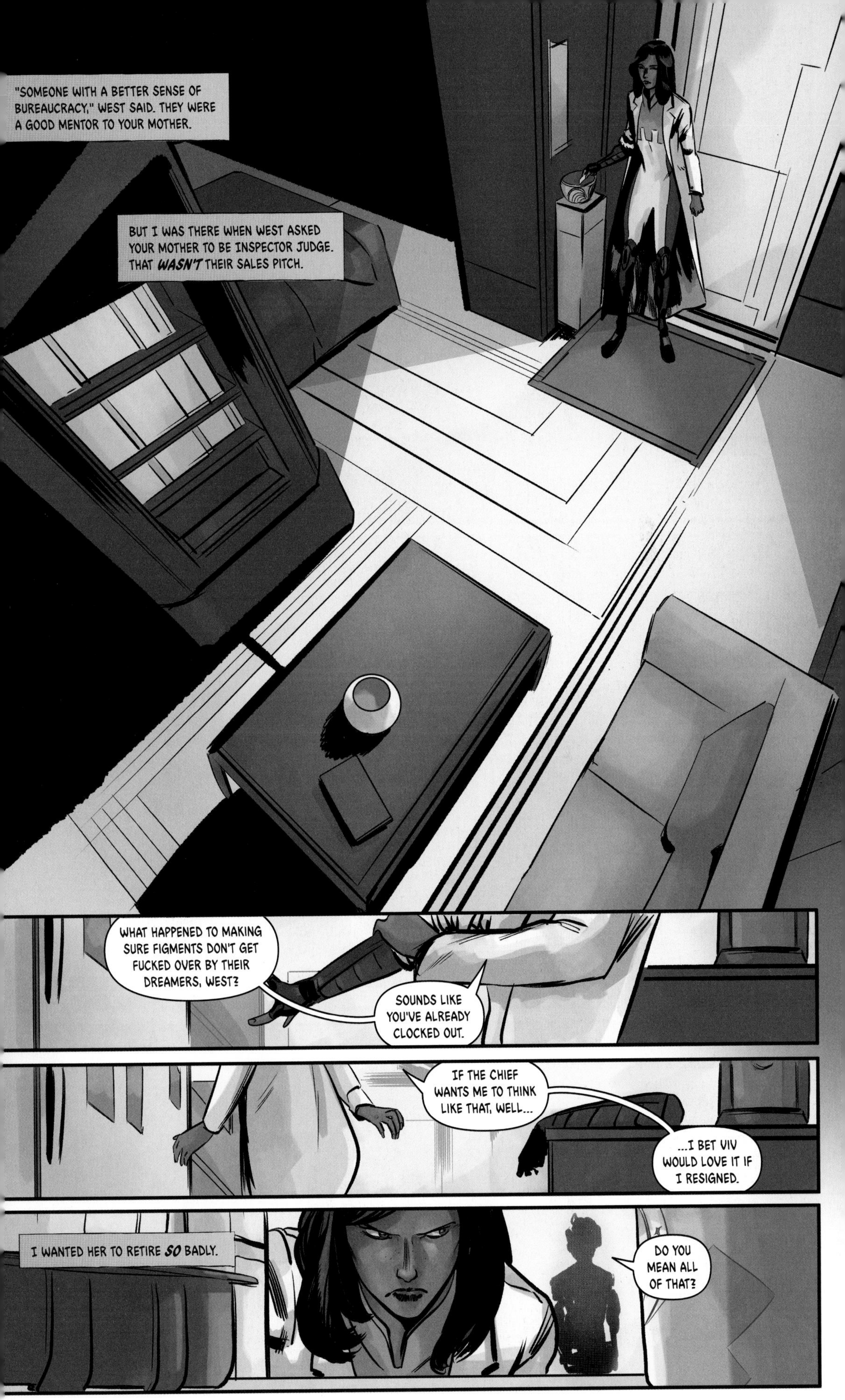
"SOMEONE WITH A BETTER SENSE OF BUREAUCRACY," WEST SAID. THEY WERE A GOOD MENTOR TO YOUR MOTHER.
BUT I WAS THERE WHEN WEST ASKED YOUR MOTHER TO BE INSPECTOR JUDGE. THAT *WASN'T* THEIR SALES PITCH.
WHAT HAPPENED TO MAKING SURE FIGMENTS DON'T GET FUCKED OVER BY THEIR DREAMERS, WEST?
SOUNDS LIKE YOU'VE ALREADY CLOCKED OUT.
IF THE CHIEF WANTS ME TO THINK LIKE THAT, WELL...
...I BET VIV WOULD LOVE IT IF I RESIGNED.
I WANTED HER TO RETIRE *SO* BADLY.
DO YOU MEAN ALL OF THAT?

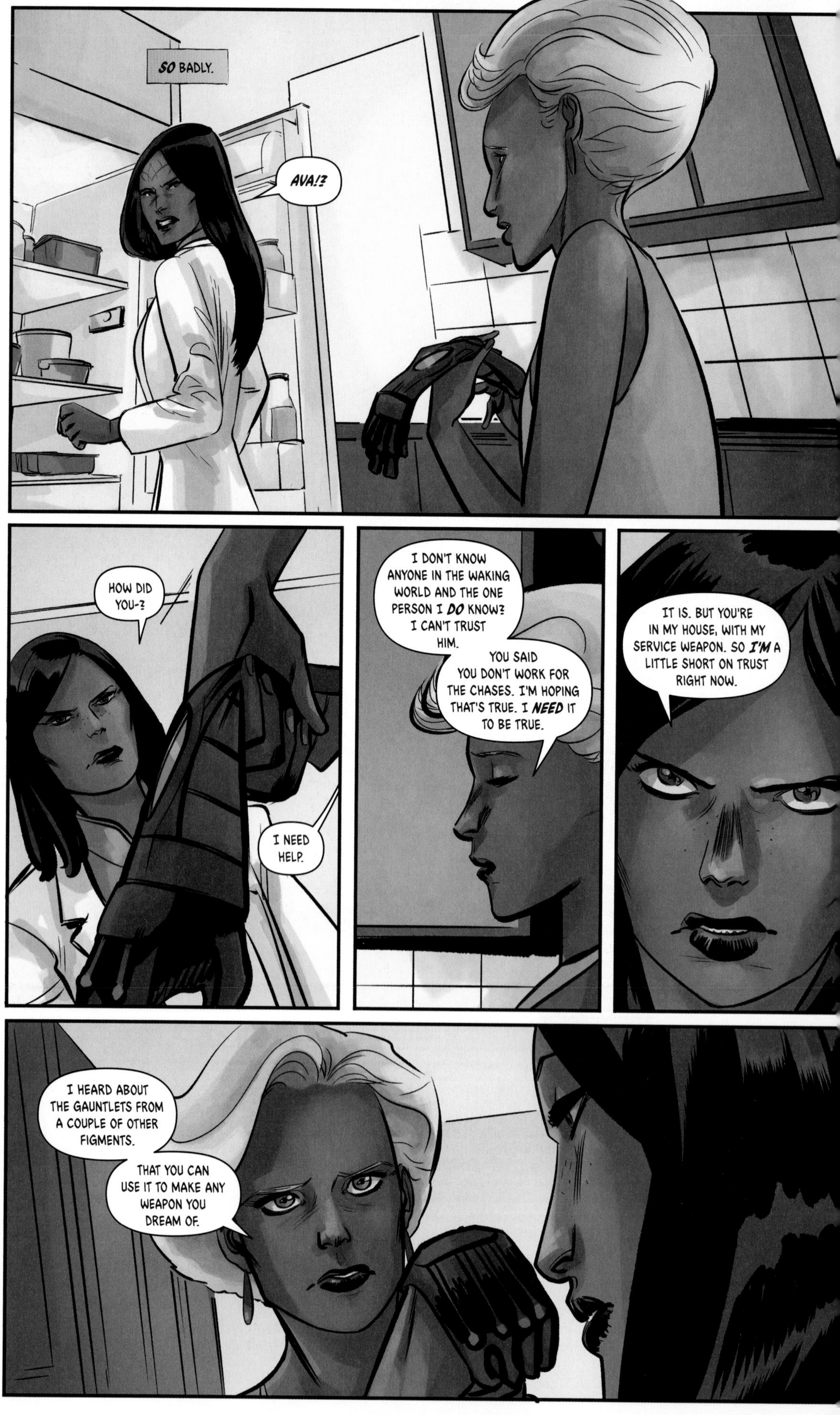

SO BADLY.
AVA!?
HOW DID YOU-?
I NEED HELP.
I DON'T KNOW ANYONE IN THE WAKING WORLD AND THE ONE PERSON I DO KNOW? I CAN'T TRUST HIM.
YOU SAID YOU DON'T WORK FOR THE CHASES. I'M HOPING THAT'S TRUE. I NEED IT TO BE TRUE.
IT IS. BUT YOU'RE IN MY HOUSE, WITH MY SERVICE WEAPON. SO I'M A LITTLE SHORT ON TRUST RIGHT NOW.
I HEARD ABOUT THE GAUNTLETS FROM A COUPLE OF OTHER FIGMENTS.
THAT YOU CAN USE IT TO MAKE ANY WEAPON YOU DREAM OF.

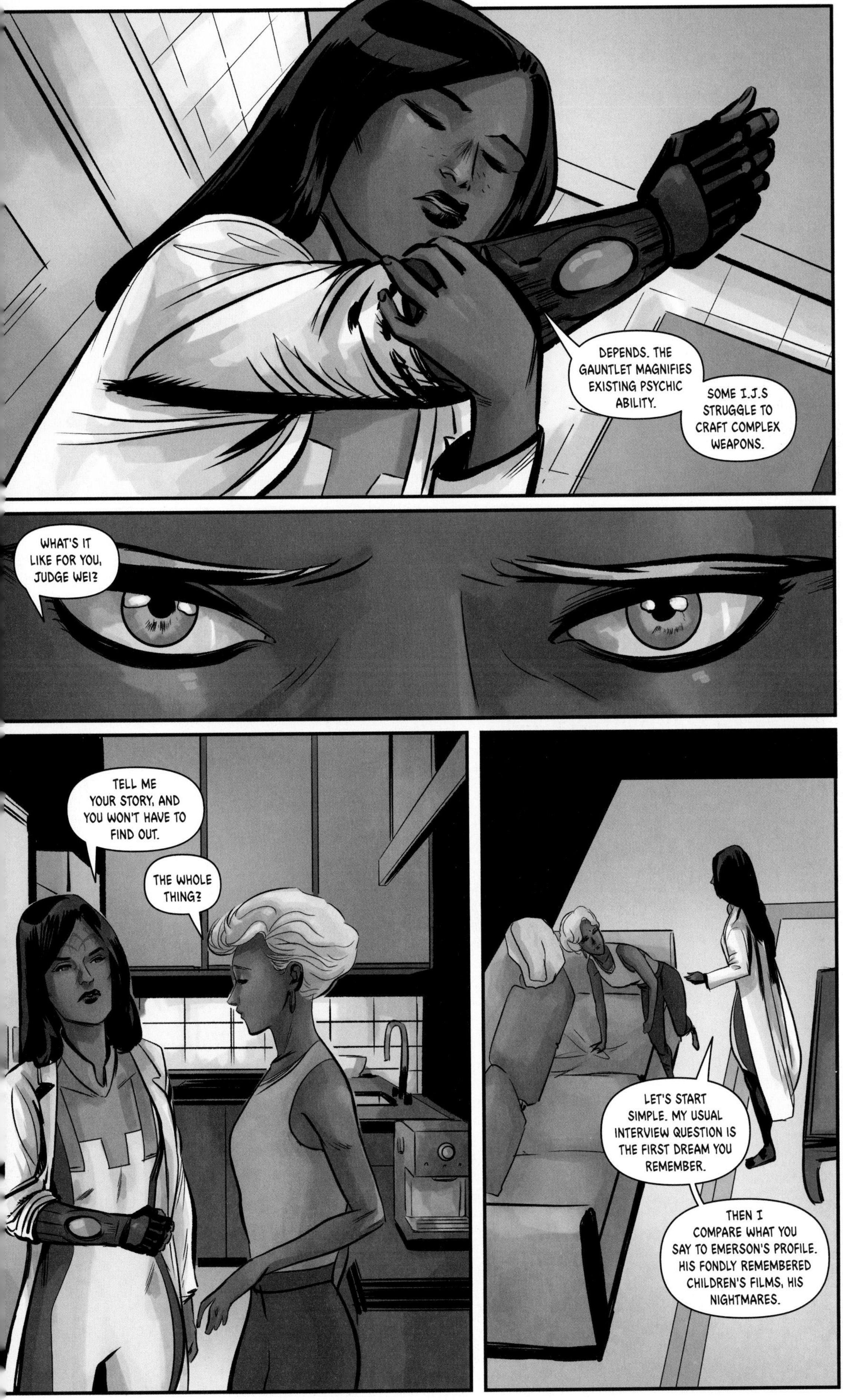
DEPENDS. THE GAUNTLET MAGNIFIES EXISTING PSYCHIC ABILITY.
SOME I.J.S STRUGGLE TO CRAFT COMPLEX WEAPONS.
WHAT'S IT LIKE FOR YOU, JUDGE WEI?
TELL ME YOUR STORY, AND YOU WON'T HAVE TO FIND OUT.
THE WHOLE THING?
LET'S START SIMPLE. MY USUAL INTERVIEW QUESTION IS THE FIRST DREAM YOU REMEMBER.
THEN I COMPARE WHAT YOU SAY TO EMERSON'S PROFILE. HIS FONDLY REMEMBERED CHILDREN'S FILMS, HIS NIGHTMARES.

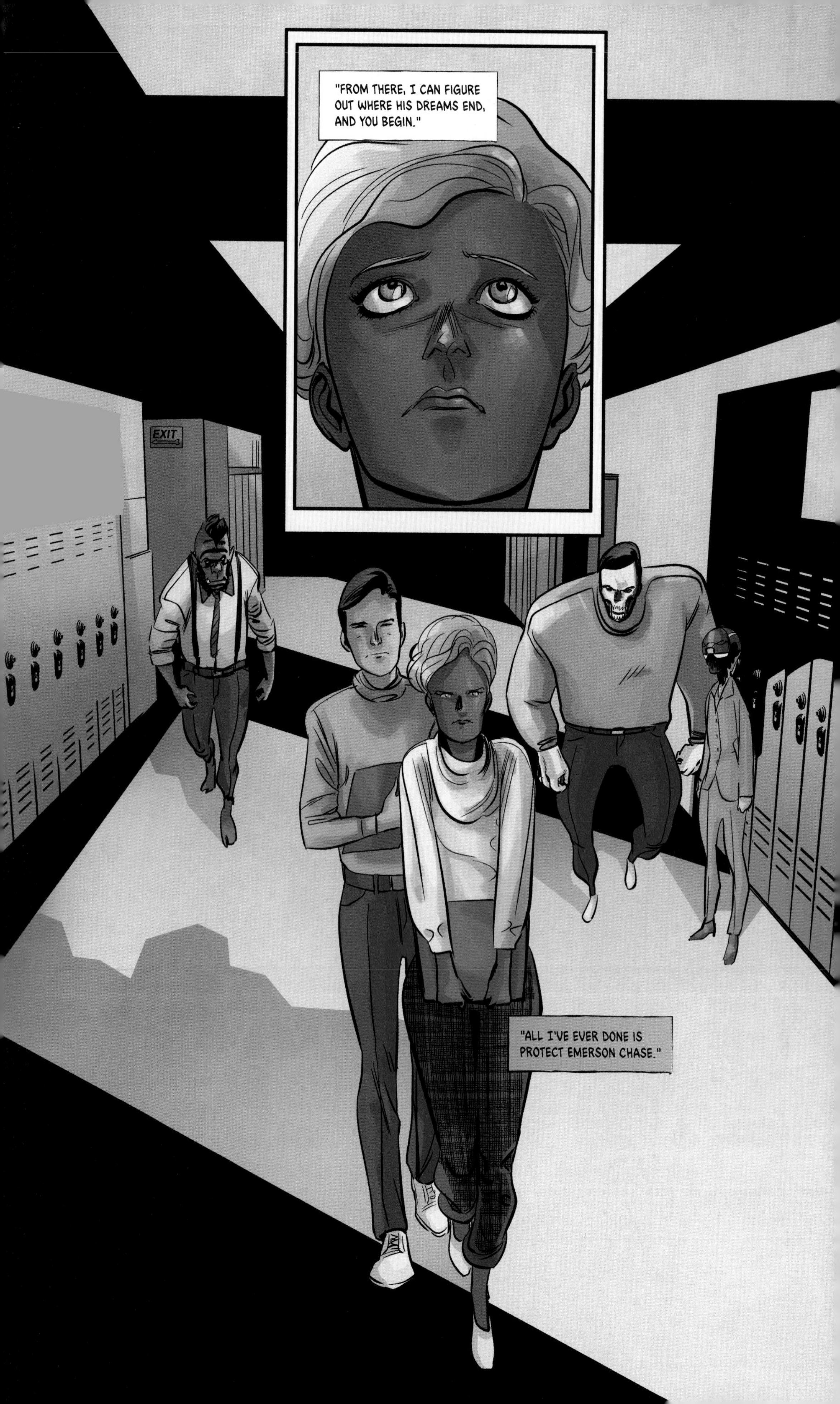
"FROM THERE, I CAN FIGURE OUT WHERE HIS DREAMS END, AND YOU BEGIN."
EXIT
"ALL I'VE EVER DONE IS PROTECT EMERSON CHASE."

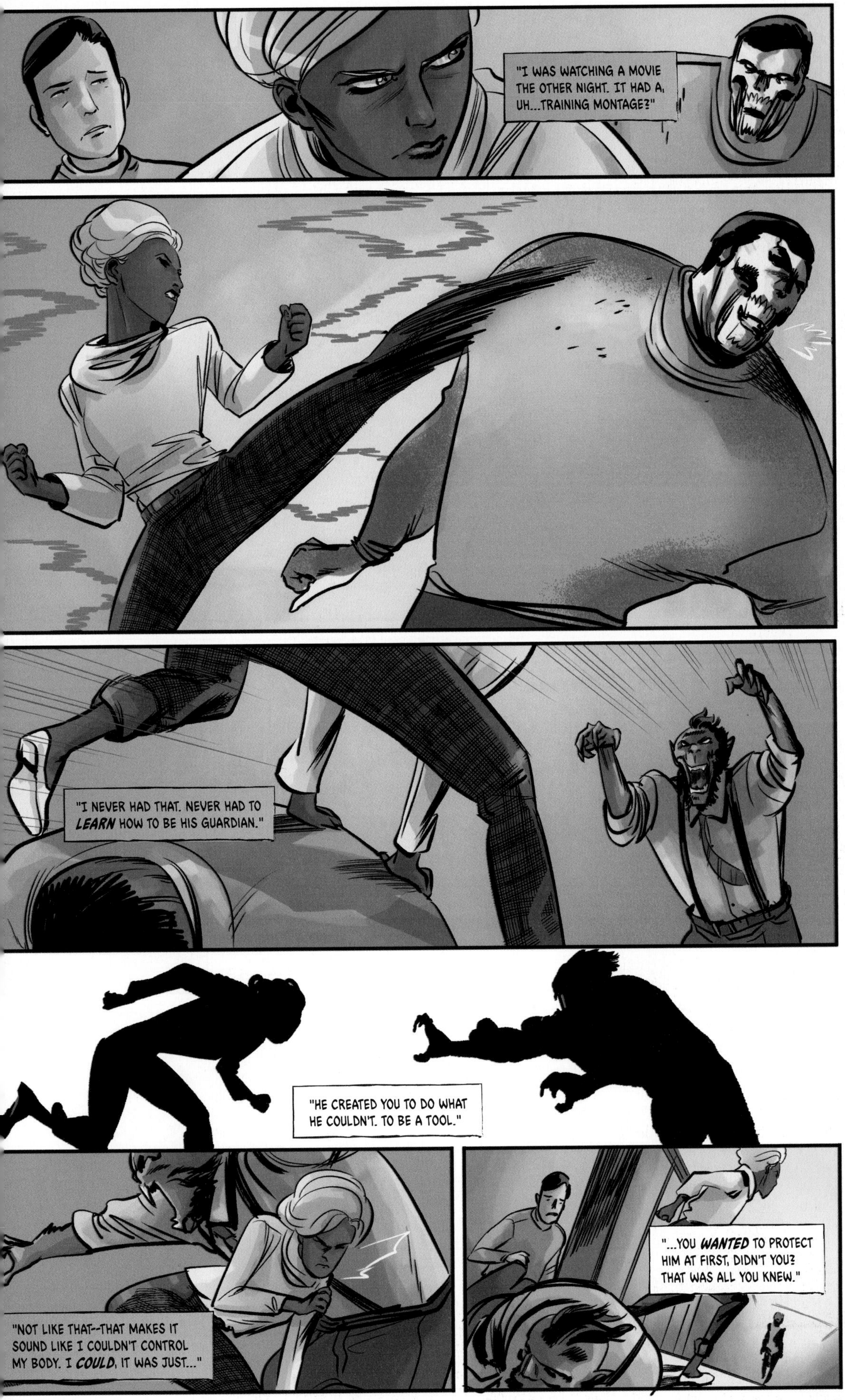

"I WAS WATCHING A MOVIE THE OTHER NIGHT. IT HAD A, UH...TRAINING MONTAGE?"
"I NEVER HAD THAT. NEVER HAD TO *LEARN* HOW TO BE HIS GUARDIAN."
"HE CREATED YOU TO DO WHAT HE COULDN'T. TO BE A TOOL."
"NOT LIKE THAT--THAT MAKES IT SOUND LIKE I COULDN'T CONTROL MY BODY. I *COULD*, IT WAS JUST..."
"...YOU *WANTED* TO PROTECT HIM AT FIRST, DIDN'T YOU? THAT WAS ALL YOU KNEW."

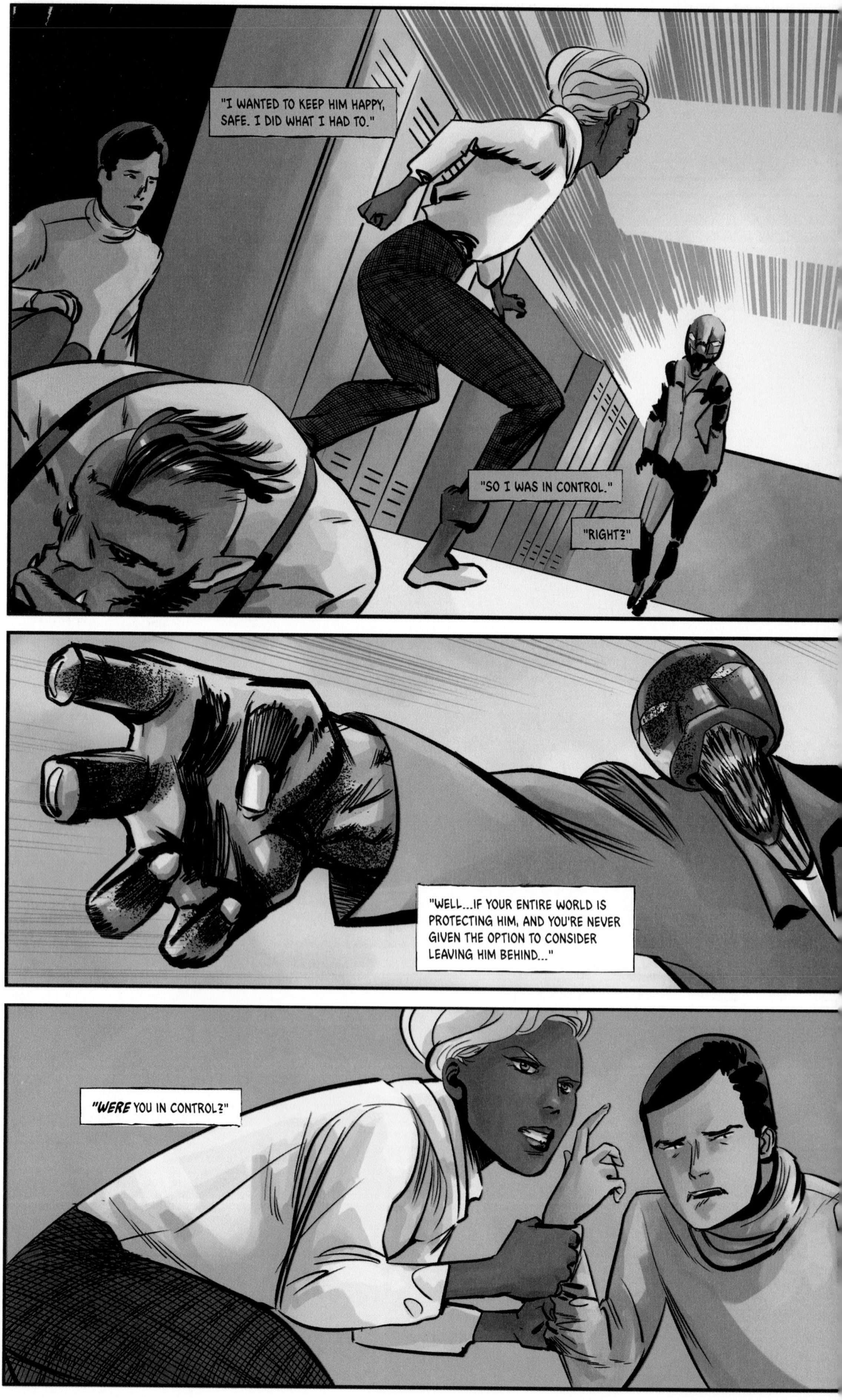
"I WANTED TO KEEP HIM HAPPY, SAFE. I DID WHAT I HAD TO."
"SO I WAS IN CONTROL."
"RIGHT?"
"WELL...IF YOUR ENTIRE WORLD IS PROTECTING HIM, AND YOU'RE NEVER GIVEN THE OPTION TO CONSIDER LEAVING HIM BEHIND..."
"*WERE* YOU IN CONTROL?"

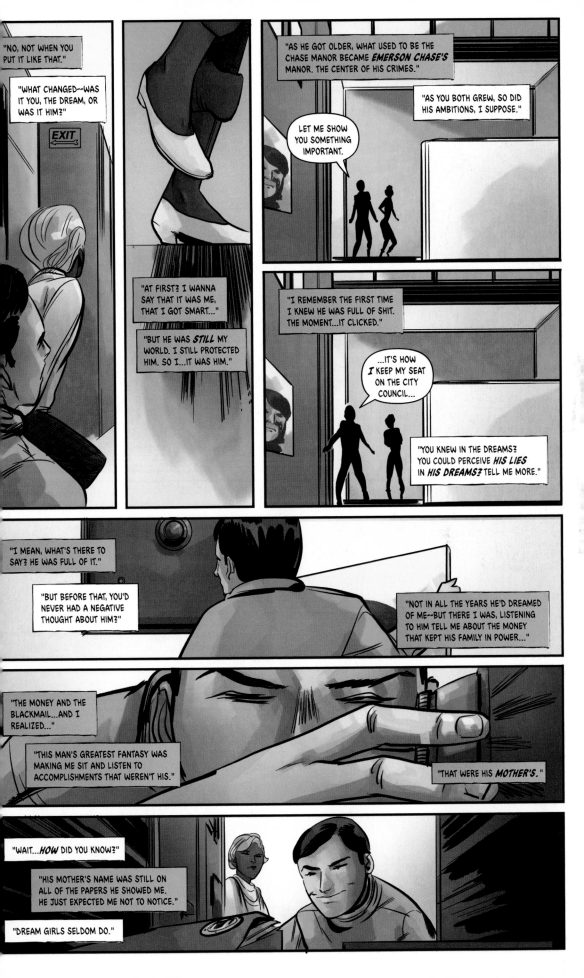

"NO, NOT WHEN YOU PUT IT LIKE THAT."

"WHAT CHANGED--WAS IT YOU, THE DREAM, OR WAS IT HIM?"

EXIT

"AT FIRST? I WANNA SAY THAT IT WAS ME, THAT I GOT SMART..."

"BUT HE WAS *STILL* MY WORLD. I STILL PROTECTED HIM. SO I...IT WAS HIM."

"AS HE GOT OLDER, WHAT USED TO BE THE CHASE MANOR BECAME *EMERSON CHASE'S* MANOR. THE CENTER OF HIS CRIMES."

"AS YOU BOTH GREW, SO DID HIS AMBITIONS, I SUPPOSE."

LET ME SHOW YOU SOMETHING IMPORTANT.

"I REMEMBER THE FIRST TIME I KNEW HE WAS FULL OF SHIT. THE MOMENT...IT CLICKED."

...IT'S HOW *I* KEEP MY SEAT ON THE CITY COUNCIL...

"YOU KNEW IN THE DREAMS? YOU COULD PERCEIVE *HIS LIES* IN *HIS DREAMS?* TELL ME MORE."

"I MEAN, WHAT'S THERE TO SAY? HE WAS FULL OF IT."

"BUT BEFORE THAT, YOU'D NEVER HAD A NEGATIVE THOUGHT ABOUT HIM?"

"NOT IN ALL THE YEARS HE'D DREAMED OF ME--BUT THERE I WAS, LISTENING TO HIM TELL ME ABOUT THE MONEY THAT KEPT HIS FAMILY IN POWER..."

"THE MONEY AND THE BLACKMAIL...AND I REALIZED..."

"THIS MAN'S GREATEST FANTASY WAS MAKING ME SIT AND LISTEN TO ACCOMPLISHMENTS THAT WEREN'T HIS."

"THAT WERE HIS *MOTHER'S.*"

"WAIT...*HOW* DID YOU KNOW?"

"HIS MOTHER'S NAME WAS STILL ON ALL OF THE PAPERS HE SHOWED ME. HE JUST EXPECTED ME NOT TO NOTICE."

"DREAM GIRLS SELDOM DO."

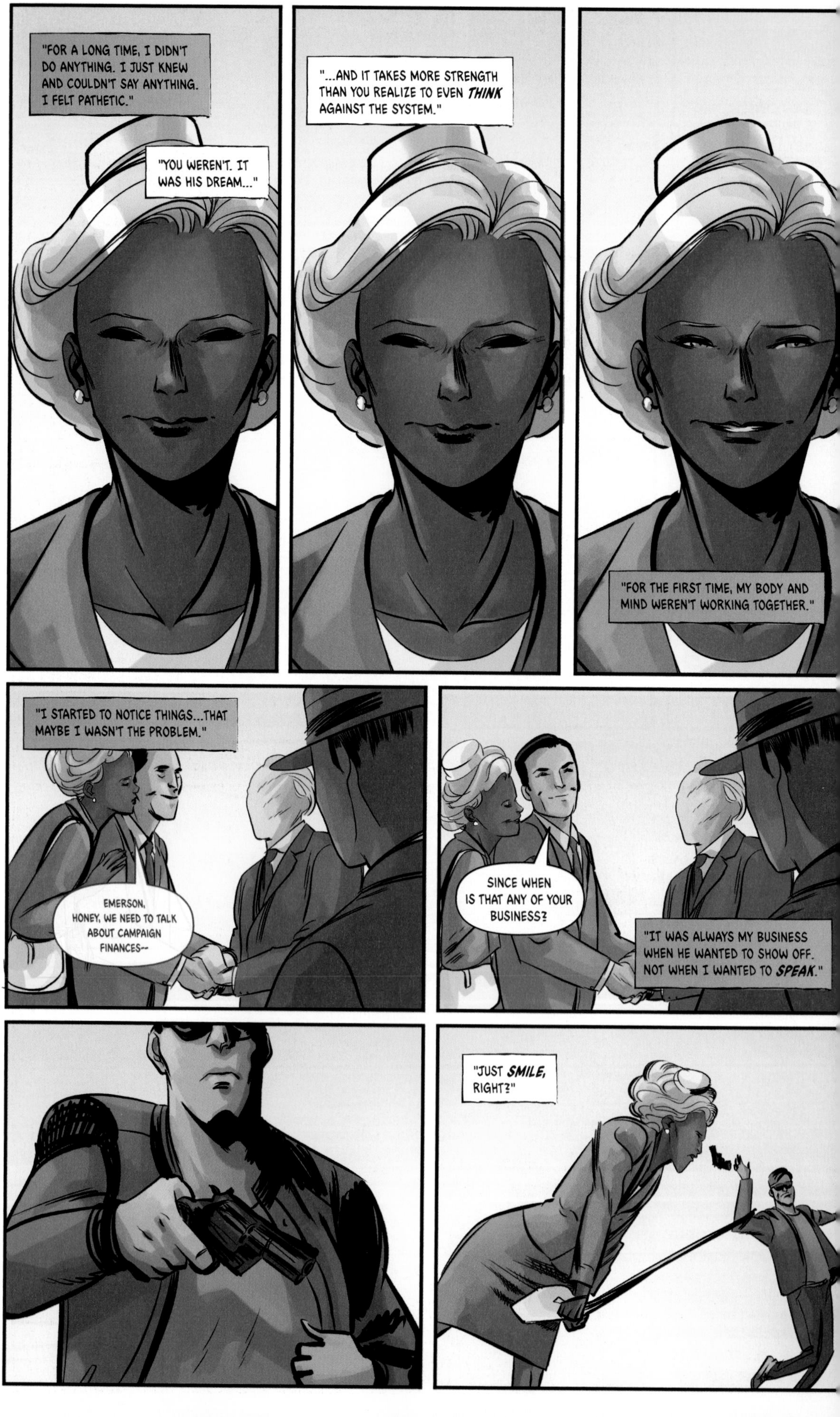
"FOR A LONG TIME, I DIDN'T DO ANYTHING. I JUST KNEW AND COULDN'T SAY ANYTHING. I FELT PATHETIC."
"YOU WEREN'T. IT WAS HIS DREAM..."
"...AND IT TAKES MORE STRENGTH THAN YOU REALIZE TO EVEN THINK AGAINST THE SYSTEM."
"FOR THE FIRST TIME, MY BODY AND MIND WEREN'T WORKING TOGETHER."
"I STARTED TO NOTICE THINGS...THAT MAYBE I WASN'T THE PROBLEM."
EMERSON, HONEY, WE NEED TO TALK ABOUT CAMPAIGN FINANCES--
SINCE WHEN IS THAT ANY OF YOUR BUSINESS?
"IT WAS ALWAYS MY BUSINESS WHEN HE WANTED TO SHOW OFF. NOT WHEN I WANTED TO SPEAK."
"JUST SMILE, RIGHT?"

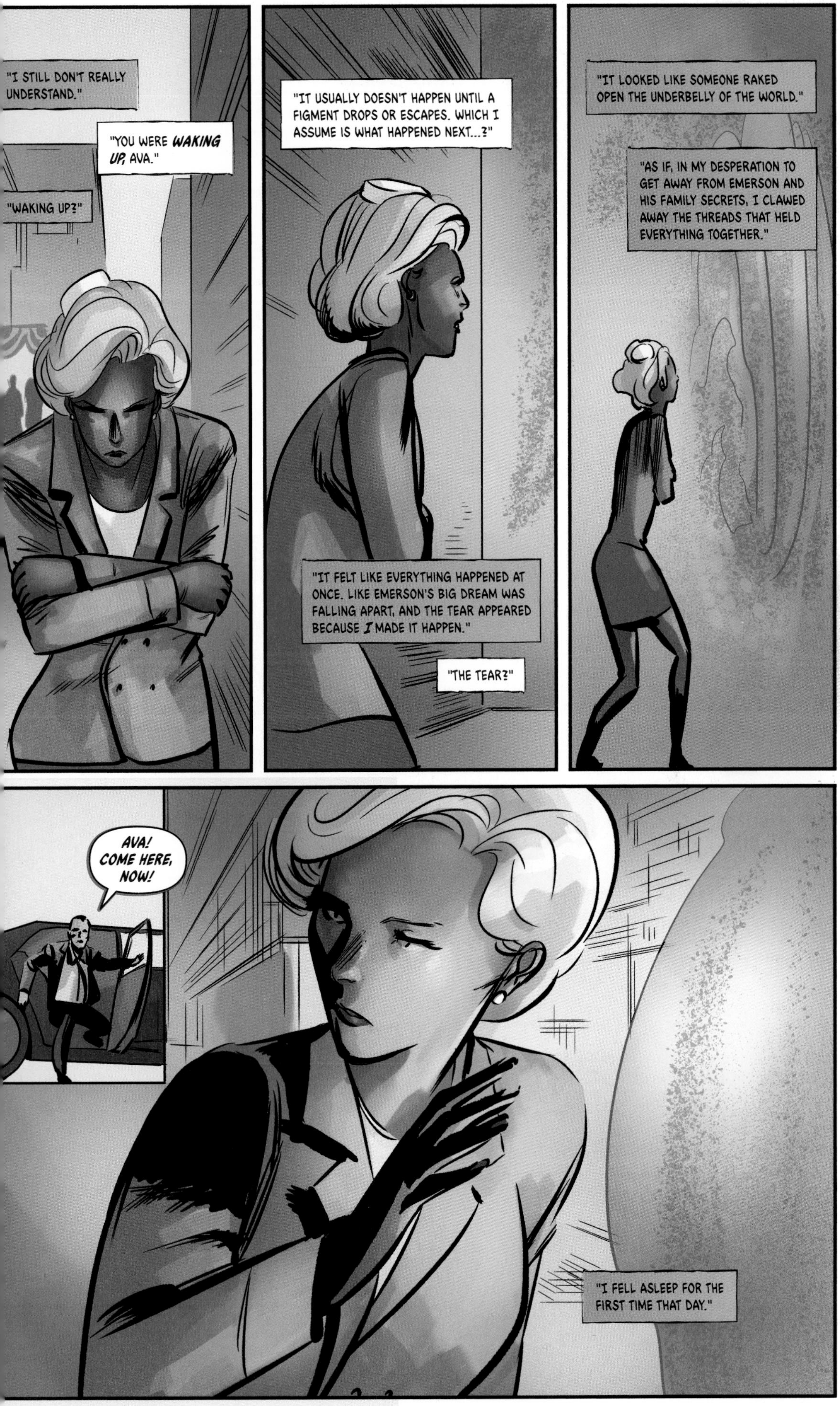
"I STILL DON'T REALLY UNDERSTAND."
"YOU WERE *WAKING UP*, AVA."
"WAKING UP?"
"IT USUALLY DOESN'T HAPPEN UNTIL A FIGMENT DROPS OR ESCAPES. WHICH I ASSUME IS WHAT HAPPENED NEXT...?"
"IT FELT LIKE EVERYTHING HAPPENED AT ONCE. LIKE EMERSON'S BIG DREAM WAS FALLING APART, AND THE TEAR APPEARED BECAUSE *I* MADE IT HAPPEN."
"THE TEAR?"
"IT LOOKED LIKE SOMEONE RAKED OPEN THE UNDERBELLY OF THE WORLD."
"AS IF, IN MY DESPERATION TO GET AWAY FROM EMERSON AND HIS FAMILY SECRETS, I CLAWED AWAY THE THREADS THAT HELD EVERYTHING TOGETHER."
AVA! COME HERE, NOW!
"I FELL ASLEEP FOR THE FIRST TIME THAT DAY."

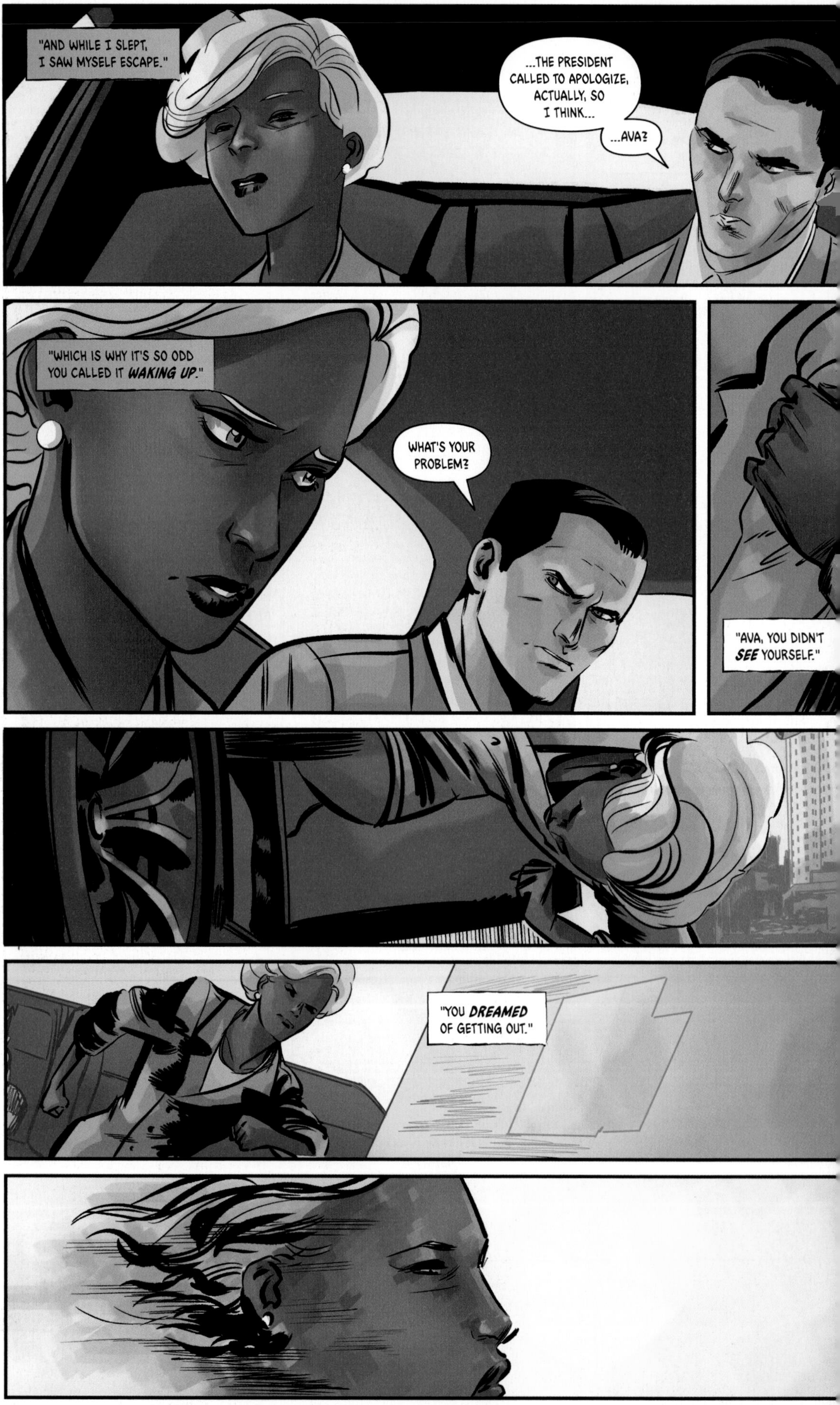
"AND WHILE I SLEPT, I SAW MYSELF ESCAPE."
...THE PRESIDENT CALLED TO APOLOGIZE, ACTUALLY, SO I THINK...
...AVA?
"WHICH IS WHY IT'S SO ODD YOU CALLED IT *WAKING UP*."
WHAT'S YOUR PROBLEM?
"AVA, YOU DIDN'T *SEE* YOURSELF."
"YOU *DREAMED* OF GETTING OUT."

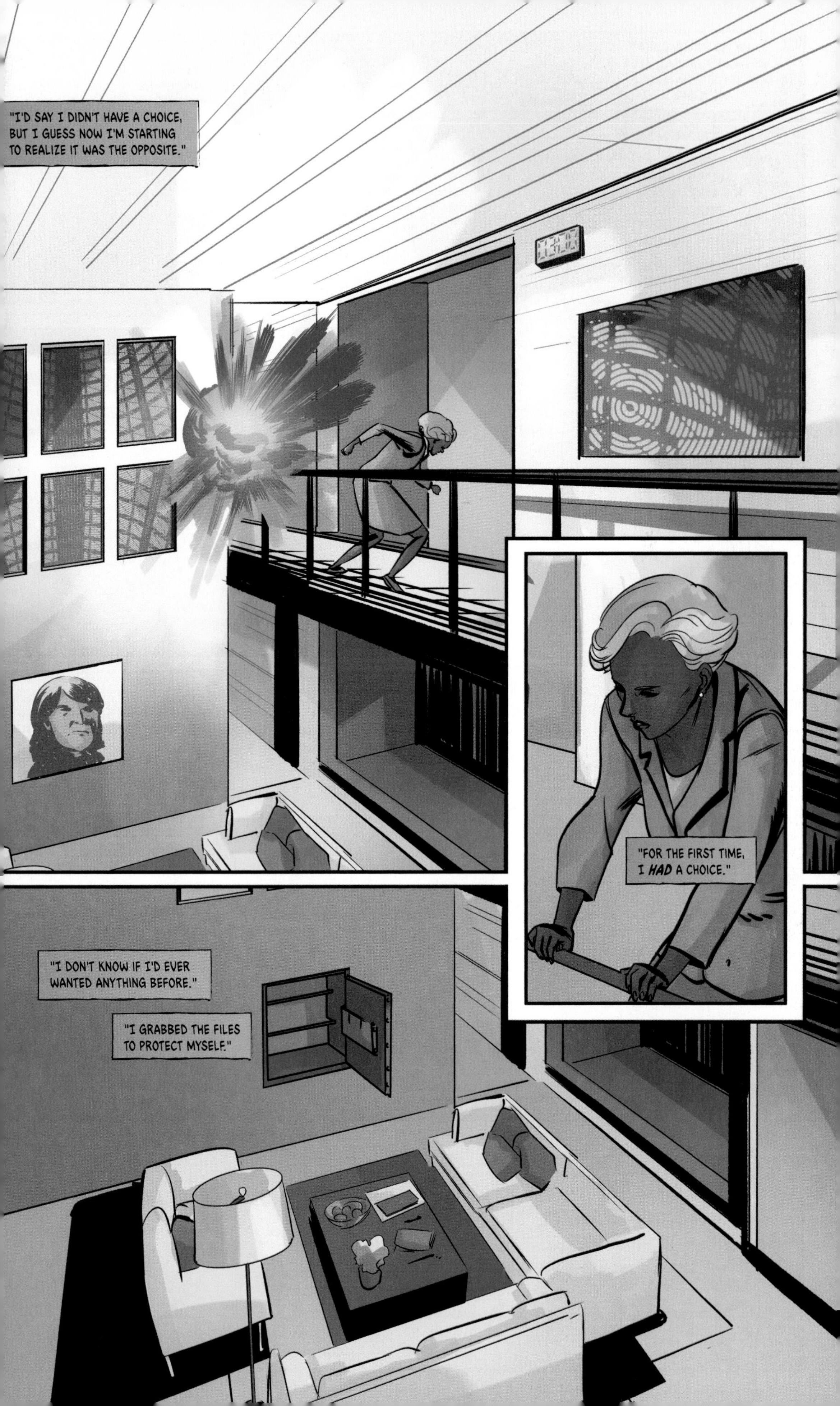
"I'D SAY I DIDN'T HAVE A CHOICE, BUT I GUESS NOW I'M STARTING TO REALIZE IT WAS THE OPPOSITE."
"FOR THE FIRST TIME, I *HAD* A CHOICE."
"I DON'T KNOW IF I'D EVER WANTED ANYTHING BEFORE."
"I GRABBED THE FILES TO PROTECT MYSELF."

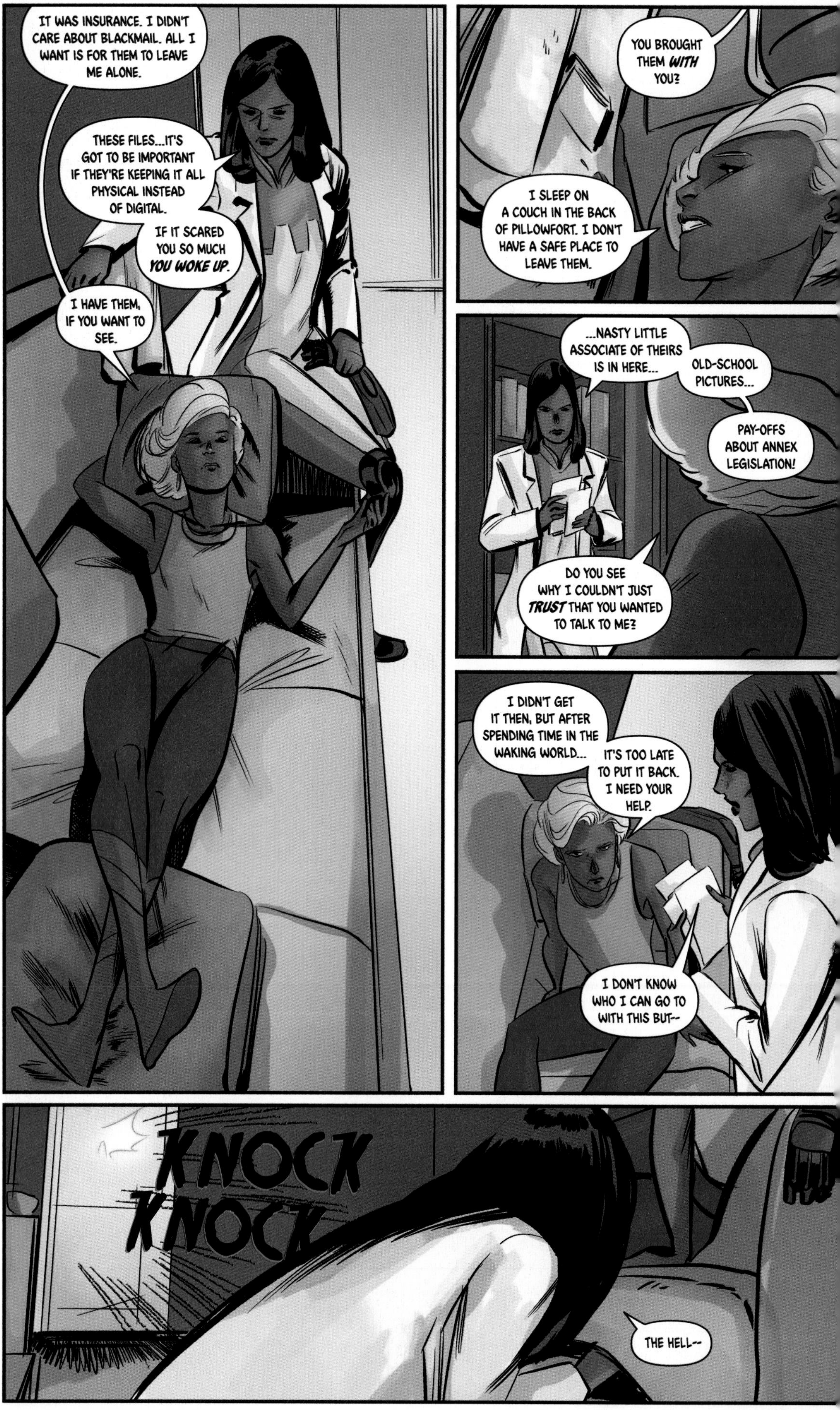
IT WAS INSURANCE. I DIDN'T CARE ABOUT BLACKMAIL. ALL I WANT IS FOR THEM TO LEAVE ME ALONE.
THESE FILES...IT'S GOT TO BE IMPORTANT IF THEY'RE KEEPING IT ALL PHYSICAL INSTEAD OF DIGITAL.
IF IT SCARED YOU SO MUCH *YOU WOKE UP*.
I HAVE THEM, IF YOU WANT TO SEE.
YOU BROUGHT THEM *WITH* YOU?
I SLEEP ON A COUCH IN THE BACK OF PILLOWFORT. I DON'T HAVE A SAFE PLACE TO LEAVE THEM.
...NASTY LITTLE ASSOCIATE OF THEIRS IS IN HERE...
OLD-SCHOOL PICTURES...
PAY-OFFS ABOUT ANNEX LEGISLATION!
DO YOU SEE WHY I COULDN'T JUST *TRUST* THAT YOU WANTED TO TALK TO ME?
I DIDN'T GET IT THEN, BUT AFTER SPENDING TIME IN THE WAKING WORLD...
IT'S TOO LATE TO PUT IT BACK. I NEED YOUR HELP.
I DON'T KNOW WHO I CAN GO TO WITH THIS BUT--
KNOCK KNOCK
THE HELL--

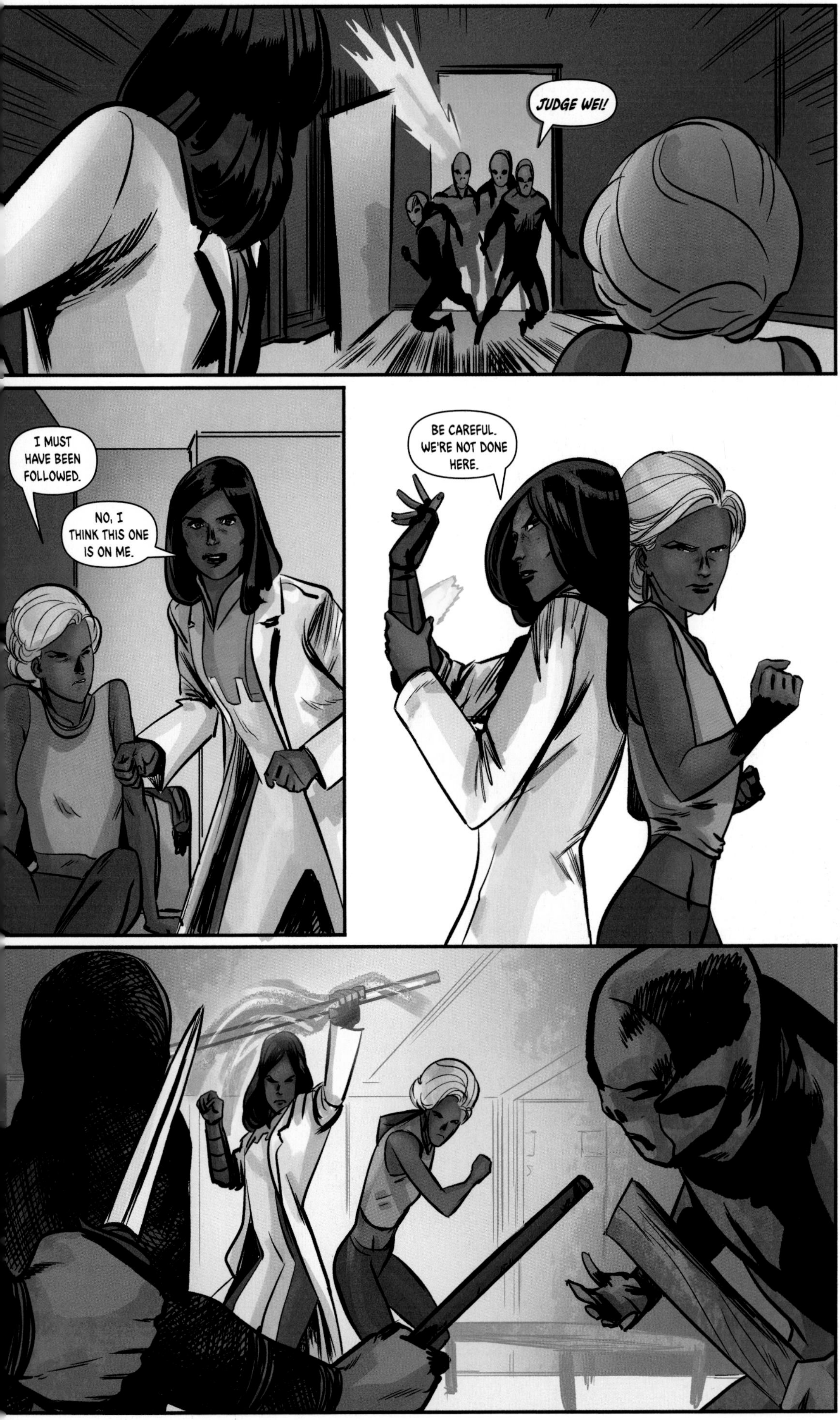
JUDGE WEI!
I MUST HAVE BEEN FOLLOWED.
NO, I THINK THIS ONE IS ON ME.
BE CAREFUL. WE'RE NOT DONE HERE.

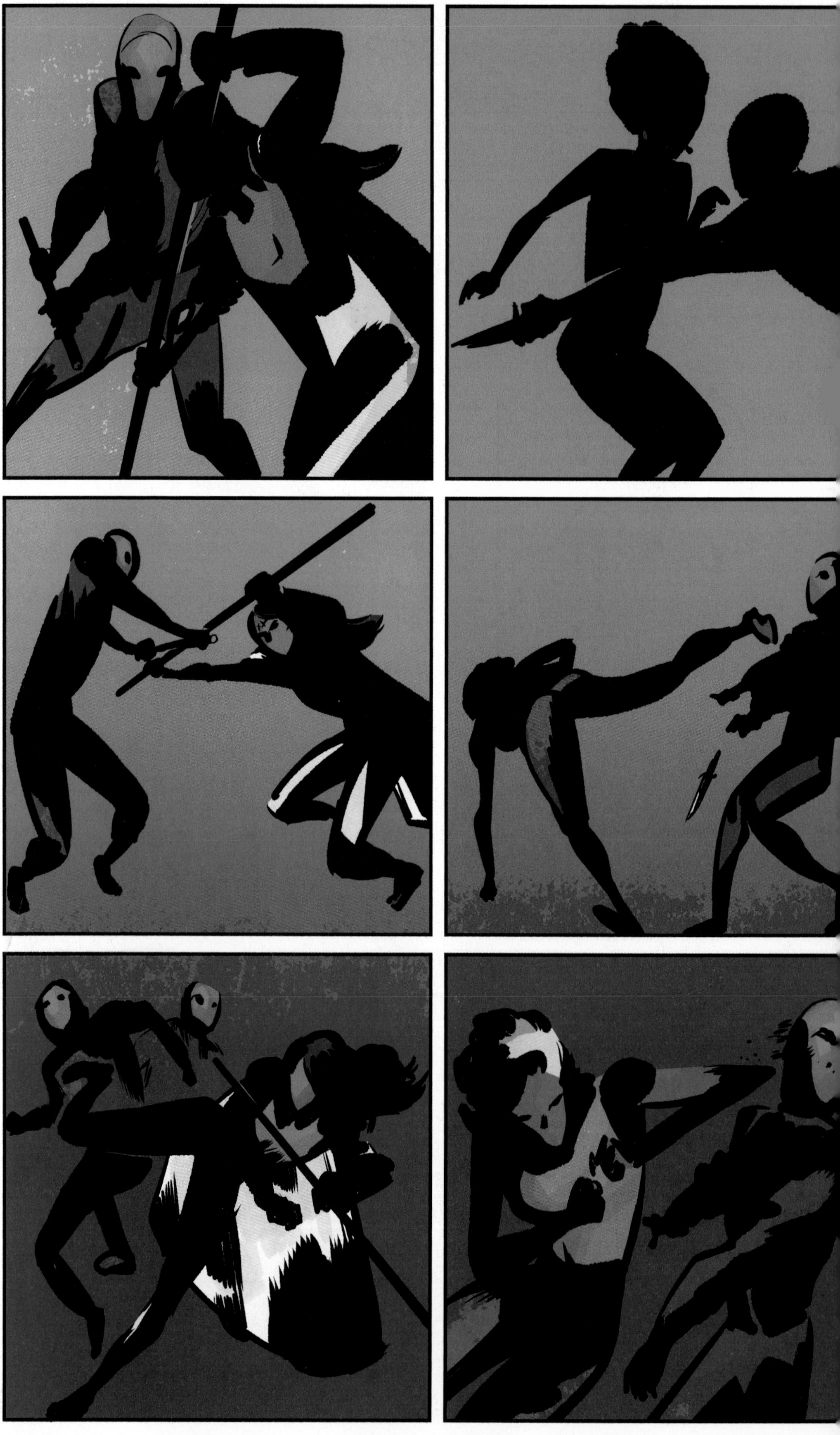

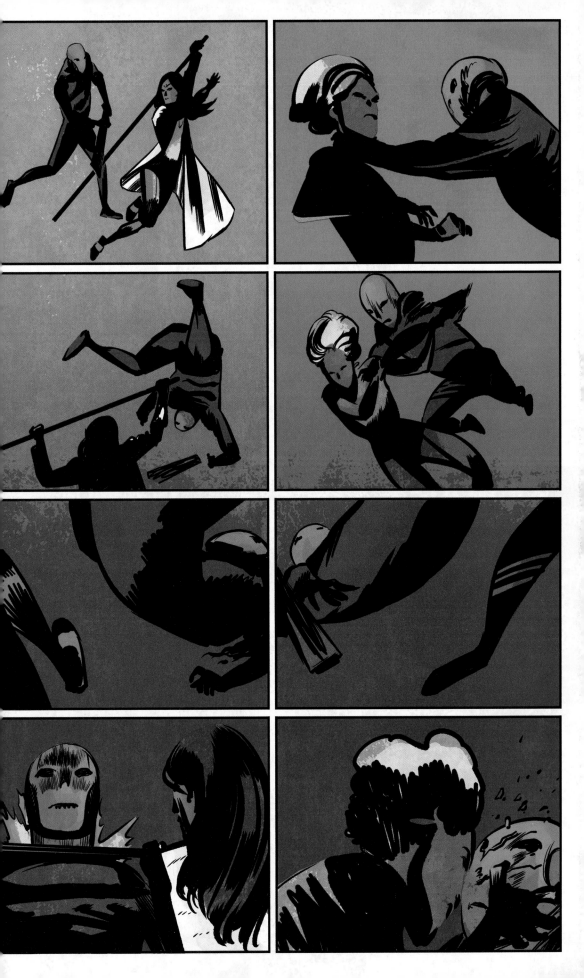

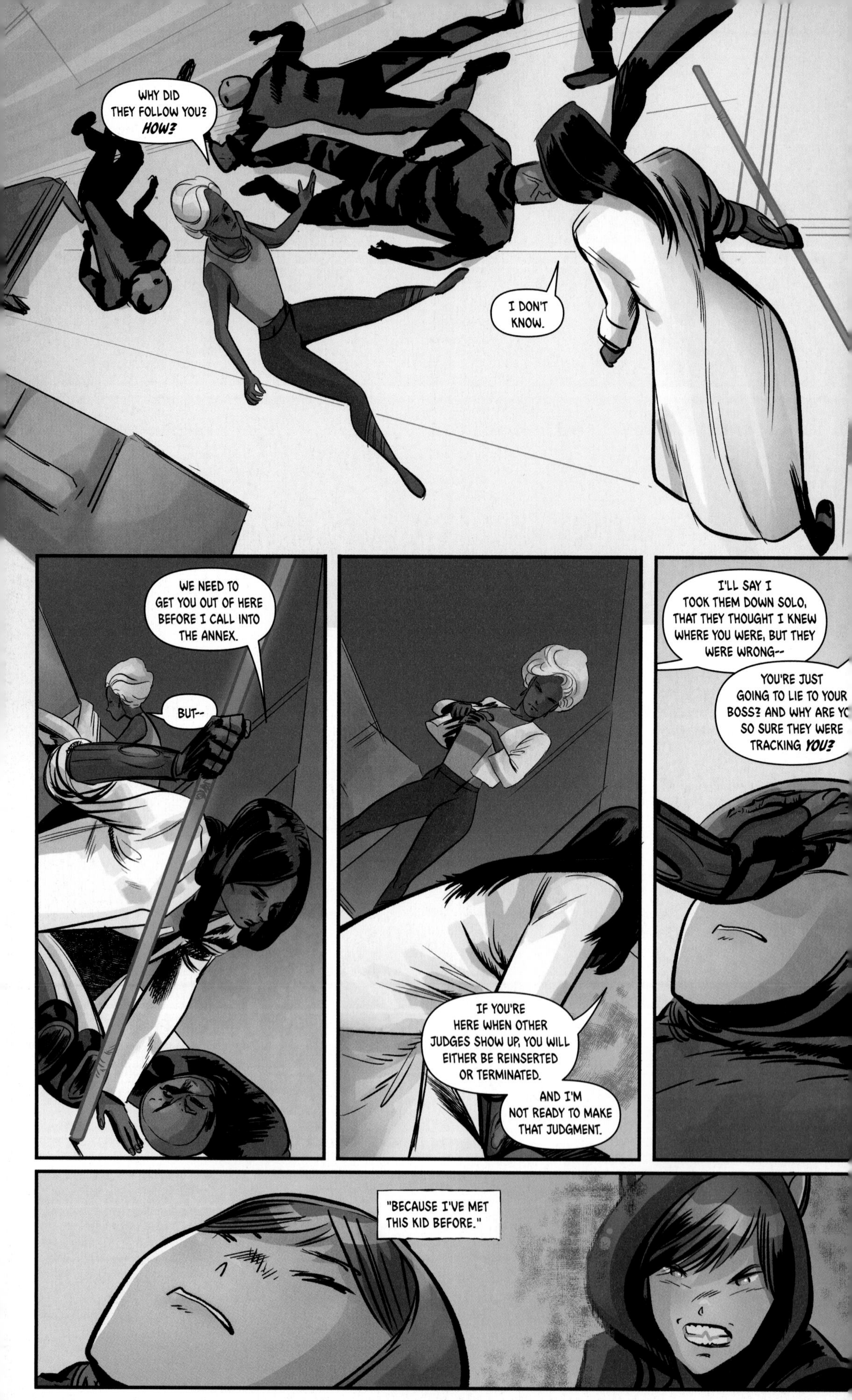
WHY DID THEY FOLLOW YOU? *HOW?*
I DON'T KNOW.
WE NEED TO GET YOU OUT OF HERE BEFORE I CALL INTO THE ANNEX.
BUT--
IF YOU'RE HERE WHEN OTHER JUDGES SHOW UP, YOU WILL EITHER BE REINSERTED OR TERMINATED.
AND I'M NOT READY TO MAKE THAT JUDGMENT.
I'LL SAY I TOOK THEM DOWN SOLO, THAT THEY THOUGHT I KNEW WHERE YOU WERE, BUT THEY WERE WRONG--
YOU'RE JUST GOING TO LIE TO YOUR BOSS? AND WHY ARE YO SO SURE THEY WERE TRACKING *YOU?*
"BECAUSE I'VE MET THIS KID BEFORE."

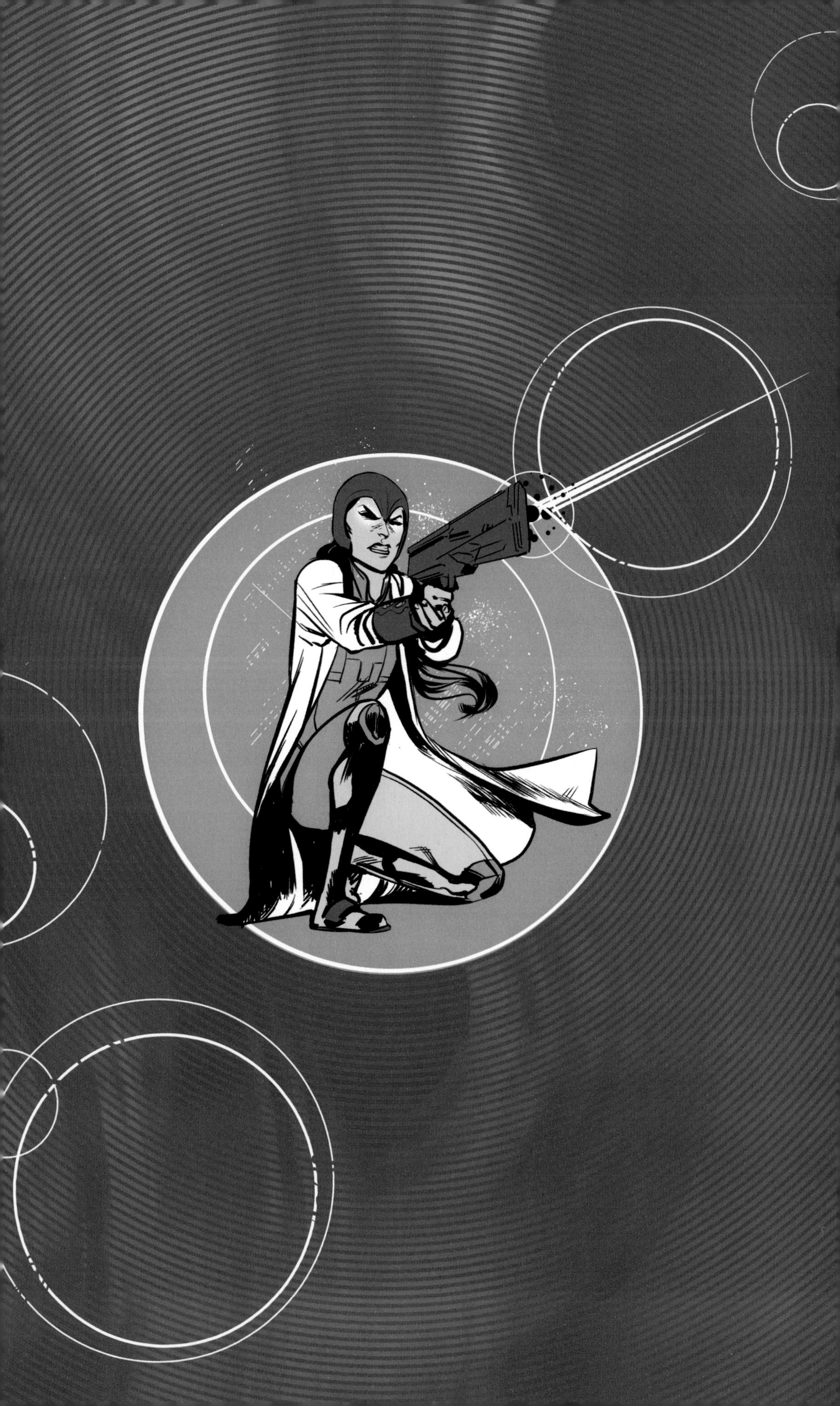

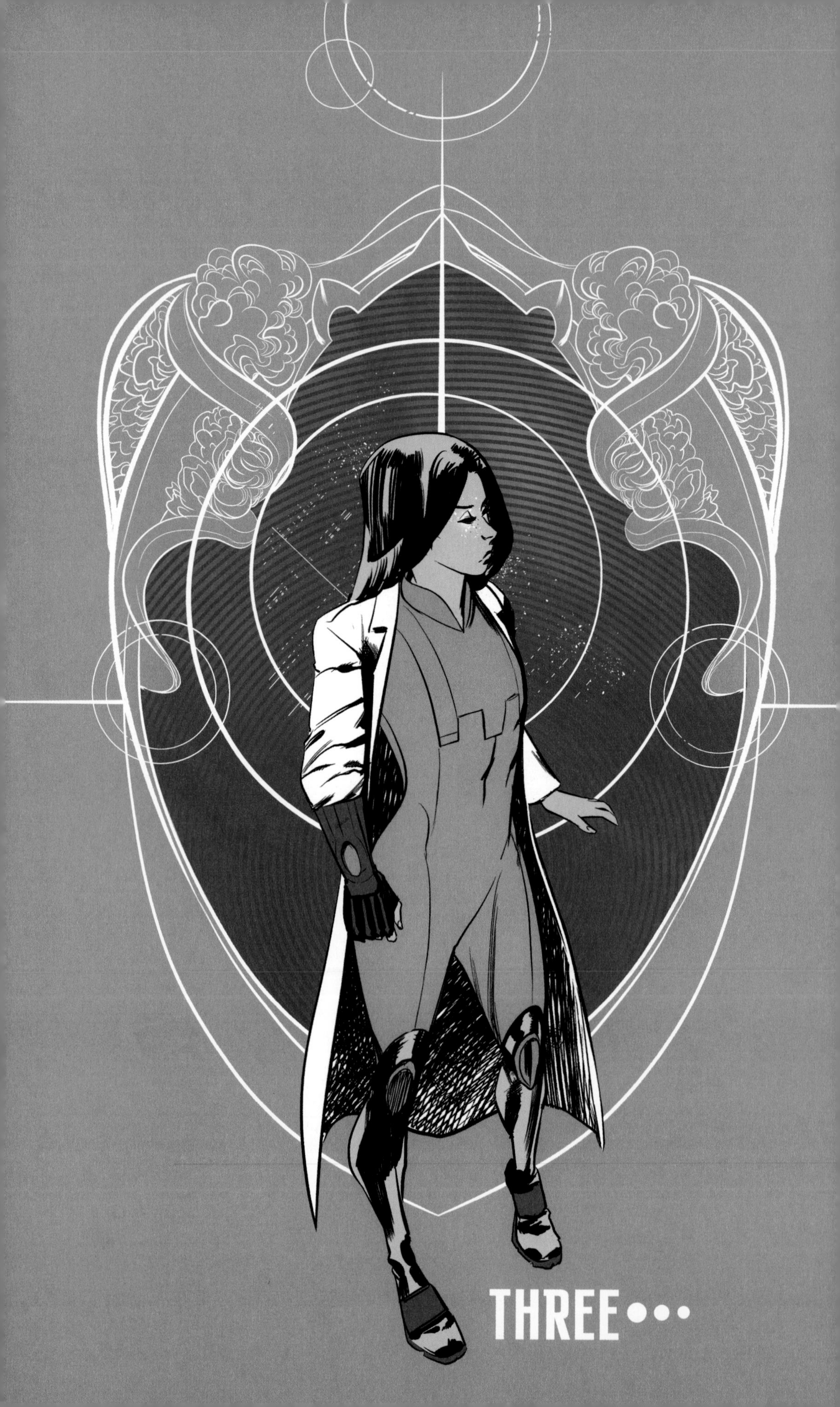

THREE•••

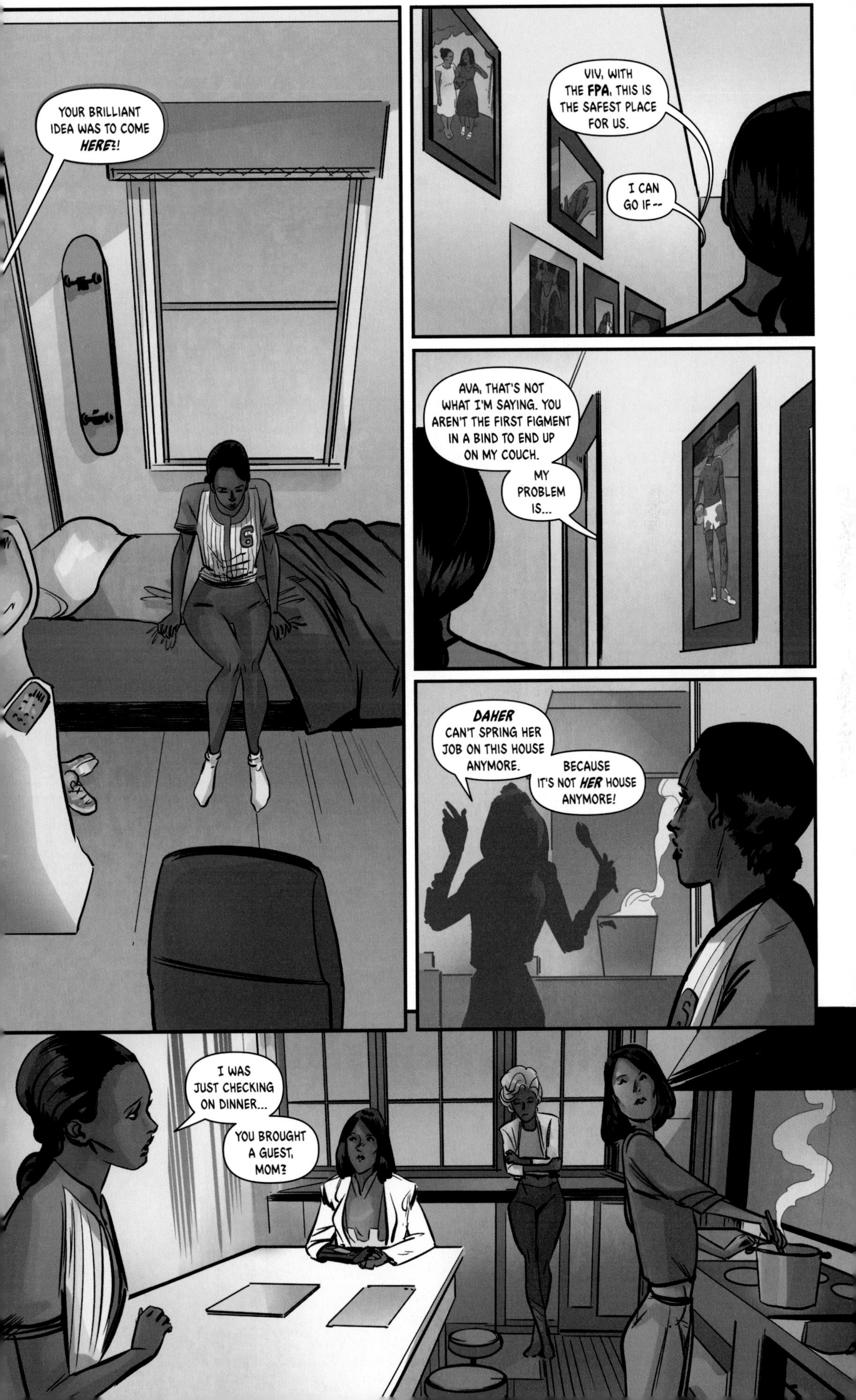
YOUR BRILLIANT IDEA WAS TO COME HERE?!
VIV, WITH THE FPA, THIS IS THE SAFEST PLACE FOR US.
I CAN GO IF--
AVA, THAT'S NOT WHAT I'M SAYING. YOU AREN'T THE FIRST FIGMENT IN A BIND TO END UP ON MY COUCH.
MY PROBLEM IS...
DAHER CAN'T SPRING HER JOB ON THIS HOUSE ANYMORE.
BECAUSE IT'S NOT HER HOUSE ANYMORE!
I WAS JUST CHECKING ON DINNER...
YOU BROUGHT A GUEST, MOM?

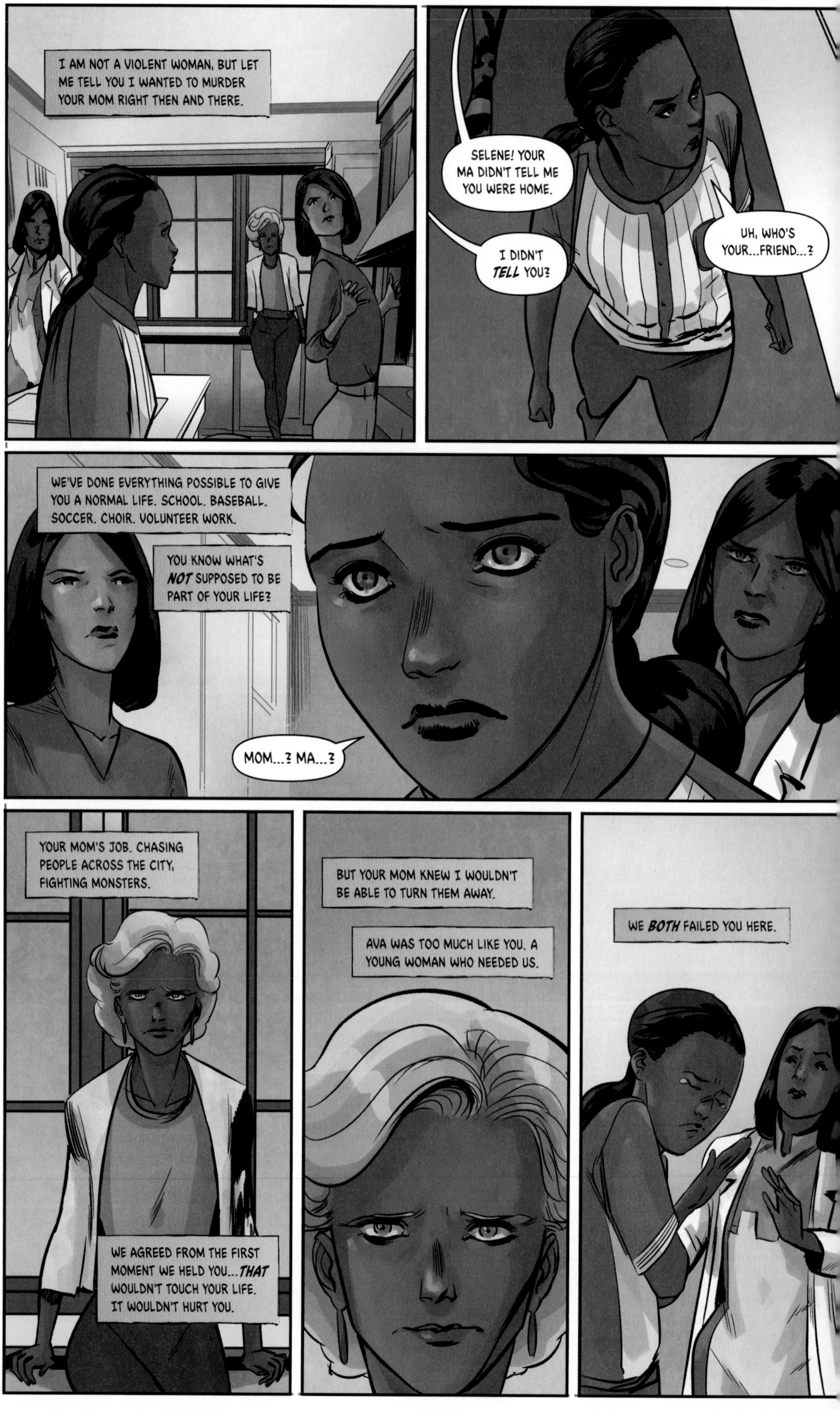
I AM NOT A VIOLENT WOMAN, BUT LET ME TELL YOU I WANTED TO MURDER YOUR MOM RIGHT THEN AND THERE.
SELENE! YOUR MA DIDN'T TELL ME YOU WERE HOME.
I DIDN'T TELL YOU?
UH, WHO'S YOUR...FRIEND...?
WE'VE DONE EVERYTHING POSSIBLE TO GIVE YOU A NORMAL LIFE. SCHOOL. BASEBALL. SOCCER. CHOIR. VOLUNTEER WORK.
YOU KNOW WHAT'S NOT SUPPOSED TO BE PART OF YOUR LIFE?
MOM...? MA...?
YOUR MOM'S JOB. CHASING PEOPLE ACROSS THE CITY, FIGHTING MONSTERS.
WE AGREED FROM THE FIRST MOMENT WE HELD YOU...THAT WOULDN'T TOUCH YOUR LIFE. IT WOULDN'T HURT YOU.
BUT YOUR MOM KNEW I WOULDN'T BE ABLE TO TURN THEM AWAY.
AVA WAS TOO MUCH LIKE YOU. A YOUNG WOMAN WHO NEEDED US.
WE BOTH FAILED YOU HERE.

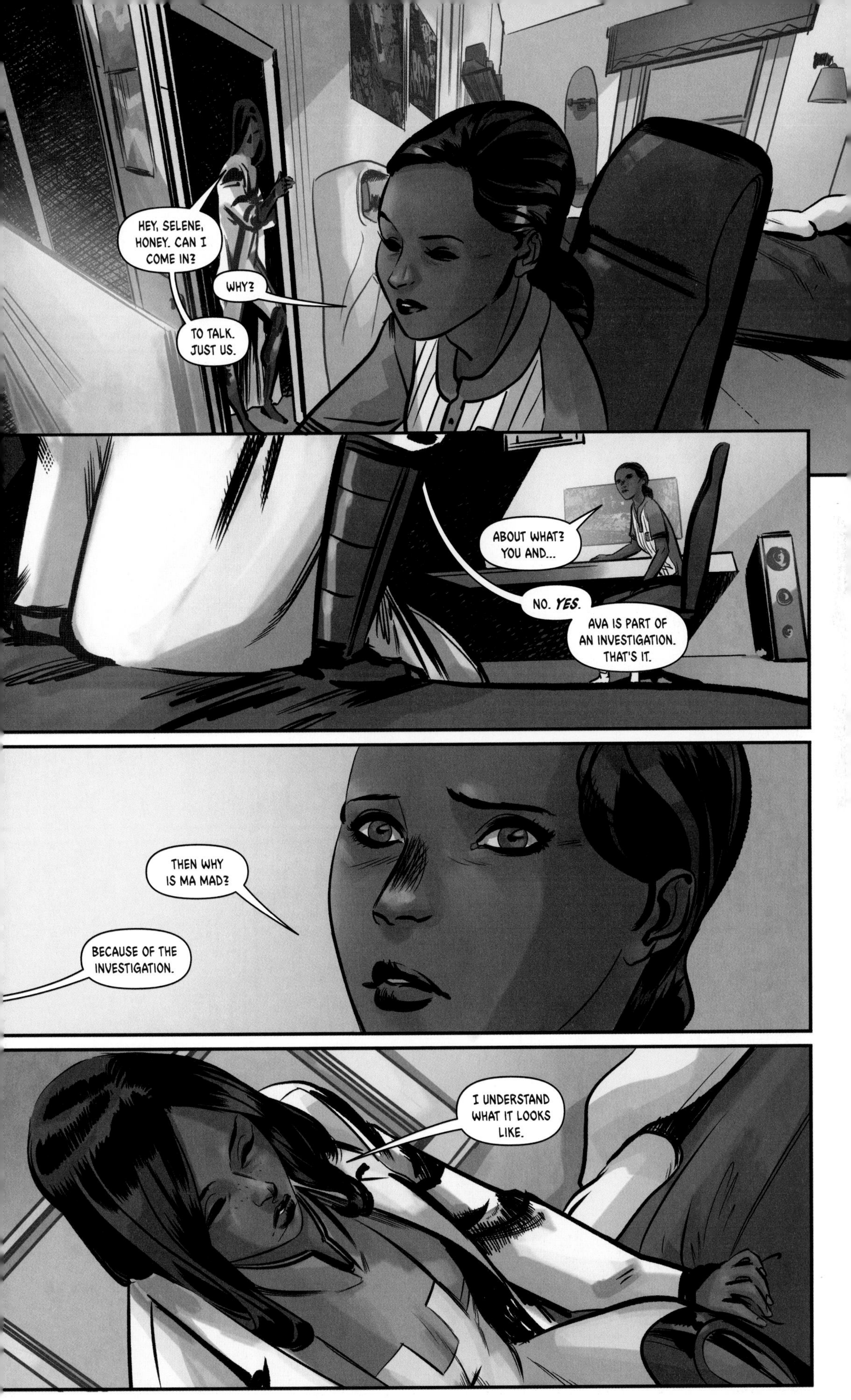
HEY, SELENE, HONEY. CAN I COME IN?
WHY?
TO TALK. JUST US.
ABOUT WHAT? YOU AND...
NO. YES.
AVA IS PART OF AN INVESTIGATION. THAT'S IT.
THEN WHY IS MA MAD?
BECAUSE OF THE INVESTIGATION.
I UNDERSTAND WHAT IT LOOKS LIKE.

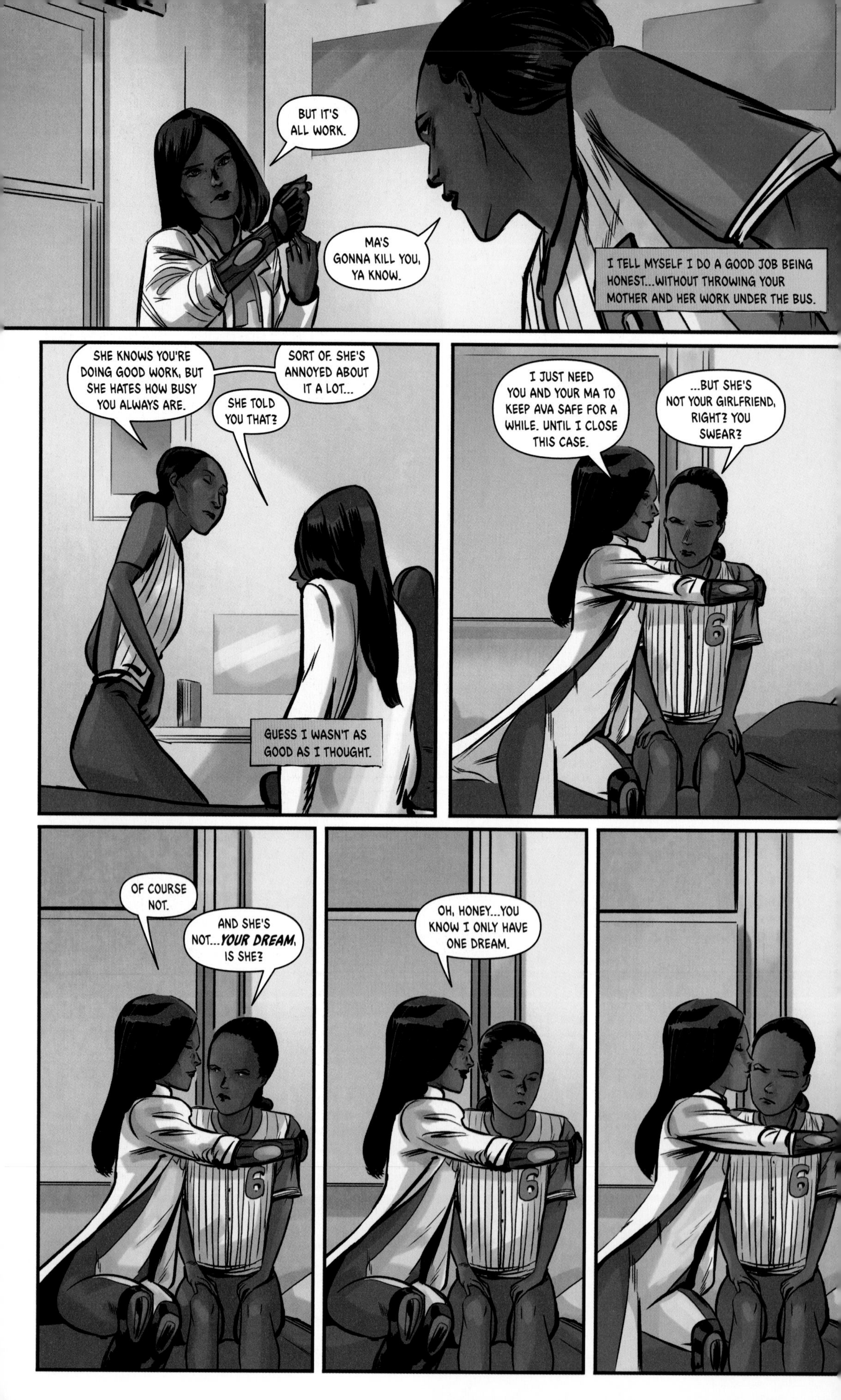
BUT IT'S ALL WORK.
MA'S GONNA KILL YOU, YA KNOW.
I TELL MYSELF I DO A GOOD JOB BEING HONEST...WITHOUT THROWING YOUR MOTHER AND HER WORK UNDER THE BUS.
SHE KNOWS YOU'RE DOING GOOD WORK, BUT SHE HATES HOW BUSY YOU ALWAYS ARE.
SORT OF. SHE'S ANNOYED ABOUT IT A LOT...
SHE TOLD YOU THAT?
GUESS I WASN'T AS GOOD AS I THOUGHT.
I JUST NEED YOU AND YOUR MA TO KEEP AVA SAFE FOR A WHILE. UNTIL I CLOSE THIS CASE.
...BUT SHE'S NOT YOUR GIRLFRIEND, RIGHT? YOU SWEAR?
OF COURSE NOT.
AND SHE'S NOT...YOUR DREAM, IS SHE?
OH, HONEY...YOU KNOW I ONLY HAVE ONE DREAM.

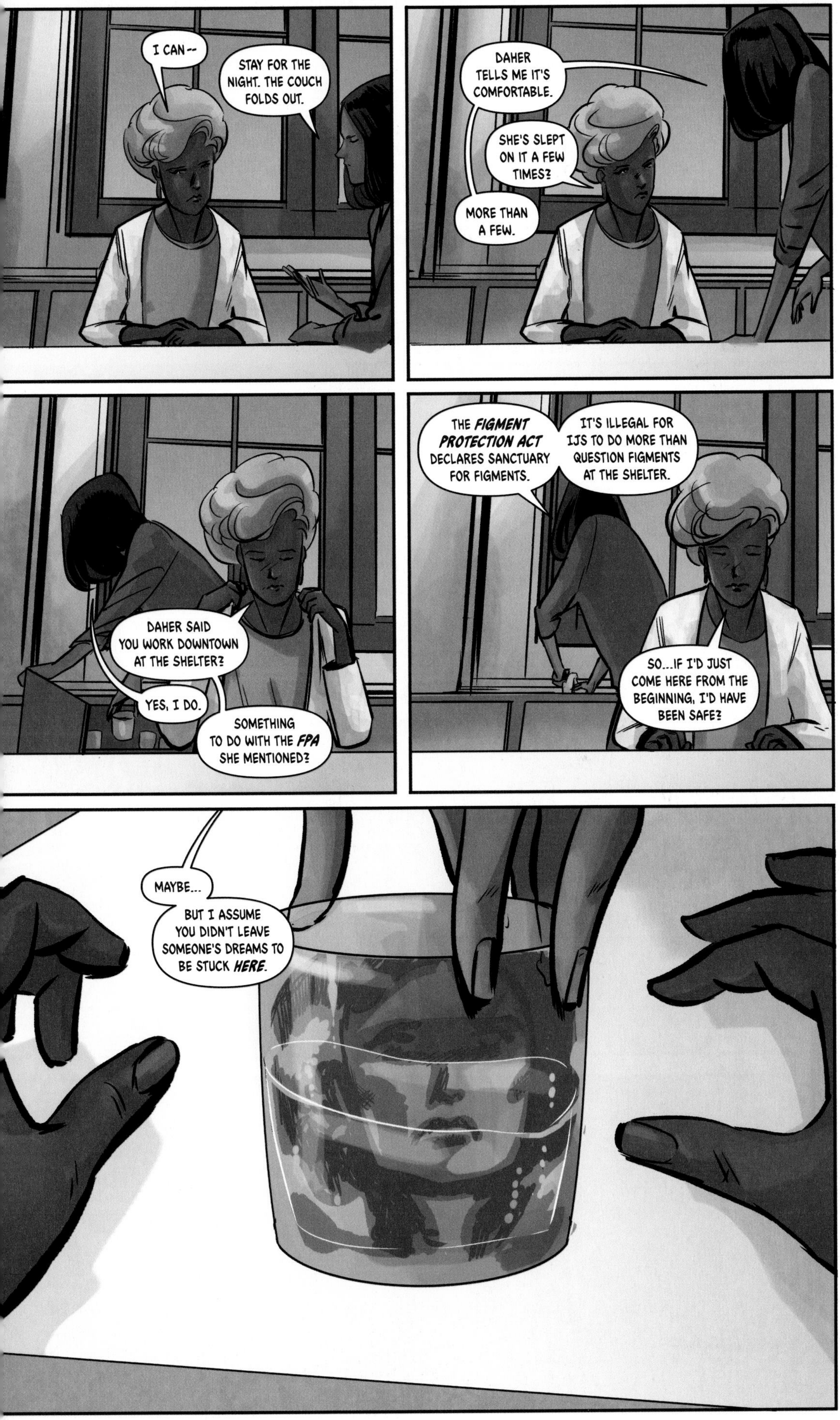
I CAN--
STAY FOR THE NIGHT. THE COUCH FOLDS OUT.
DAHER TELLS ME IT'S COMFORTABLE.
SHE'S SLEPT ON IT A FEW TIMES?
MORE THAN A FEW.
DAHER SAID YOU WORK DOWNTOWN AT THE SHELTER?
YES, I DO.
SOMETHING TO DO WITH THE *FPA* SHE MENTIONED?
THE *FIGMENT PROTECTION ACT* DECLARES SANCTUARY FOR FIGMENTS.
IT'S ILLEGAL FOR IJS TO DO MORE THAN QUESTION FIGMENTS AT THE SHELTER.
SO...IF I'D JUST COME HERE FROM THE BEGINNING, I'D HAVE BEEN SAFE?
MAYBE...
BUT I ASSUME YOU DIDN'T LEAVE SOMEONE'S DREAMS TO BE STUCK *HERE*.

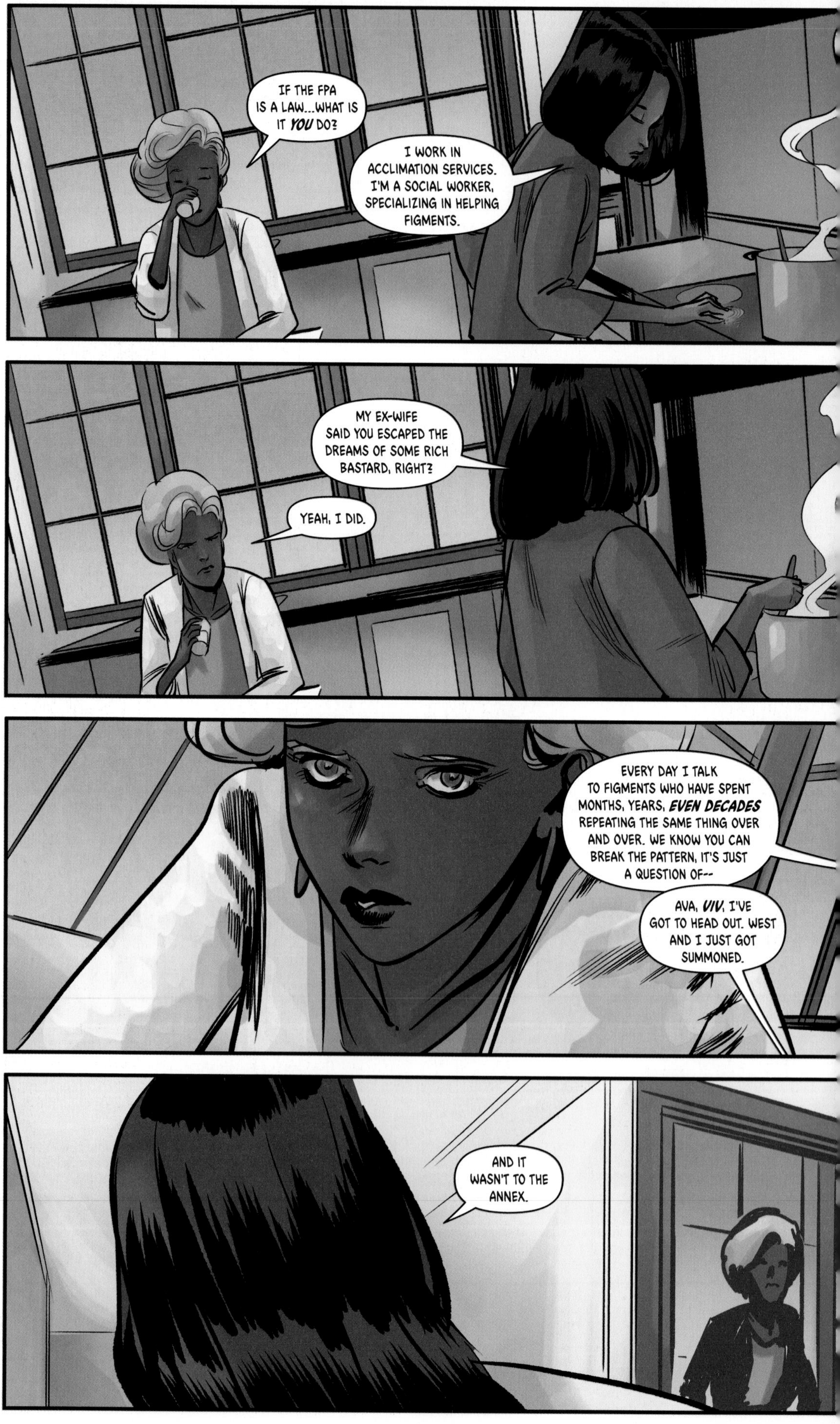
IF THE FPA IS A LAW...WHAT IS IT YOU DO?
I WORK IN ACCLIMATION SERVICES. I'M A SOCIAL WORKER, SPECIALIZING IN HELPING FIGMENTS.
MY EX-WIFE SAID YOU ESCAPED THE DREAMS OF SOME RICH BASTARD, RIGHT?
YEAH, I DID.
EVERY DAY I TALK TO FIGMENTS WHO HAVE SPENT MONTHS, YEARS, EVEN DECADES REPEATING THE SAME THING OVER AND OVER. WE KNOW YOU CAN BREAK THE PATTERN, IT'S JUST A QUESTION OF--
AVA, VIV, I'VE GOT TO HEAD OUT. WEST AND I JUST GOT SUMMONED.
AND IT WASN'T TO THE ANNEX.

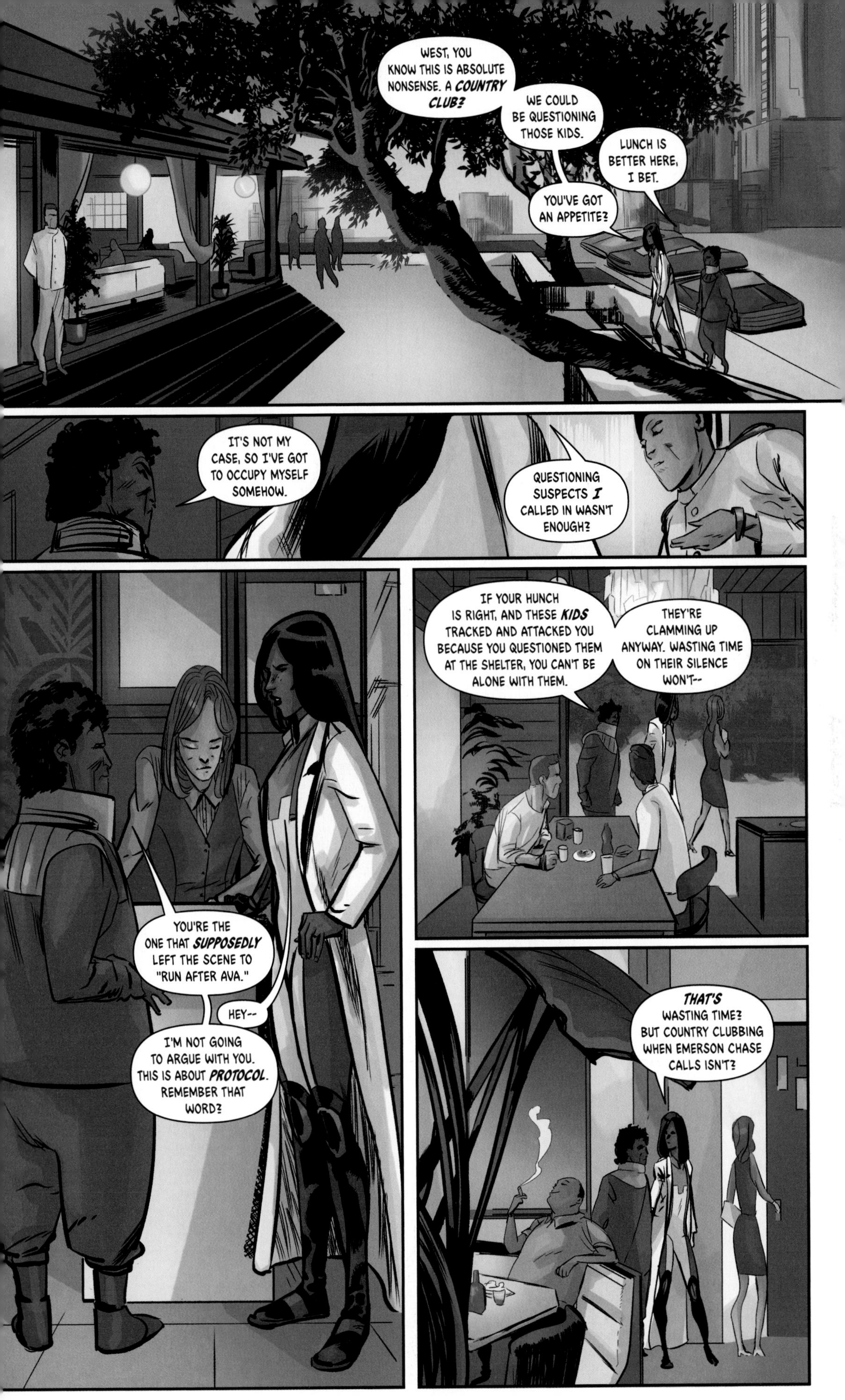

WEST, YOU KNOW THIS IS ABSOLUTE NONSENSE. A COUNTRY CLUB?
WE COULD BE QUESTIONING THOSE KIDS.
LUNCH IS BETTER HERE, I BET.
YOU'VE GOT AN APPETITE?
IT'S NOT MY CASE, SO I'VE GOT TO OCCUPY MYSELF SOMEHOW.
QUESTIONING SUSPECTS I CALLED IN WASN'T ENOUGH?
YOU'RE THE ONE THAT SUPPOSEDLY LEFT THE SCENE TO "RUN AFTER AVA."
HEY--
I'M NOT GOING TO ARGUE WITH YOU. THIS IS ABOUT PROTOCOL. REMEMBER THAT WORD?
IF YOUR HUNCH IS RIGHT, AND THESE KIDS TRACKED AND ATTACKED YOU BECAUSE YOU QUESTIONED THEM AT THE SHELTER, YOU CAN'T BE ALONE WITH THEM.
THEY'RE CLAMMING UP ANYWAY. WASTING TIME ON THEIR SILENCE WON'T--
THAT'S WASTING TIME? BUT COUNTRY CLUBBING WHEN EMERSON CHASE CALLS ISN'T?

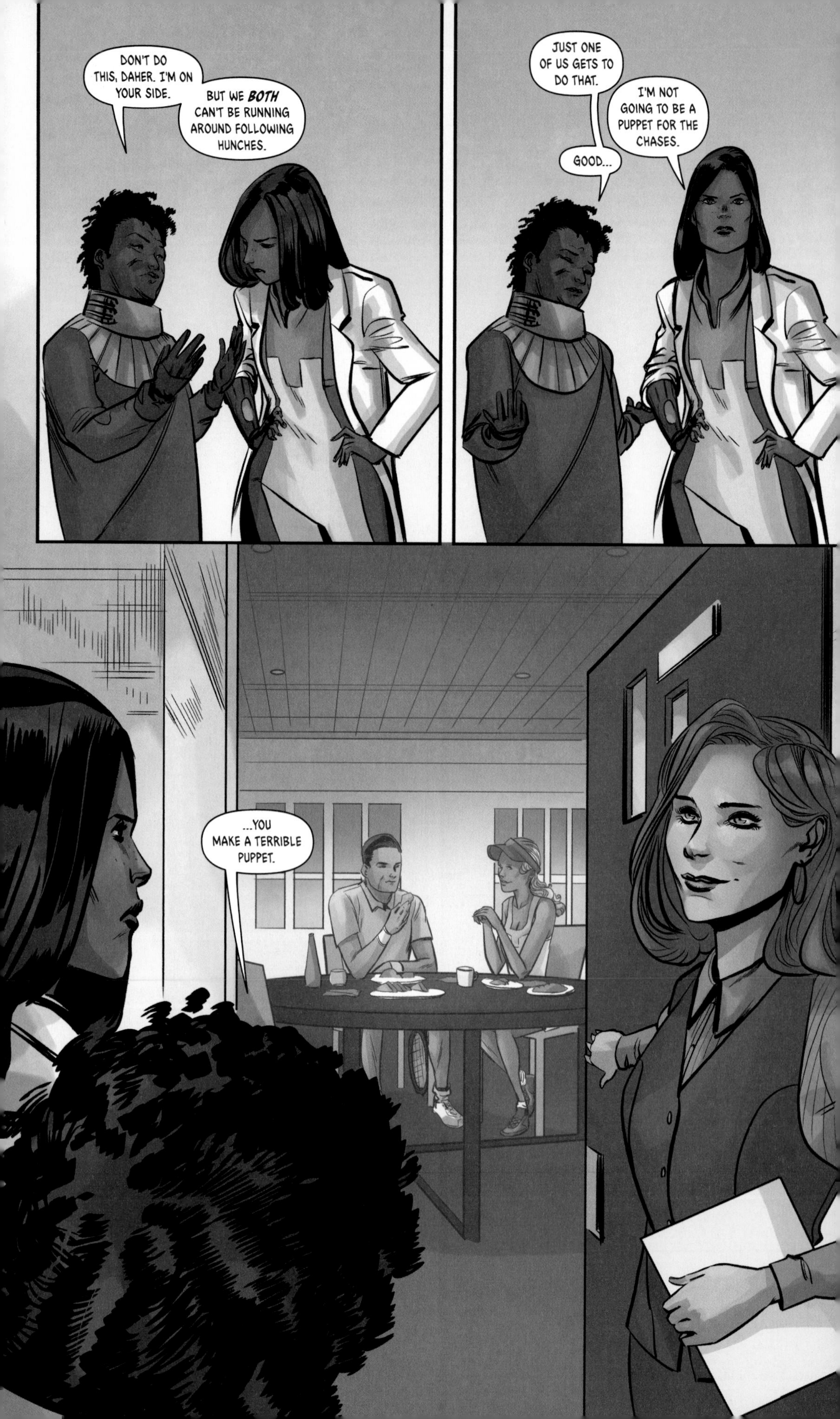
DON'T DO THIS, DAHER. I'M ON YOUR SIDE.
BUT WE BOTH CAN'T BE RUNNING AROUND FOLLOWING HUNCHES.
JUST ONE OF US GETS TO DO THAT.
GOOD...
I'M NOT GOING TO BE A PUPPET FOR THE CHASES.
...YOU MAKE A TERRIBLE PUPPET.

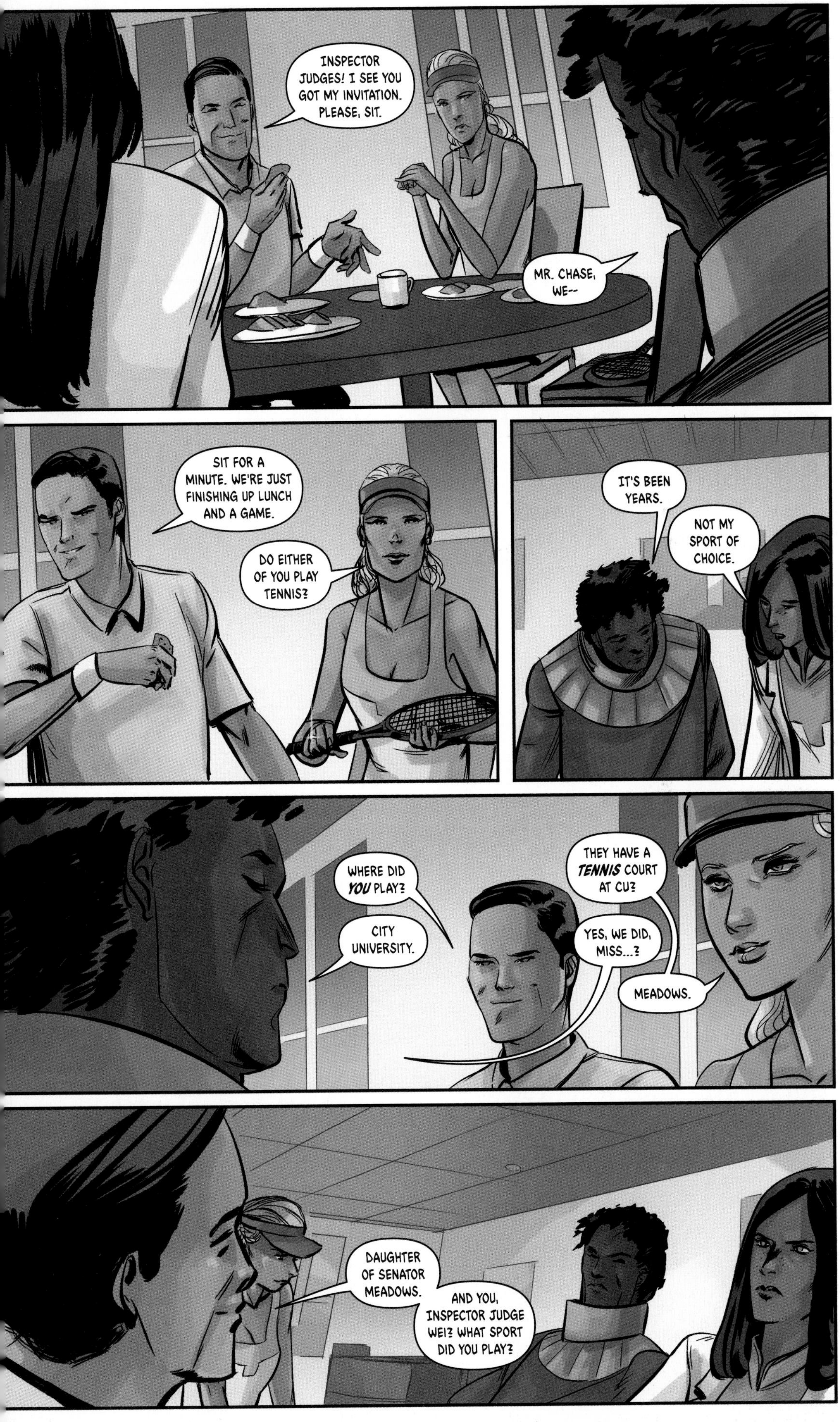
INSPECTOR JUDGES! I SEE YOU GOT MY INVITATION. PLEASE, SIT.
MR. CHASE, WE--
SIT FOR A MINUTE. WE'RE JUST FINISHING UP LUNCH AND A GAME.
DO EITHER OF YOU PLAY TENNIS?
IT'S BEEN YEARS.
NOT MY SPORT OF CHOICE.
WHERE DID YOU PLAY?
CITY UNIVERSITY.
THEY HAVE A TENNIS COURT AT CU?
YES, WE DID, MISS...?
MEADOWS.
DAUGHTER OF SENATOR MEADOWS.
AND YOU, INSPECTOR JUDGE WEI? WHAT SPORT DID YOU PLAY?

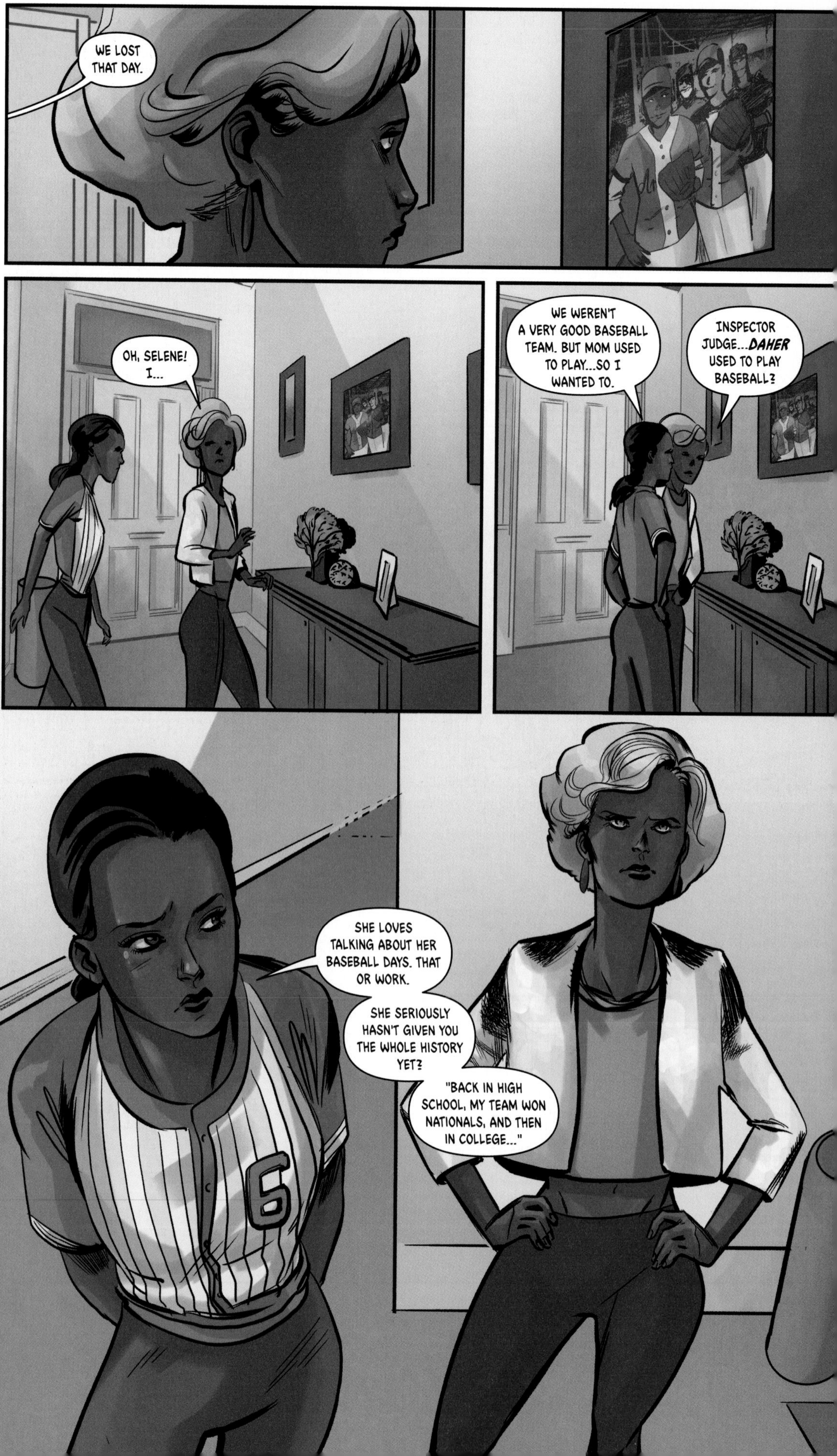
WE LOST THAT DAY.
OH, SELENE! I...
WE WEREN'T A VERY GOOD BASEBALL TEAM. BUT MOM USED TO PLAY...SO I WANTED TO.
INSPECTOR JUDGE...DAHER USED TO PLAY BASEBALL?
SHE LOVES TALKING ABOUT HER BASEBALL DAYS. THAT OR WORK.
SHE SERIOUSLY HASN'T GIVEN YOU THE WHOLE HISTORY YET?
"BACK IN HIGH SCHOOL, MY TEAM WON NATIONALS, AND THEN IN COLLEGE..."

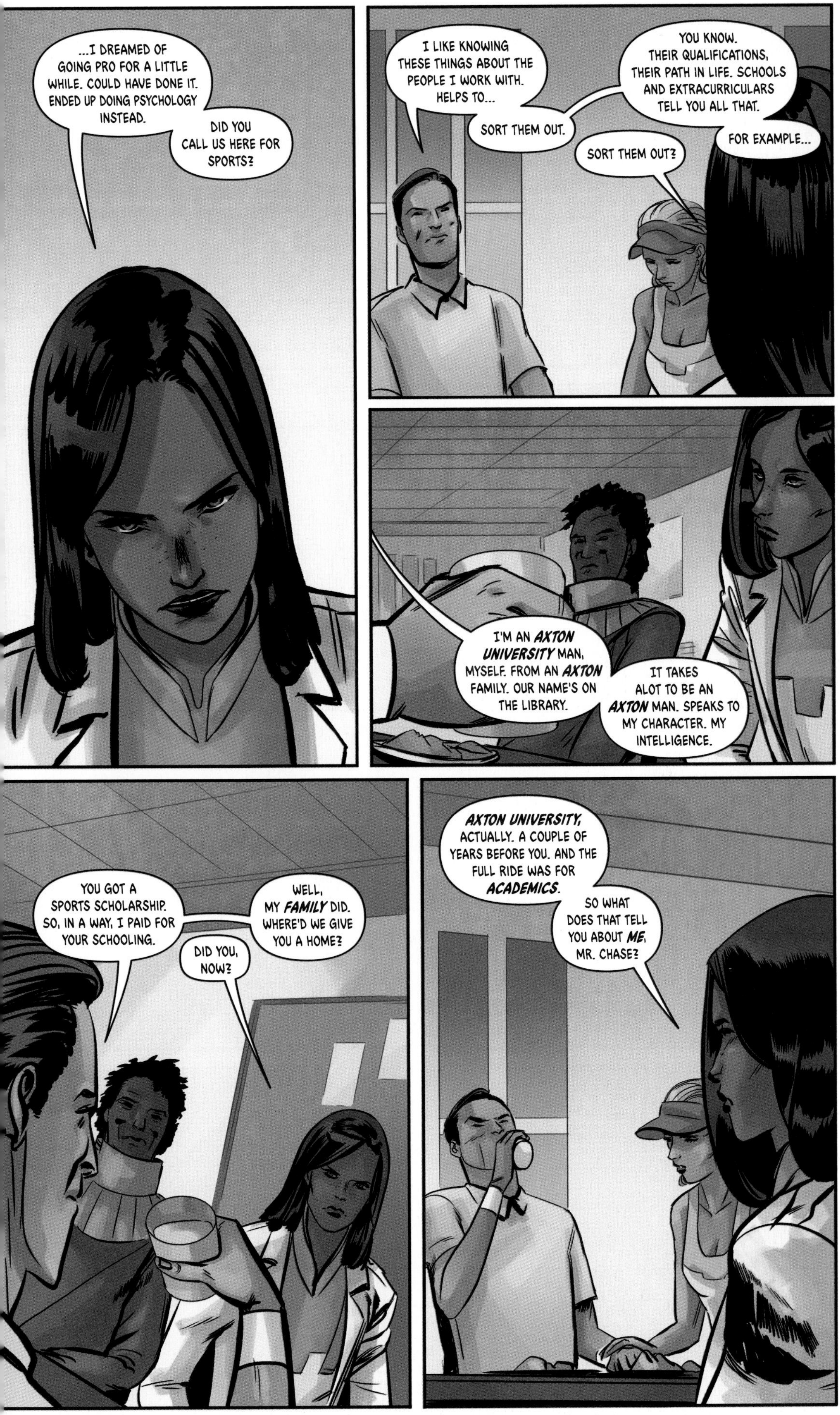
...I DREAMED OF GOING PRO FOR A LITTLE WHILE. COULD HAVE DONE IT. ENDED UP DOING PSYCHOLOGY INSTEAD.
DID YOU CALL US HERE FOR SPORTS?
I LIKE KNOWING THESE THINGS ABOUT THE PEOPLE I WORK WITH. HELPS TO...
SORT THEM OUT.
SORT THEM OUT?
YOU KNOW. THEIR QUALIFICATIONS, THEIR PATH IN LIFE. SCHOOLS AND EXTRACURRICULARS TELL YOU ALL THAT.
FOR EXAMPLE...
I'M AN AXTON UNIVERSITY MAN, MYSELF. FROM AN AXTON FAMILY. OUR NAME'S ON THE LIBRARY.
IT TAKES ALOT TO BE AN AXTON MAN. SPEAKS TO MY CHARACTER. MY INTELLIGENCE.
YOU GOT A SPORTS SCHOLARSHIP. SO, IN A WAY, I PAID FOR YOUR SCHOOLING.
DID YOU, NOW?
WELL, MY FAMILY DID. WHERE'D WE GIVE YOU A HOME?
AXTON UNIVERSITY, ACTUALLY. A COUPLE OF YEARS BEFORE YOU. AND THE FULL RIDE WAS FOR ACADEMICS.
SO WHAT DOES THAT TELL YOU ABOUT ME, MR. CHASE?

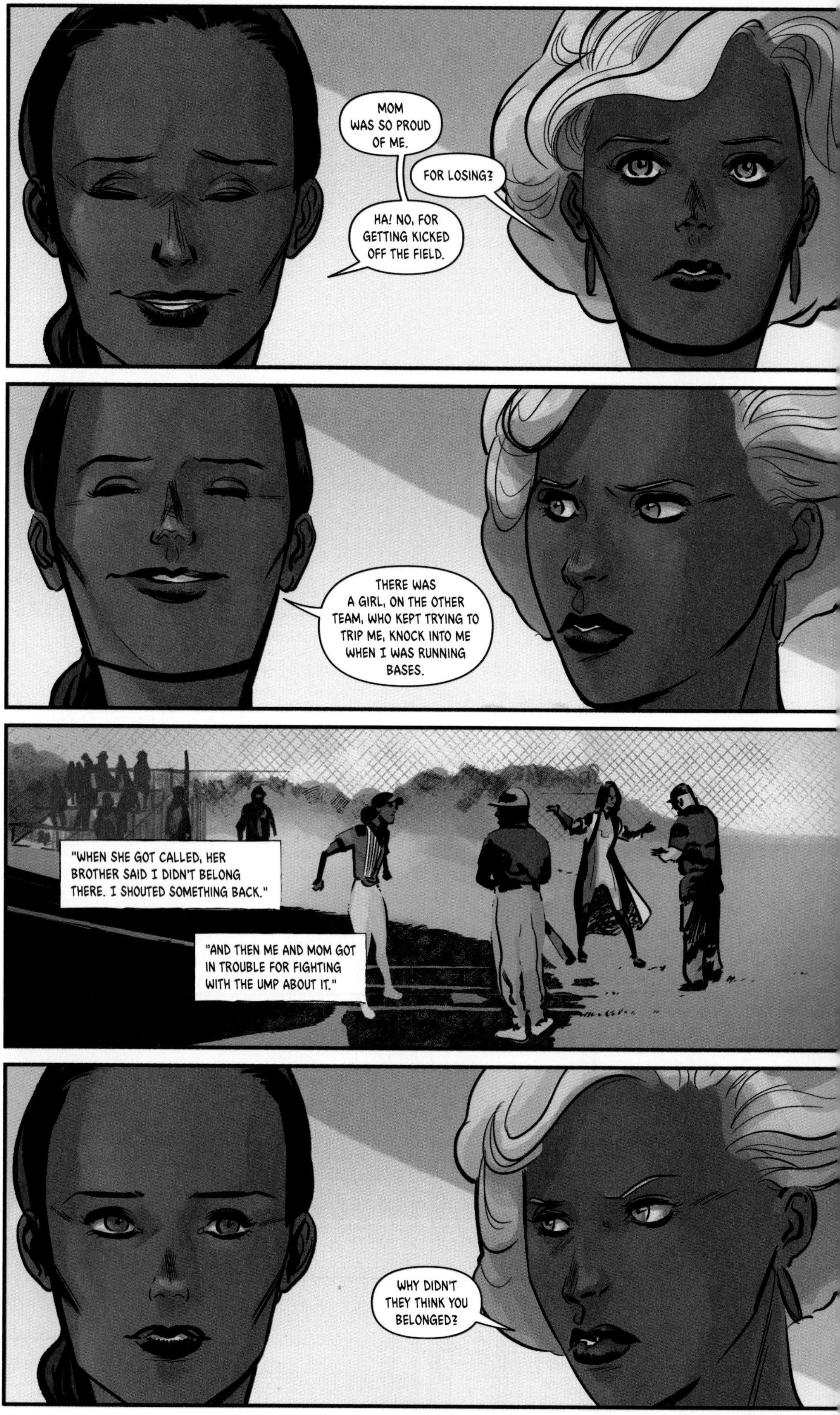
MOM WAS SO PROUD OF ME.
FOR LOSING?
HA! NO, FOR GETTING KICKED OFF THE FIELD.
THERE WAS A GIRL, ON THE OTHER TEAM, WHO KEPT TRYING TO TRIP ME, KNOCK INTO ME WHEN I WAS RUNNING BASES.
"WHEN SHE GOT CALLED, HER BROTHER SAID I DIDN'T BELONG THERE. I SHOUTED SOMETHING BACK."
"AND THEN ME AND MOM GOT IN TROUBLE FOR FIGHTING WITH THE UMP ABOUT IT."
WHY DIDN'T THEY THINK YOU BELONGED?

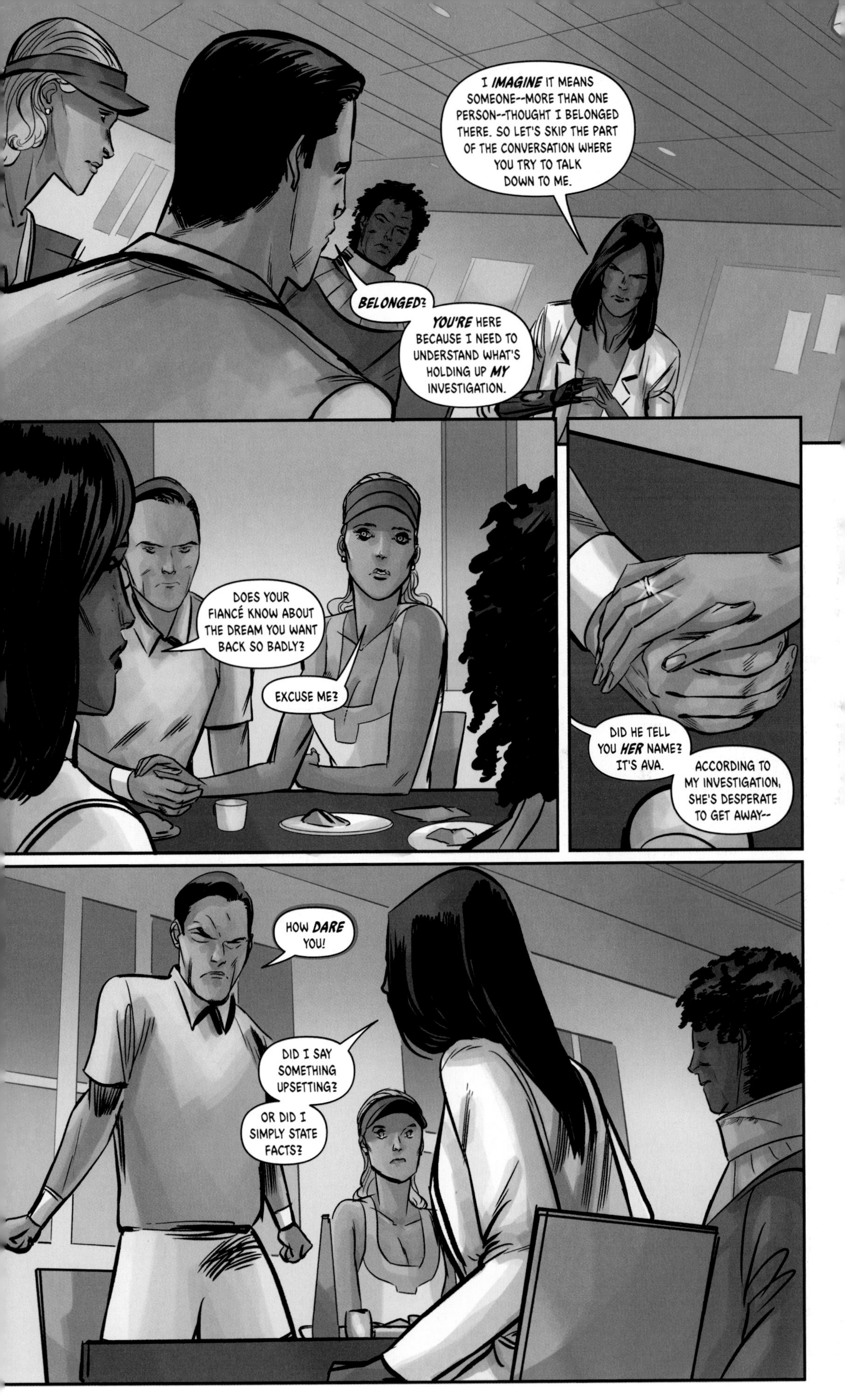
I IMAGINE IT MEANS SOMEONE--MORE THAN ONE PERSON--THOUGHT I BELONGED THERE. SO LET'S SKIP THE PART OF THE CONVERSATION WHERE YOU TRY TO TALK DOWN TO ME.
BELONGED?
YOU'RE HERE BECAUSE I NEED TO UNDERSTAND WHAT'S HOLDING UP MY INVESTIGATION.
DOES YOUR FIANCÉ KNOW ABOUT THE DREAM YOU WANT BACK SO BADLY?
EXCUSE ME?
DID HE TELL YOU HER NAME? IT'S AVA.
ACCORDING TO MY INVESTIGATION, SHE'S DESPERATE TO GET AWAY--
HOW DARE YOU!
DID I SAY SOMETHING UPSETTING?
OR DID I SIMPLY STATE FACTS?

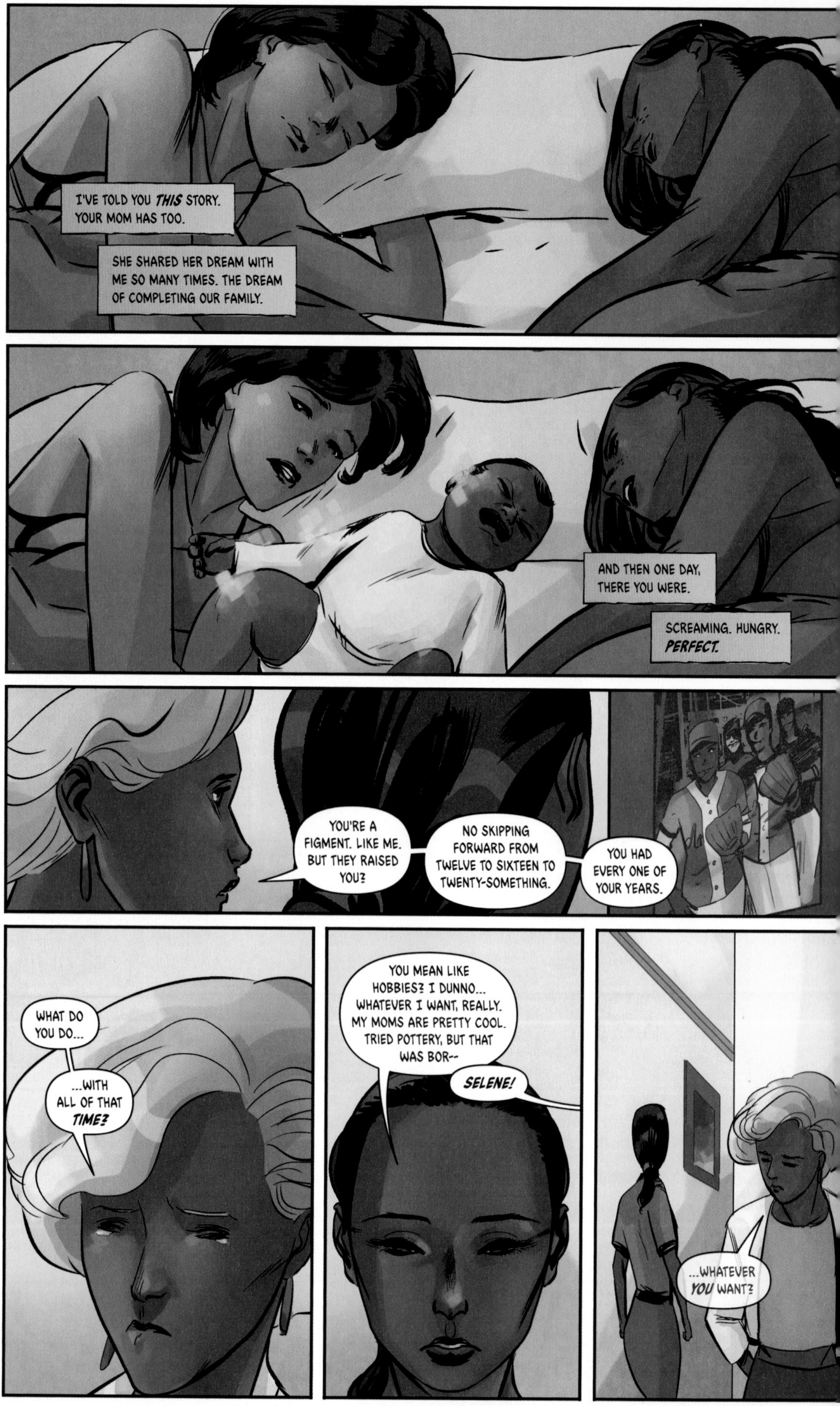
I'VE TOLD YOU *THIS* STORY. YOUR MOM HAS TOO.
SHE SHARED HER DREAM WITH ME SO MANY TIMES. THE DREAM OF COMPLETING OUR FAMILY.
AND THEN ONE DAY, THERE YOU WERE.
SCREAMING. HUNGRY. ***PERFECT.***
YOU'RE A FIGMENT. LIKE ME. BUT THEY RAISED YOU?
NO SKIPPING FORWARD FROM TWELVE TO SIXTEEN TO TWENTY-SOMETHING.
YOU HAD EVERY ONE OF YOUR YEARS.
WHAT DO YOU DO...
...WITH ALL OF THAT ***TIME?***
YOU MEAN LIKE HOBBIES? I DUNNO... WHATEVER I WANT, REALLY. MY MOMS ARE PRETTY COOL. TRIED POTTERY, BUT THAT WAS BOR--
SELENE!
...WHATEVER ***YOU*** WANT?

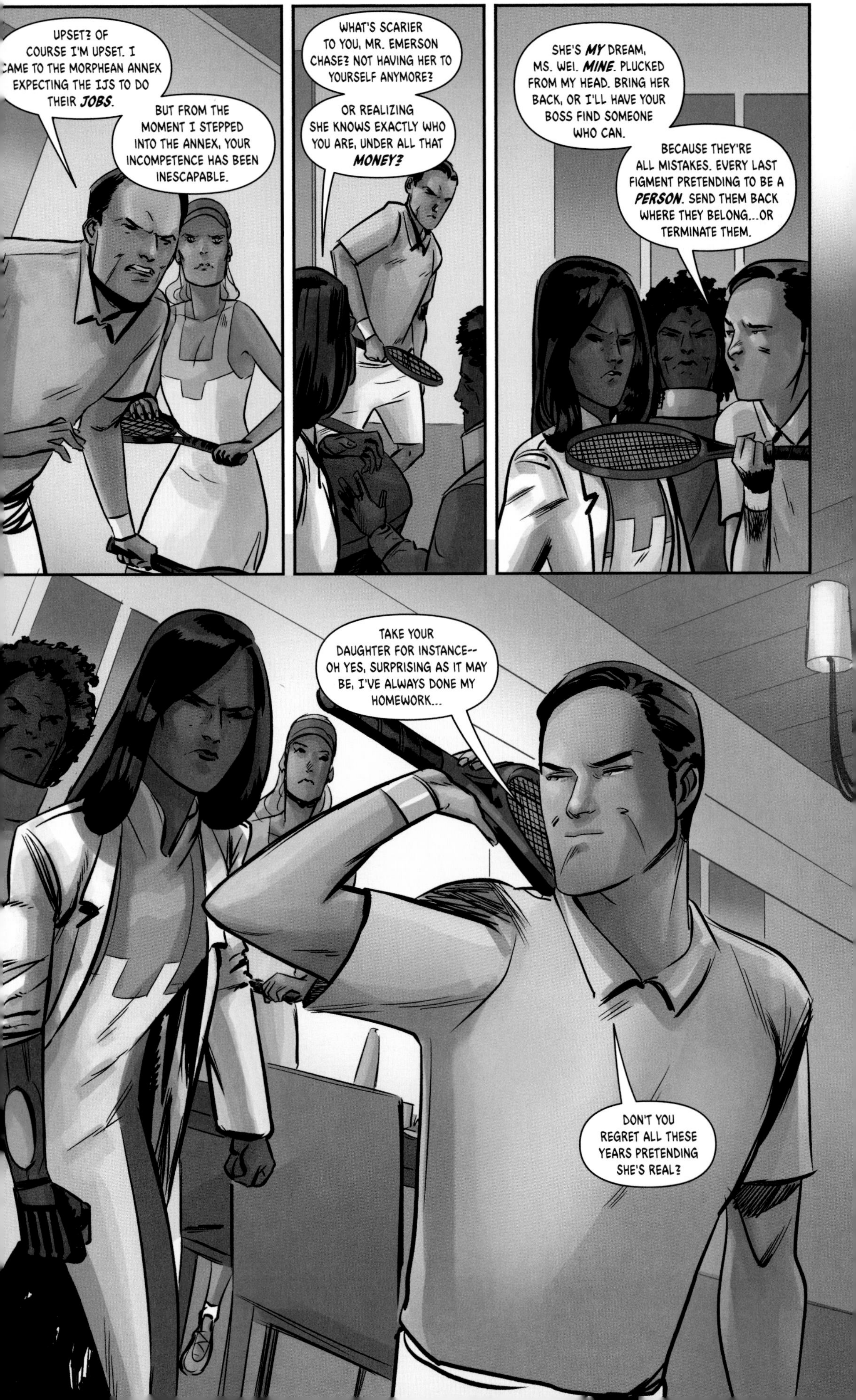
UPSET? OF COURSE I'M UPSET. I CAME TO THE MORPHEAN ANNEX EXPECTING THE IJS TO DO THEIR *JOBS*.
BUT FROM THE MOMENT I STEPPED INTO THE ANNEX, YOUR INCOMPETENCE HAS BEEN INESCAPABLE.
WHAT'S SCARIER TO YOU, MR. EMERSON CHASE? NOT HAVING HER TO YOURSELF ANYMORE?
OR REALIZING SHE KNOWS EXACTLY WHO YOU ARE, UNDER ALL THAT *MONEY?*
SHE'S *MY* DREAM, MS. WEI. *MINE*. PLUCKED FROM MY HEAD. BRING HER BACK, OR I'LL HAVE YOUR BOSS FIND SOMEONE WHO CAN.
BECAUSE THEY'RE ALL MISTAKES. EVERY LAST FIGMENT PRETENDING TO BE A *PERSON*. SEND THEM BACK WHERE THEY BELONG...OR TERMINATE THEM.
TAKE YOUR DAUGHTER FOR INSTANCE-- OH YES, SURPRISING AS IT MAY BE, I'VE ALWAYS DONE MY HOMEWORK...
DON'T YOU REGRET ALL THESE YEARS PRETENDING SHE'S REAL?

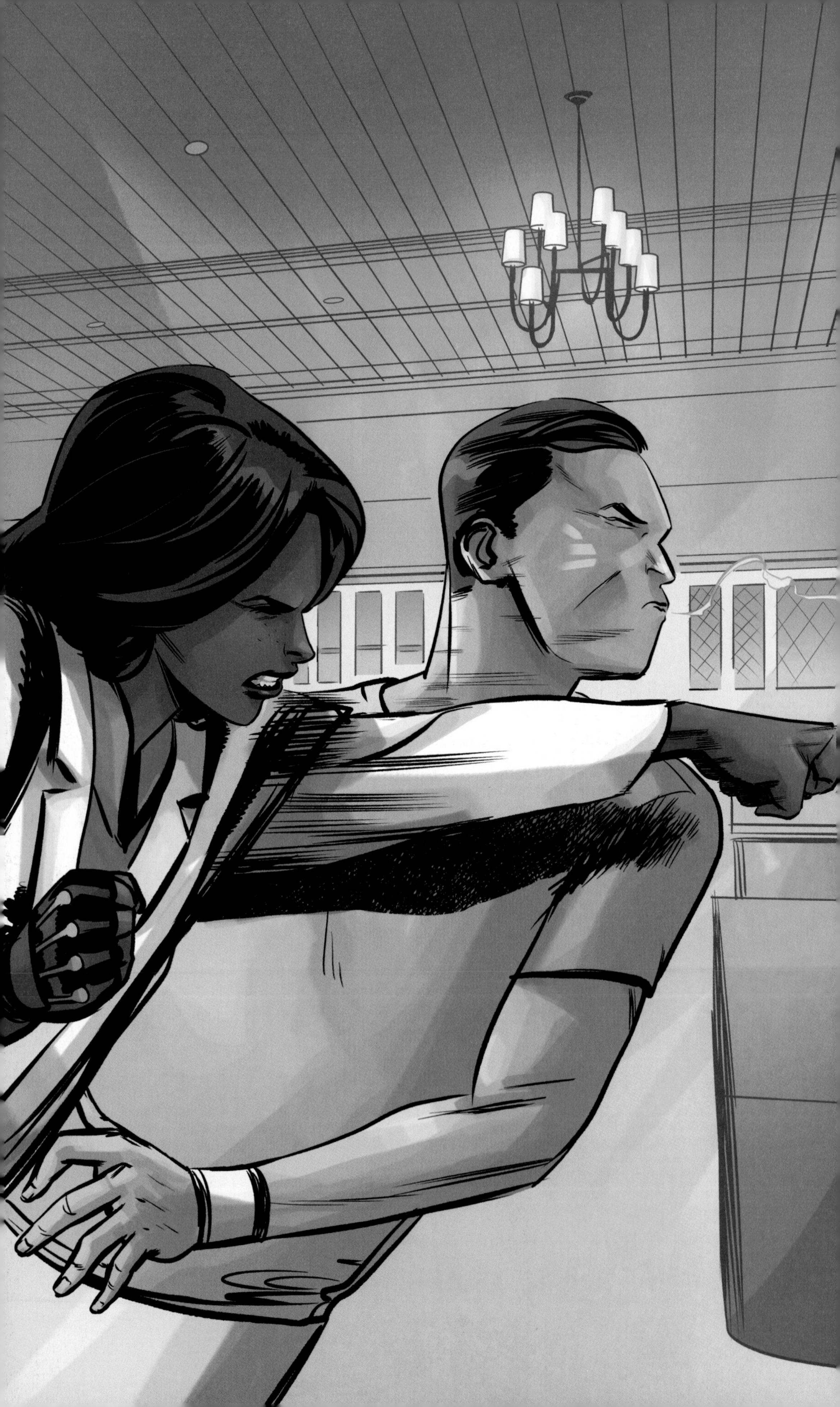

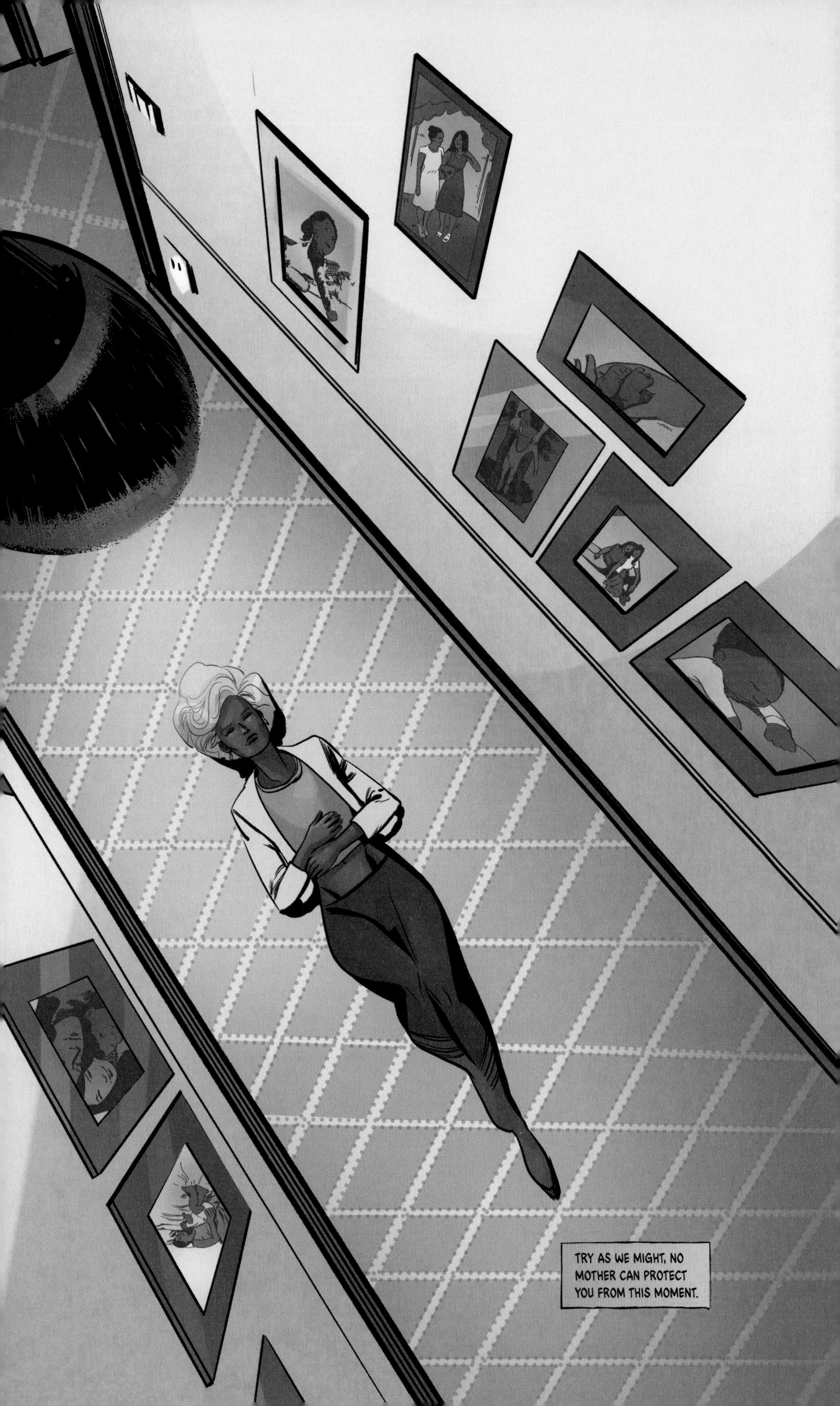
TRY AS WE MIGHT, NO
MOTHER CAN PROTECT
YOU FROM THIS MOMENT.

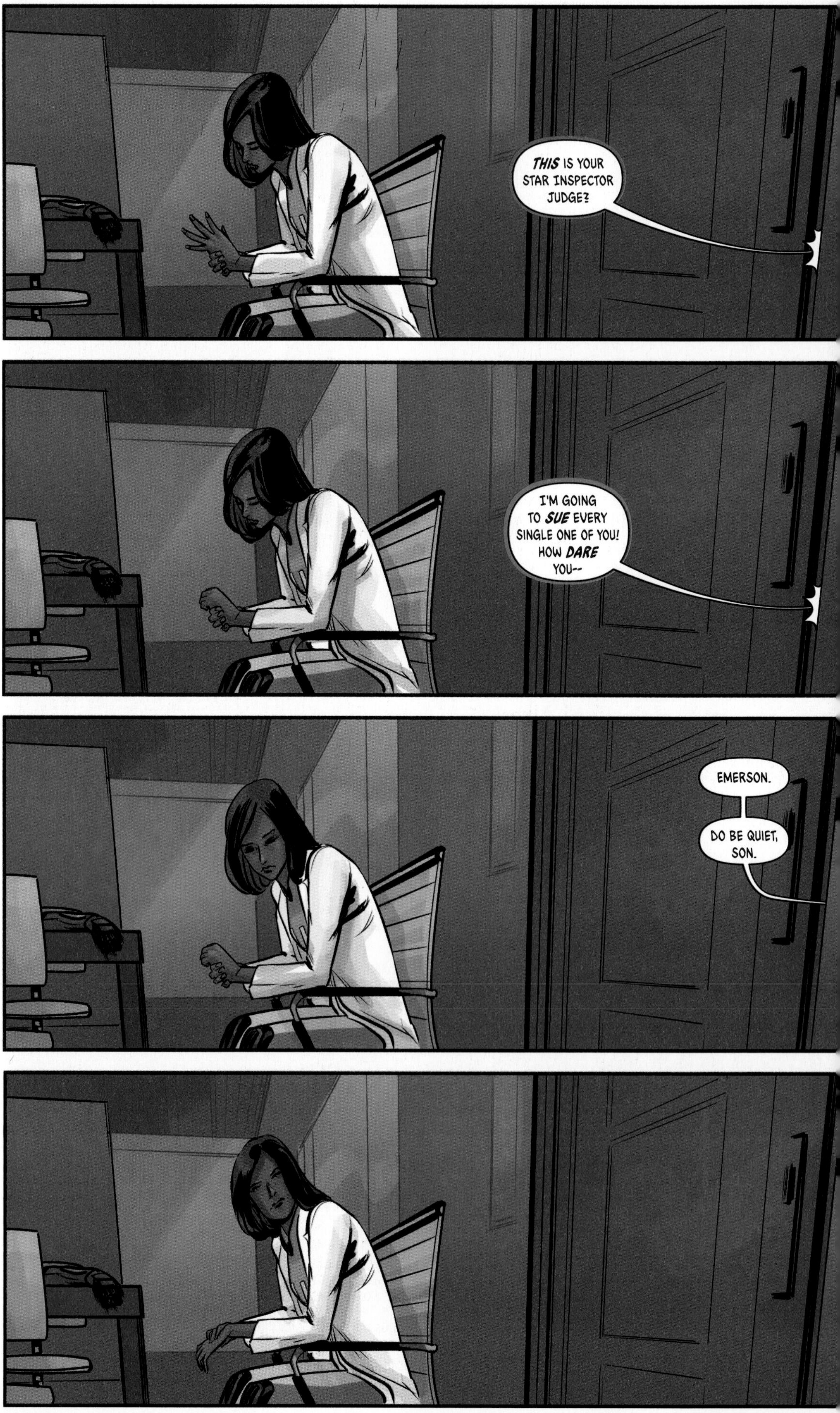
THIS IS YOUR STAR INSPECTOR JUDGE?
I'M GOING TO SUE EVERY SINGLE ONE OF YOU! HOW DARE YOU--
EMERSON.
DO BE QUIET, SON.

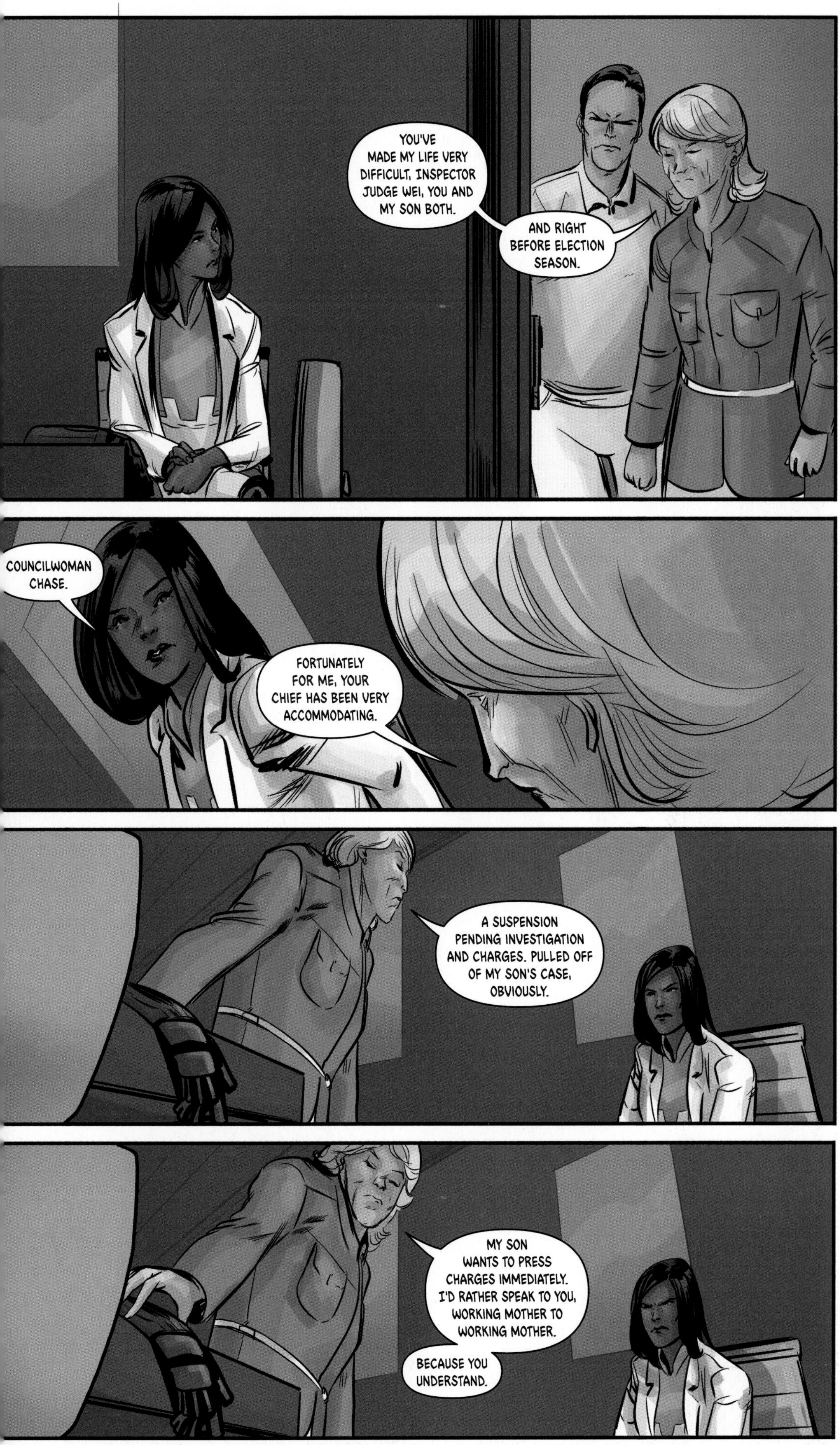
YOU'VE MADE MY LIFE VERY DIFFICULT, INSPECTOR JUDGE WEI, YOU AND MY SON BOTH.
AND RIGHT BEFORE ELECTION SEASON.
COUNCILWOMAN CHASE.
FORTUNATELY FOR ME, YOUR CHIEF HAS BEEN VERY ACCOMMODATING.
A SUSPENSION PENDING INVESTIGATION AND CHARGES. PULLED OFF OF MY SON'S CASE, OBVIOUSLY.
MY SON WANTS TO PRESS CHARGES IMMEDIATELY. I'D RATHER SPEAK TO YOU, WORKING MOTHER TO WORKING MOTHER.
BECAUSE YOU UNDERSTAND.

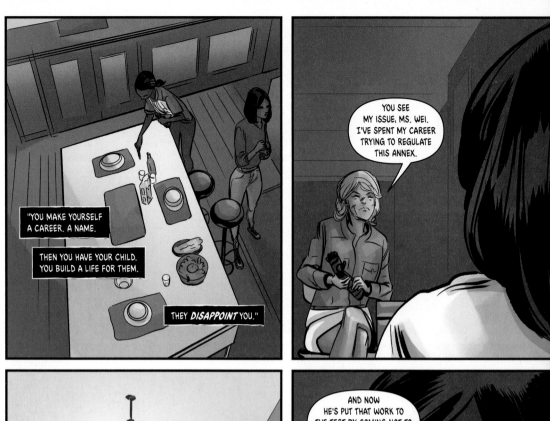

"YOU MAKE YOURSELF A CAREER. A NAME.

THEN YOU HAVE YOUR CHILD. YOU BUILD A LIFE FOR THEM.

THEY *DISAPPOINT* YOU."

YOU SEE MY ISSUE, MS. WEI. I'VE SPENT MY CAREER TRYING TO REGULATE THIS ANNEX.

"PUT A STOP TO INSPECTOR JUDGES AND THEIR POWER TO ADJUDICATE THE DREAMS OF PEOPLE LIKE MY *SON*."

AND NOW HE'S PUT THAT WORK TO THE TEST BY COMING NOT TO ME, HIS MOTHER, BUT *YOU*, TO SOLVE THINGS.

"IS THAT WHAT YOU THINK BEING A MOTHER IS?"

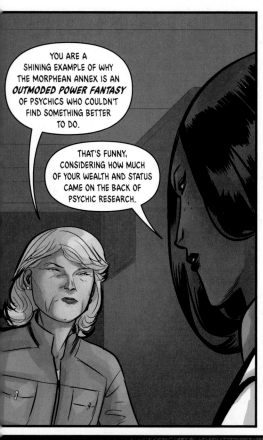
YOU ARE A SHINING EXAMPLE OF WHY THE MORPHEAN ANNEX IS AN *OUTMODED POWER FANTASY* OF PSYCHICS WHO COULDN'T FIND SOMETHING BETTER TO DO.

THAT'S FUNNY, CONSIDERING HOW MUCH OF YOUR WEALTH AND STATUS CAME ON THE BACK OF PSYCHIC RESEARCH.

IT'S UNFORTUNATE THAT YOU DO NOT UNDERSTAND, MS. WEI. WE COULD HAVE HELPED EACH OTHER.

WE COULD HAVE WORKED TOGETHER TO PRESERVE MY SON'S DREAMS.

MY DREAMS.

FUCK. YOU.

IT'S NOT *YOUR* DREAMS I'M HERE TO PROTECT.

I WAS BEING NICE. LETTING YOU SAVE FACE. I DON'T NEED YOU.

I ONLY NEED AVA. AND A LOCATION.

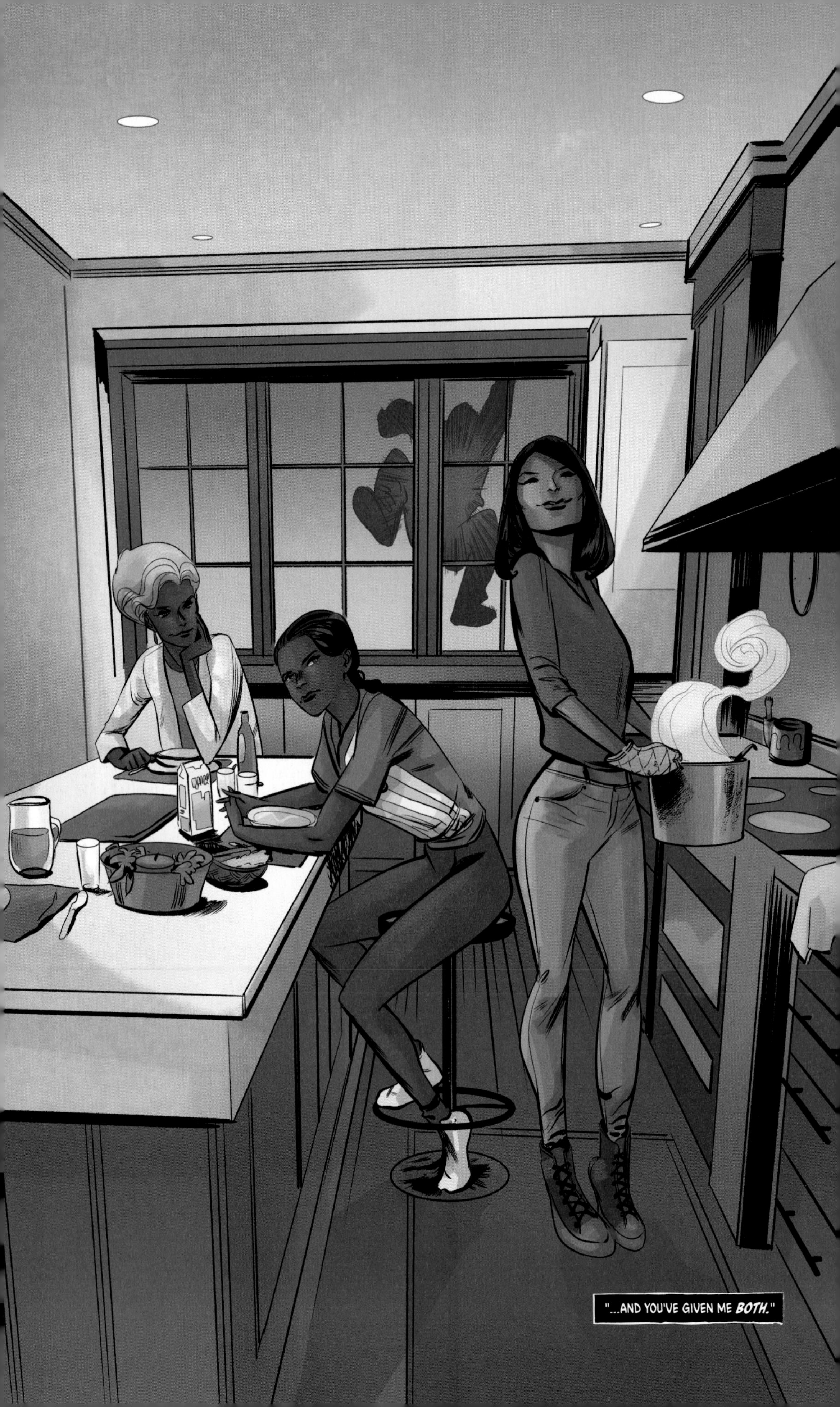
"...AND YOU'VE GIVEN ME *BOTH.*"

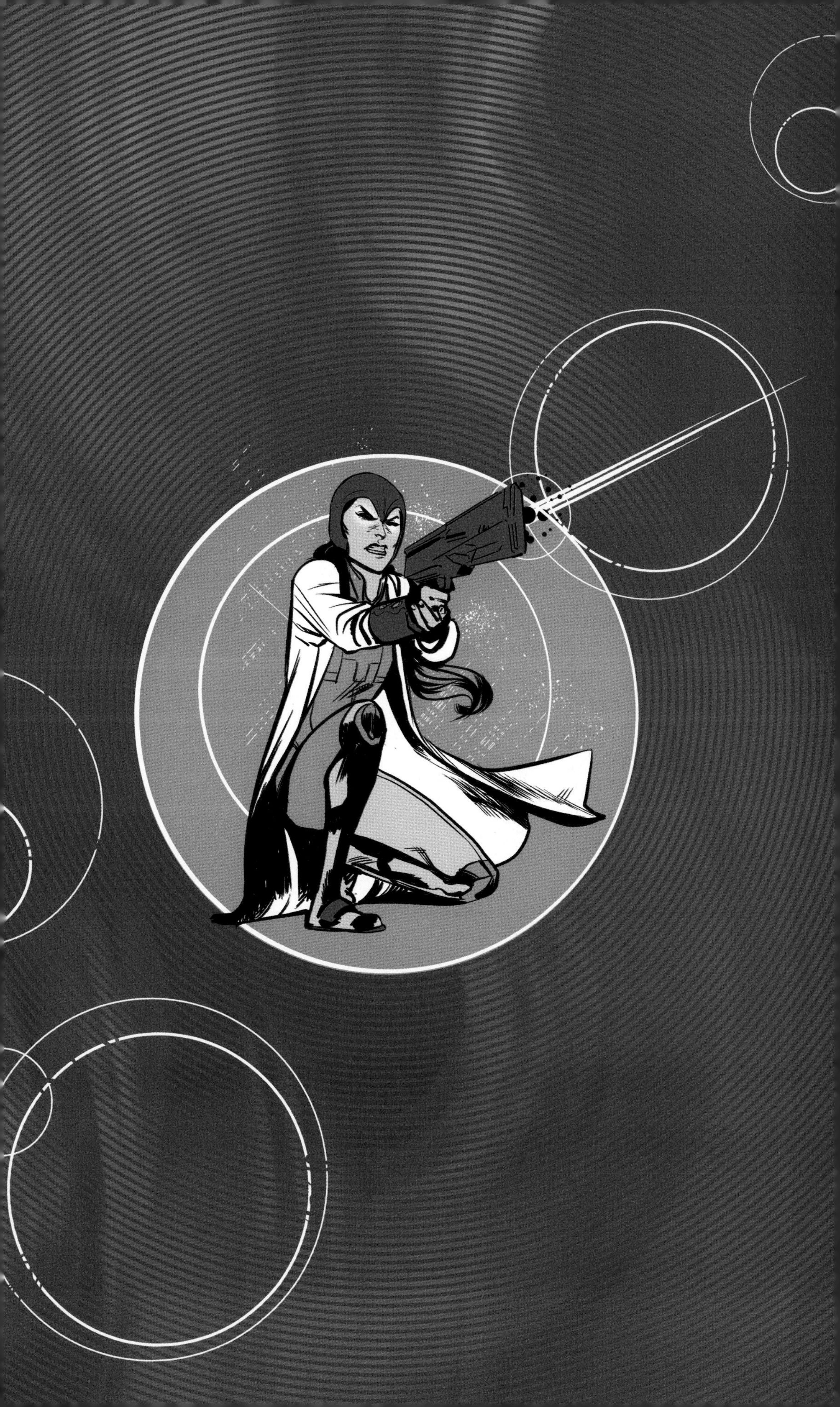

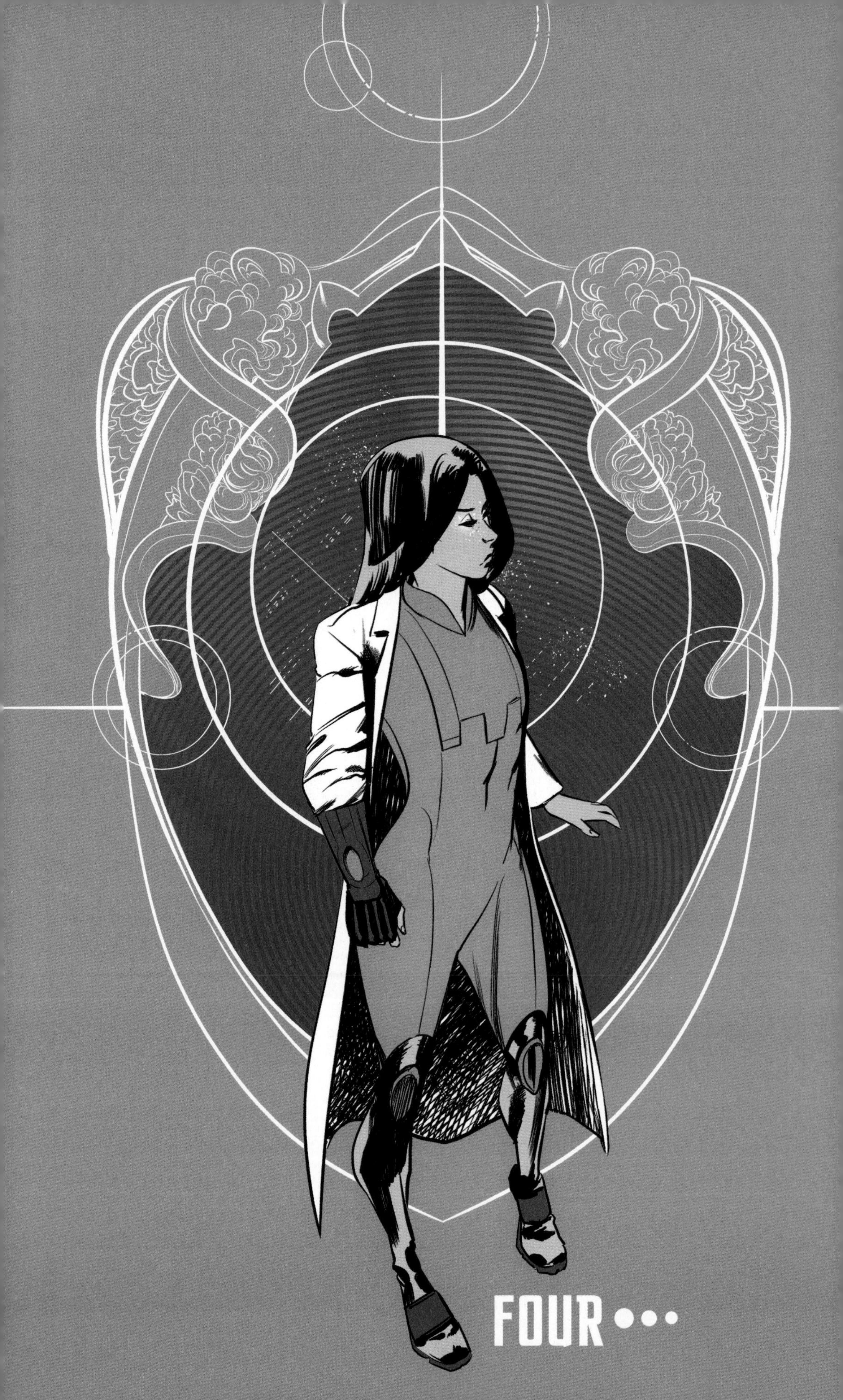

FOUR •••

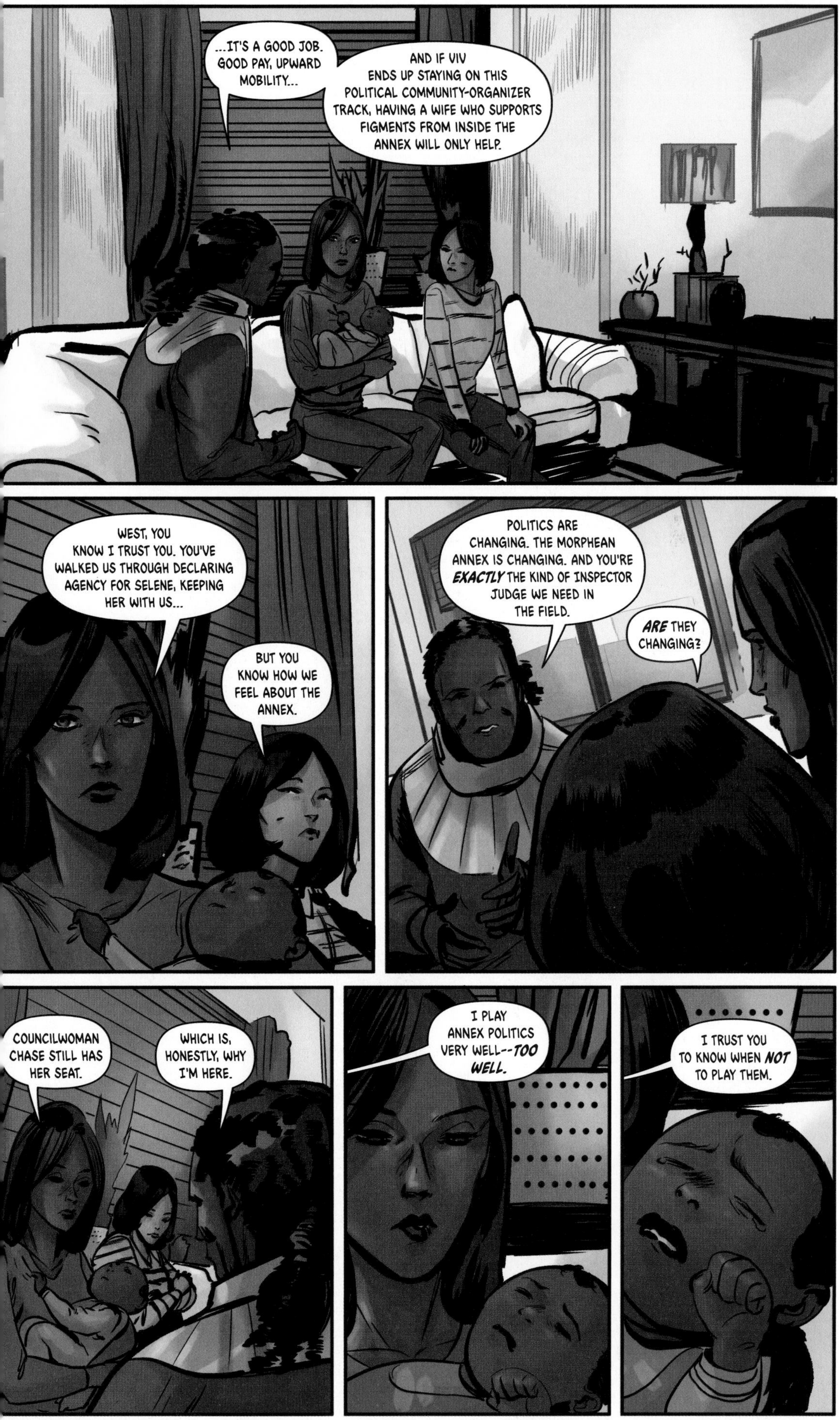

...IT'S A GOOD JOB. GOOD PAY, UPWARD MOBILITY...
AND IF VIV ENDS UP STAYING ON THIS POLITICAL COMMUNITY-ORGANIZER TRACK, HAVING A WIFE WHO SUPPORTS FIGMENTS FROM INSIDE THE ANNEX WILL ONLY HELP.
WEST, YOU KNOW I TRUST YOU. YOU'VE WALKED US THROUGH DECLARING AGENCY FOR SELENE, KEEPING HER WITH US...
BUT YOU KNOW HOW WE FEEL ABOUT THE ANNEX.
POLITICS ARE CHANGING. THE MORPHEAN ANNEX IS CHANGING. AND YOU'RE *EXACTLY* THE KIND OF INSPECTOR JUDGE WE NEED IN THE FIELD.
ARE THEY CHANGING?
COUNCILWOMAN CHASE STILL HAS HER SEAT.
WHICH IS, HONESTLY, WHY I'M HERE.
I PLAY ANNEX POLITICS VERY WELL--*TOO WELL.*
I TRUST YOU TO KNOW WHEN *NOT* TO PLAY THEM.

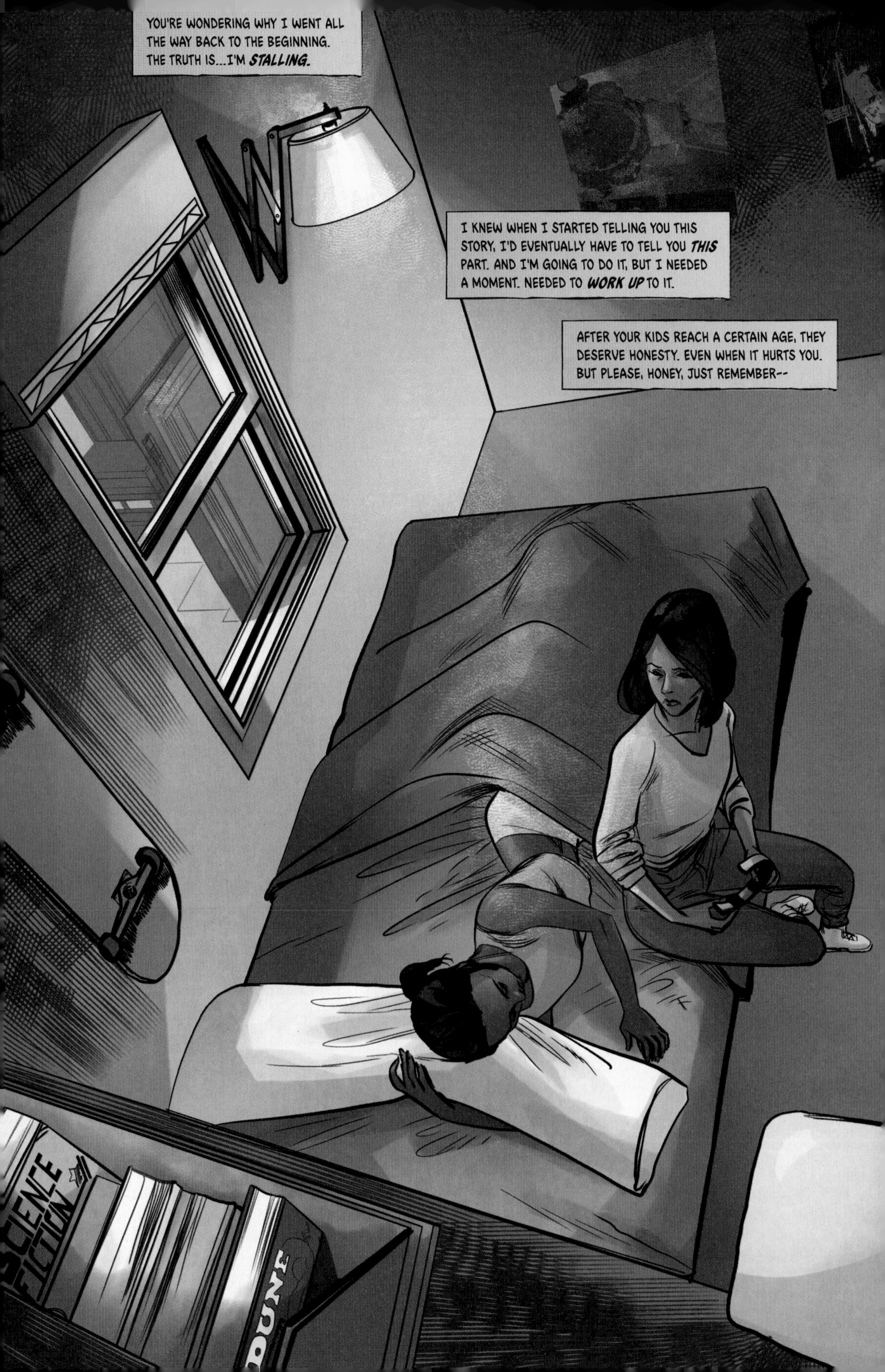
YOU'RE WONDERING WHY I WENT ALL THE WAY BACK TO THE BEGINNING. THE TRUTH IS...I'M STALLING.
I KNEW WHEN I STARTED TELLING YOU THIS STORY, I'D EVENTUALLY HAVE TO TELL YOU THIS PART. AND I'M GOING TO DO IT, BUT I NEEDED A MOMENT. NEEDED TO WORK UP TO IT.
AFTER YOUR KIDS REACH A CERTAIN AGE, THEY DESERVE HONESTY. EVEN WHEN IT HURTS YOU. BUT PLEASE, HONEY, JUST REMEMBER--
SCIENCE FICTION
DUNE

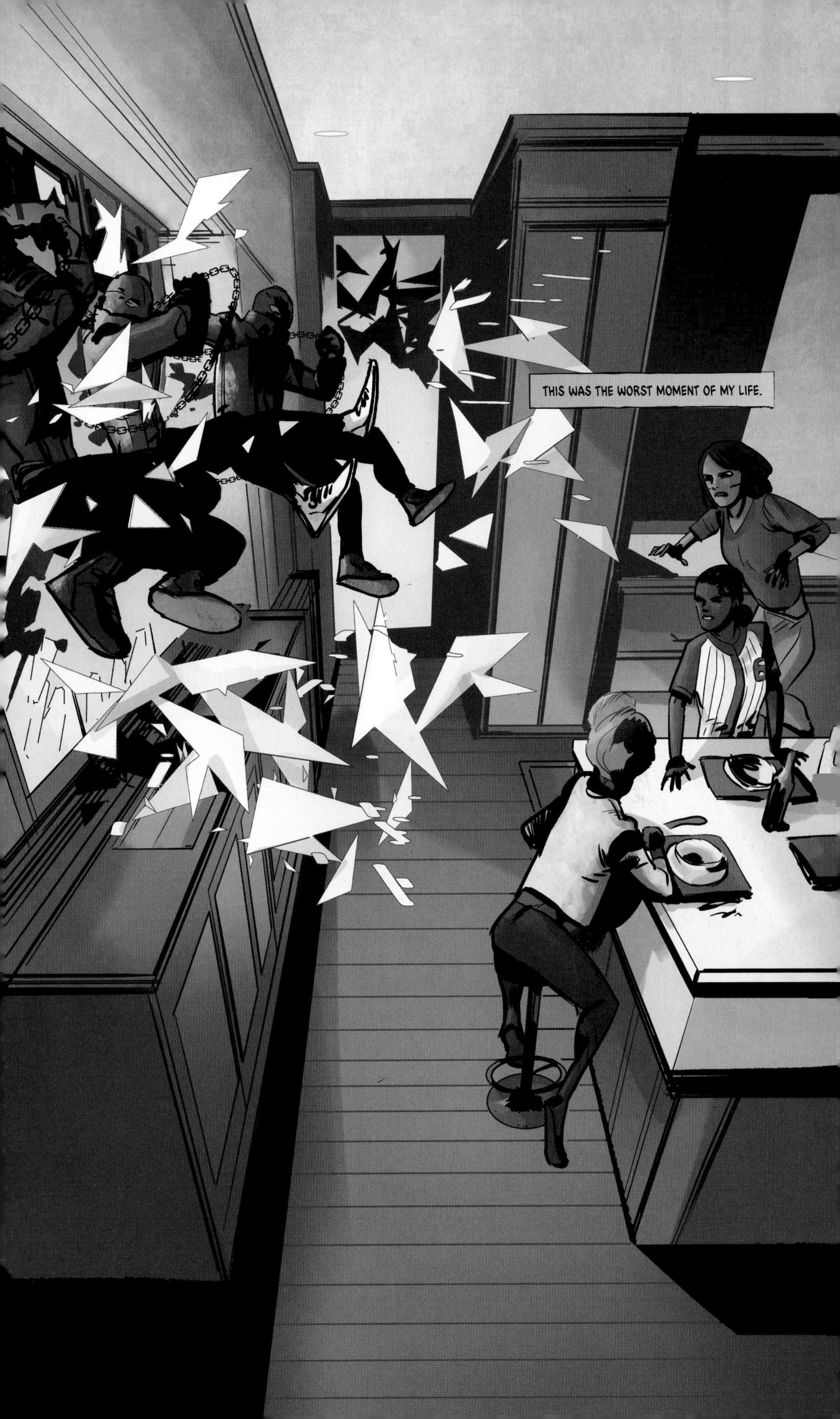
THIS WAS THE WORST MOMENT OF MY LIFE.

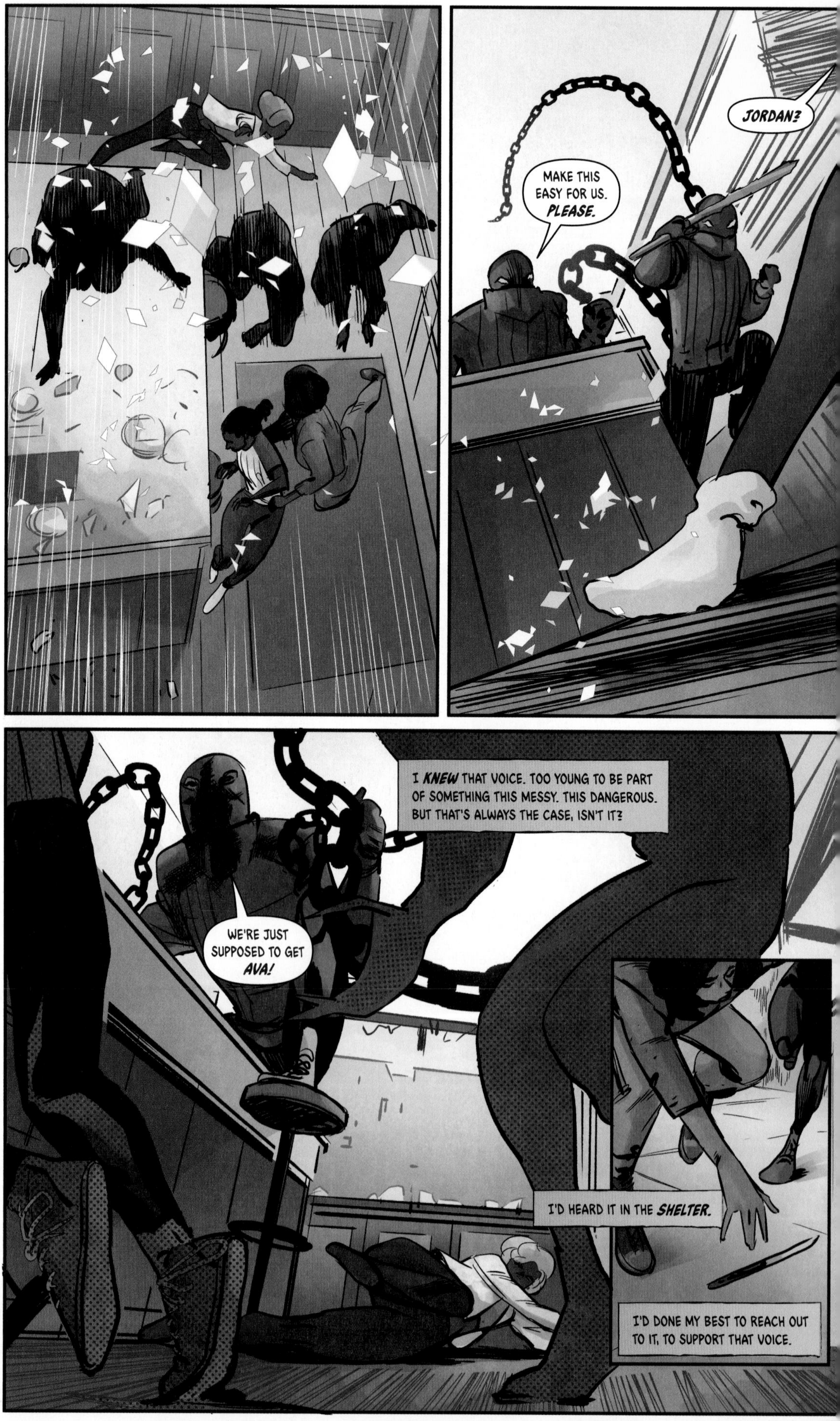
MAKE THIS EASY FOR US. PLEASE.
JORDAN?
I KNEW THAT VOICE. TOO YOUNG TO BE PART OF SOMETHING THIS MESSY. THIS DANGEROUS. BUT THAT'S ALWAYS THE CASE, ISN'T IT?
WE'RE JUST SUPPOSED TO GET AVA!
I'D HEARD IT IN THE SHELTER.
I'D DONE MY BEST TO REACH OUT TO IT, TO SUPPORT THAT VOICE.

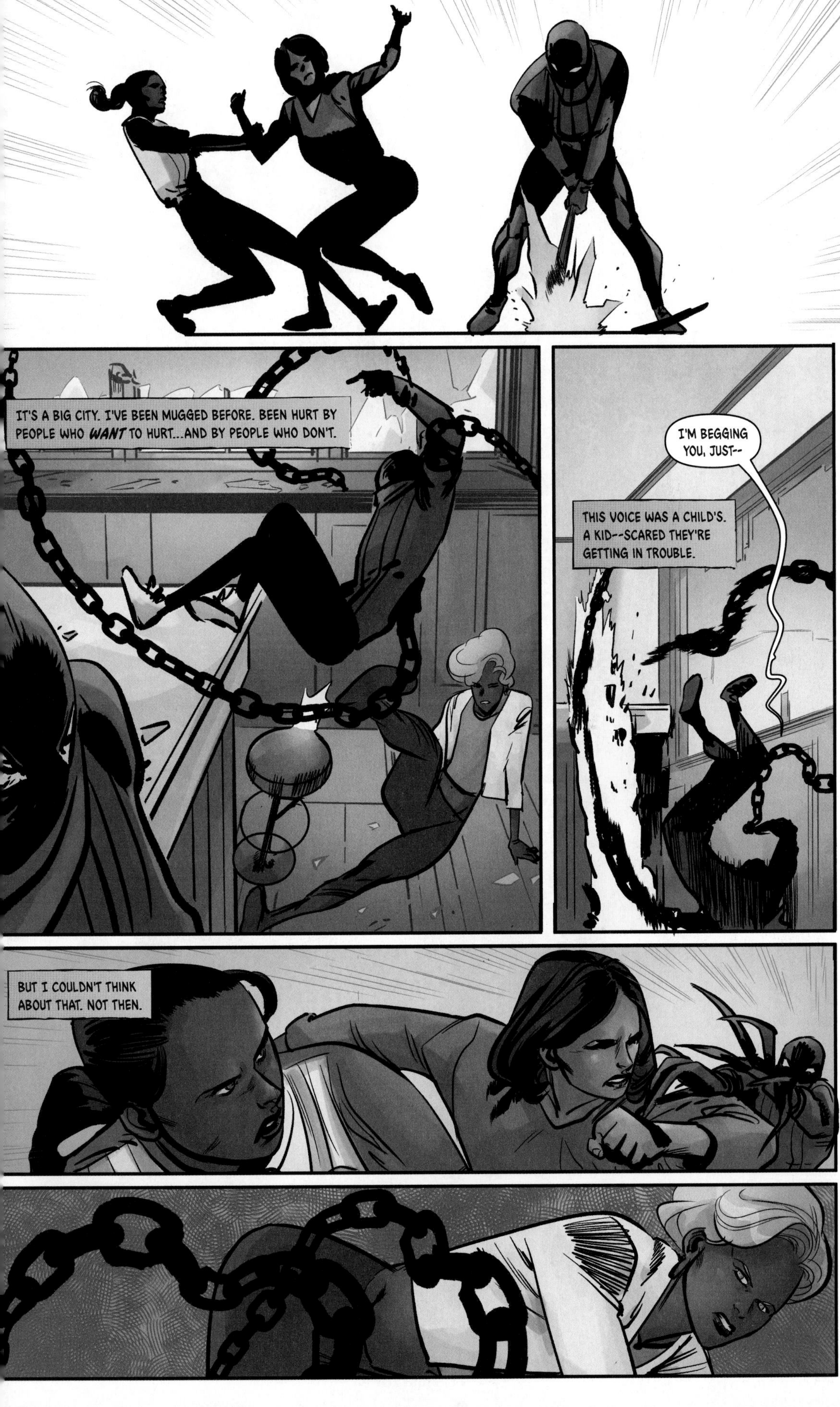

IT'S A BIG CITY. I'VE BEEN MUGGED BEFORE. BEEN HURT BY PEOPLE WHO *WANT* TO HURT...AND BY PEOPLE WHO DON'T.
I'M BEGGING YOU, JUST--
THIS VOICE WAS A CHILD'S. A KID--SCARED THEY'RE GETTING IN TROUBLE.
BUT I COULDN'T THINK ABOUT THAT. NOT THEN.

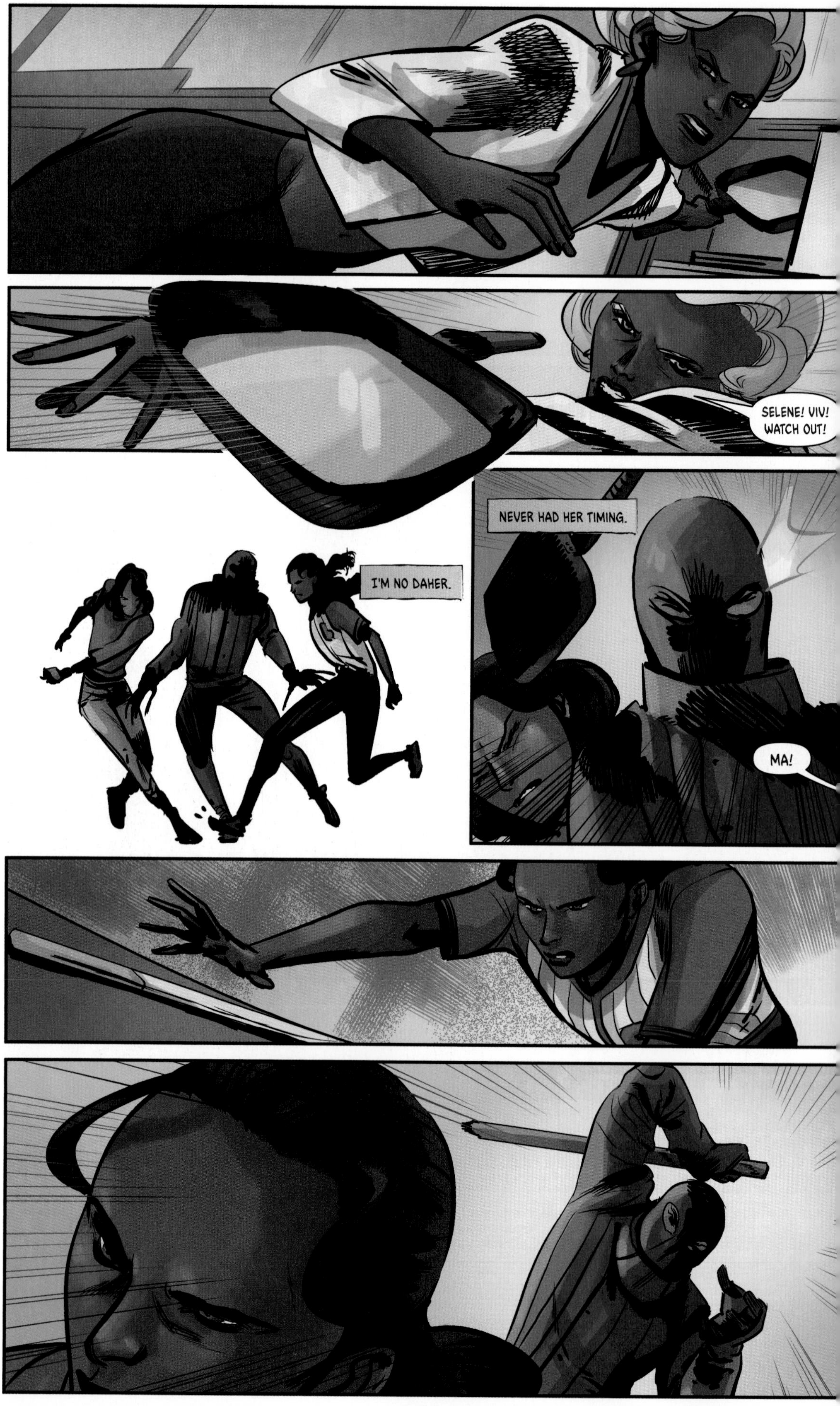
SELENE! VIV! WATCH OUT!
I'M NO DAHER.
NEVER HAD HER TIMING.
MA!

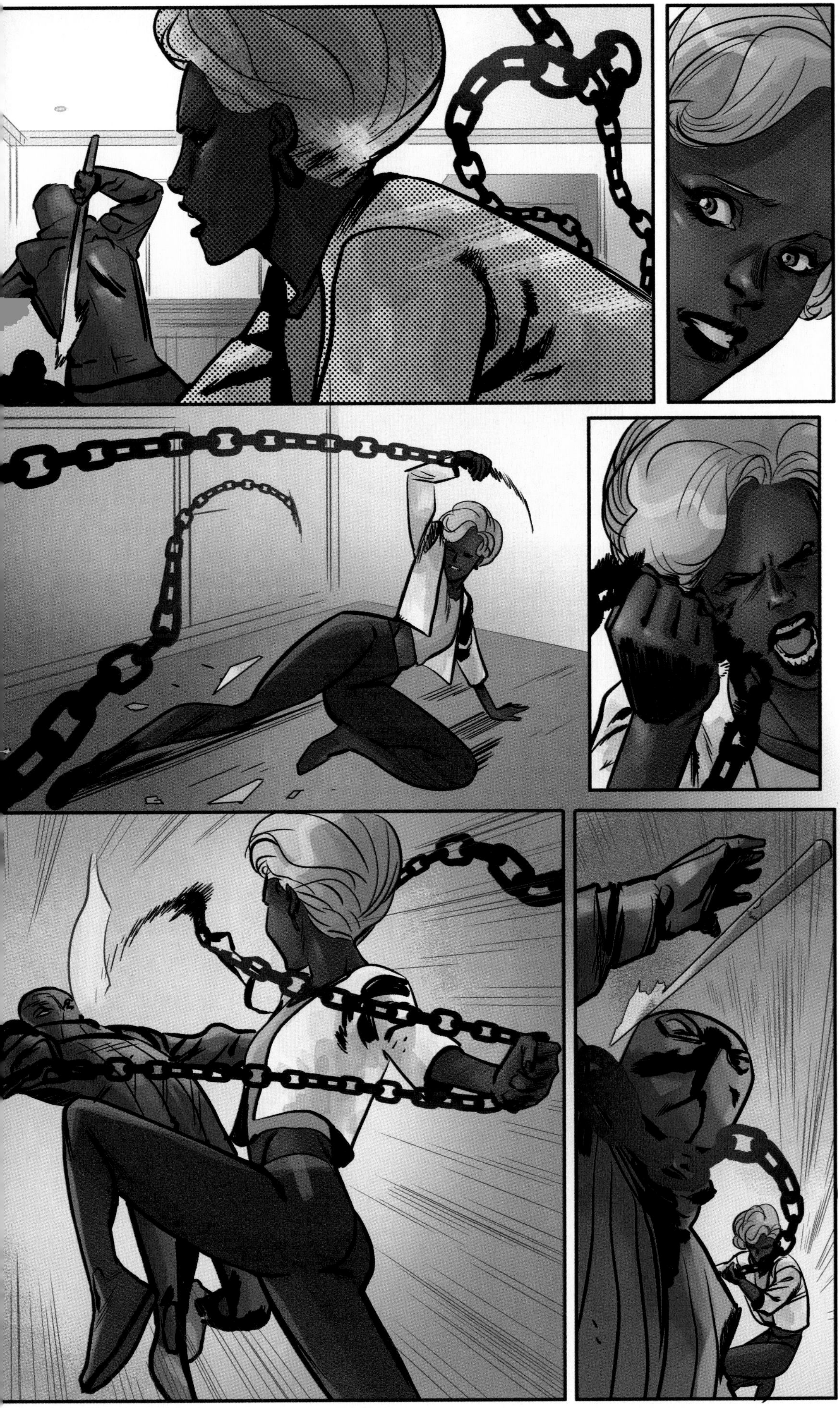

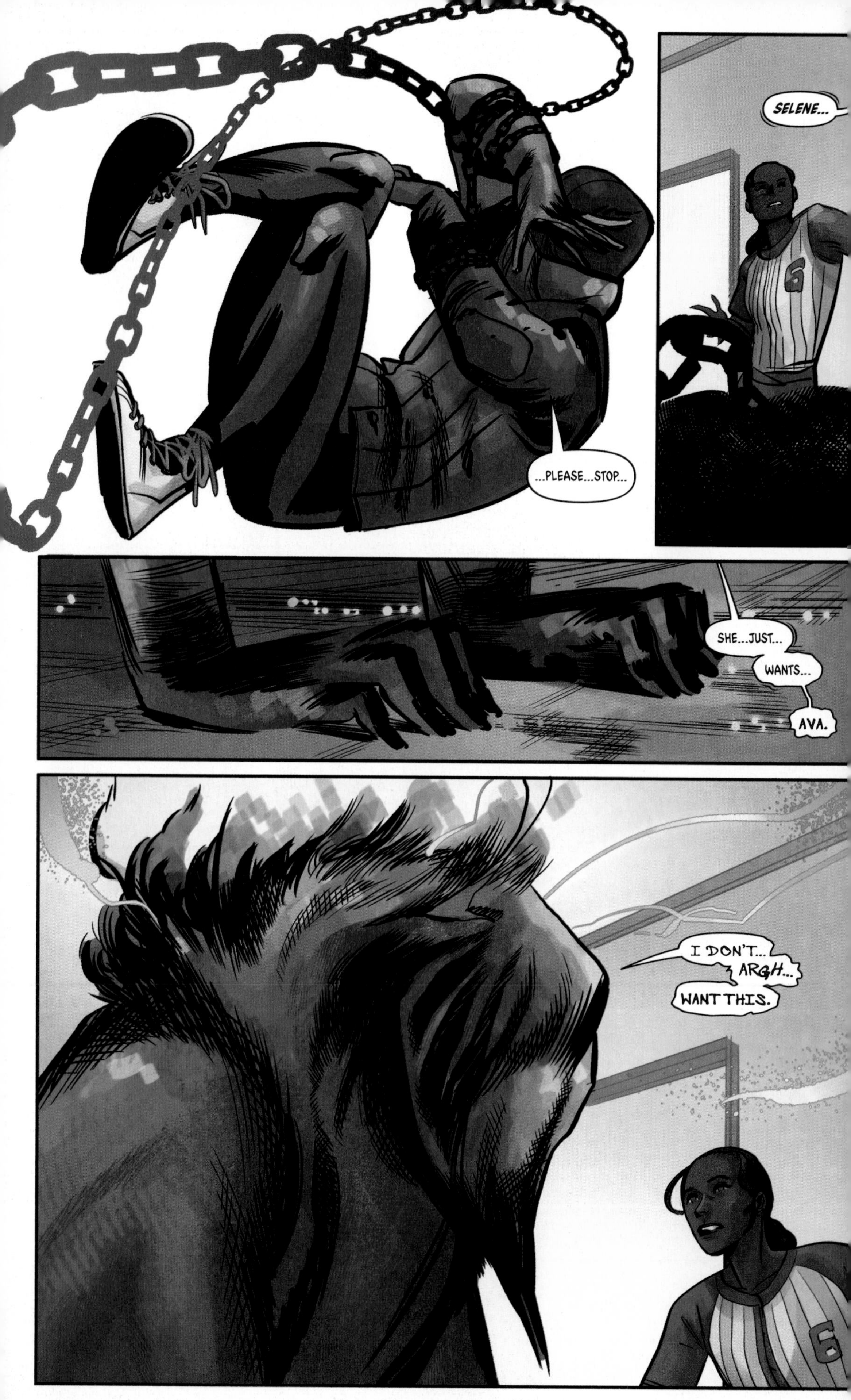
...PLEASE...STOP...
SELENE...
SHE...JUST...
WANTS...
AVA.
I DON'T...
ARGH...
WANT THIS.

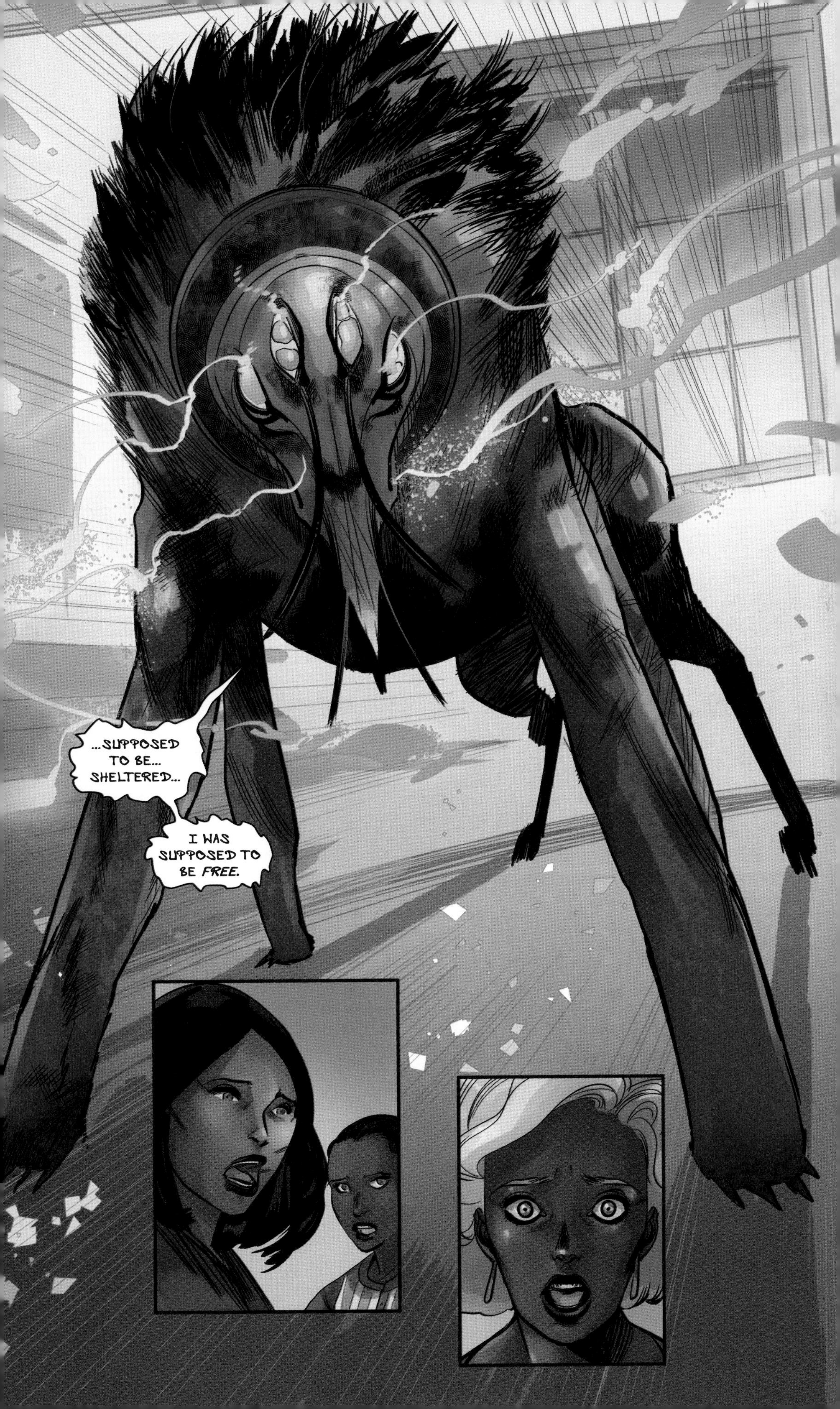
...SUPPOSED TO BE... SHELTERED...
I WAS SUPPOSED TO BE *FREE*.

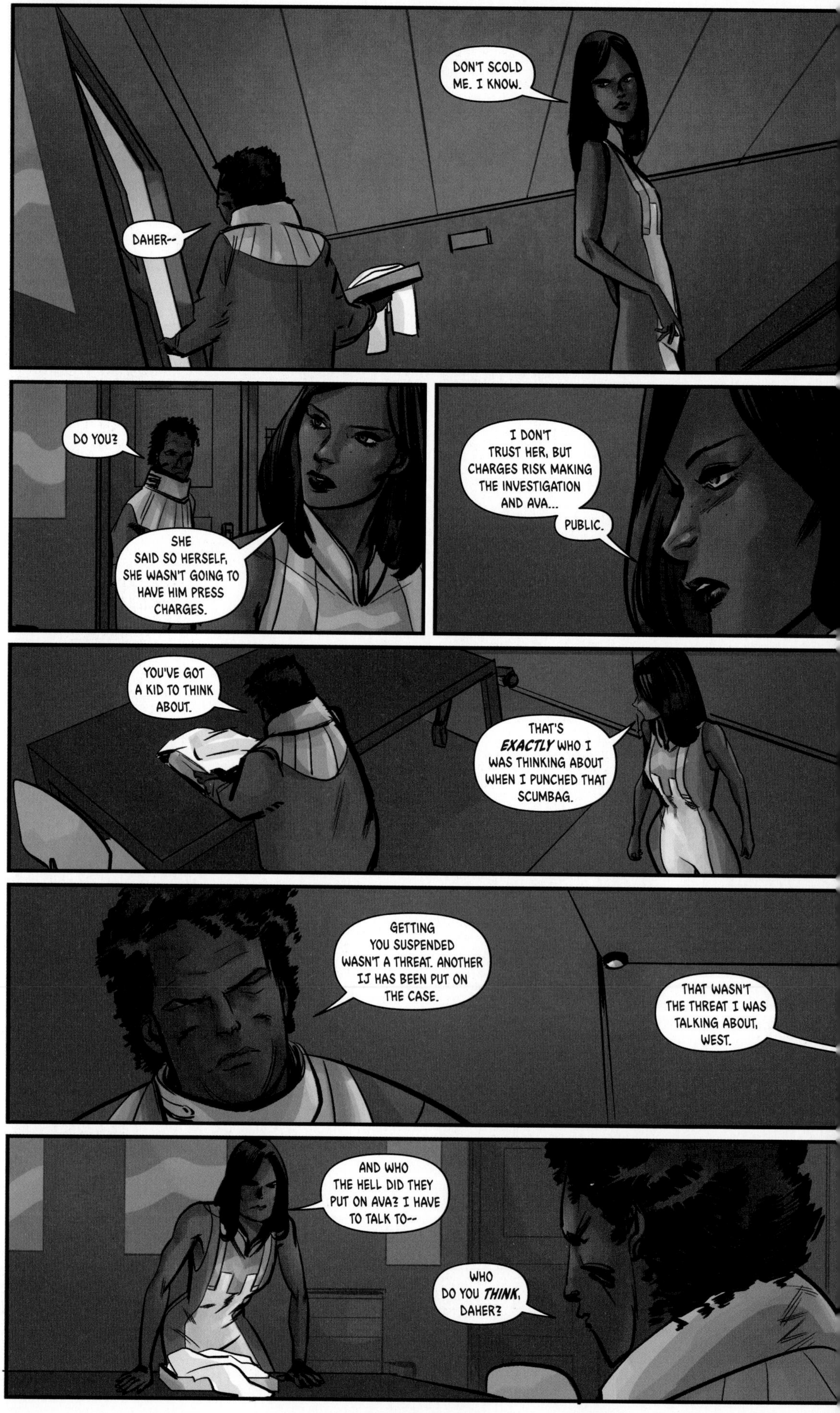
DON'T SCOLD ME. I KNOW.
DAHER--
DO YOU?
SHE SAID SO HERSELF, SHE WASN'T GOING TO HAVE HIM PRESS CHARGES.
I DON'T TRUST HER, BUT CHARGES RISK MAKING THE INVESTIGATION AND AVA...
PUBLIC.
YOU'VE GOT A KID TO THINK ABOUT.
THAT'S *EXACTLY* WHO I WAS THINKING ABOUT WHEN I PUNCHED THAT SCUMBAG.
GETTING YOU SUSPENDED WASN'T A THREAT. ANOTHER IJ HAS BEEN PUT ON THE CASE.
THAT WASN'T THE THREAT I WAS TALKING ABOUT, WEST.
AND WHO THE HELL DID THEY PUT ON AVA? I HAVE TO TALK TO--
WHO DO YOU *THINK*, DAHER?

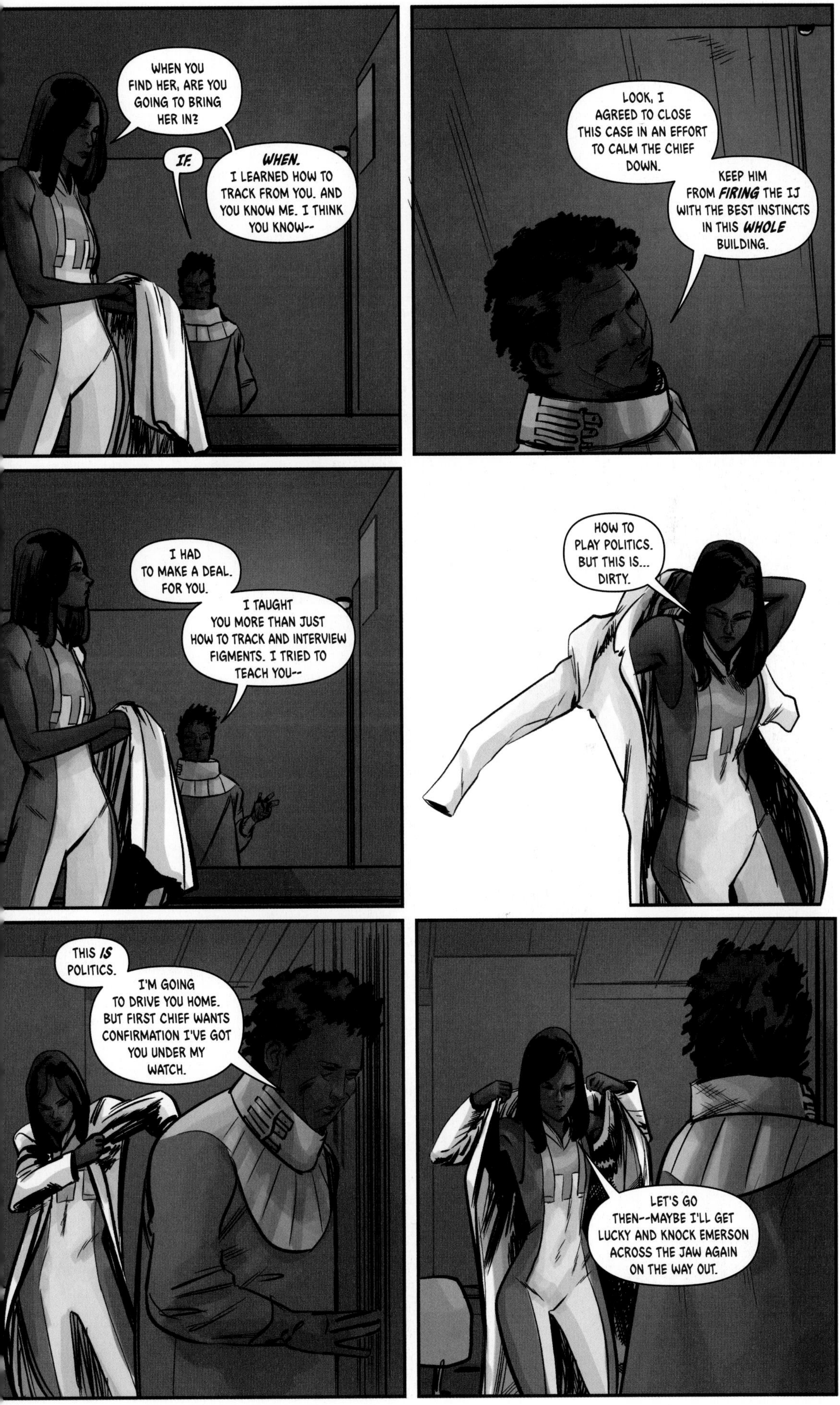
WHEN YOU FIND HER, ARE YOU GOING TO BRING HER IN?
IF.
WHEN. I LEARNED HOW TO TRACK FROM YOU. AND YOU KNOW ME. I THINK YOU KNOW--
LOOK, I AGREED TO CLOSE THIS CASE IN AN EFFORT TO CALM THE CHIEF DOWN.
KEEP HIM FROM FIRING THE IJ WITH THE BEST INSTINCTS IN THIS WHOLE BUILDING.
I HAD TO MAKE A DEAL. FOR YOU.
I TAUGHT YOU MORE THAN JUST HOW TO TRACK AND INTERVIEW FIGMENTS. I TRIED TO TEACH YOU--
HOW TO PLAY POLITICS. BUT THIS IS... DIRTY.
THIS IS POLITICS.
I'M GOING TO DRIVE YOU HOME. BUT FIRST CHIEF WANTS CONFIRMATION I'VE GOT YOU UNDER MY WATCH.
LET'S GO THEN--MAYBE I'LL GET LUCKY AND KNOCK EMERSON ACROSS THE JAW AGAIN ON THE WAY OUT.

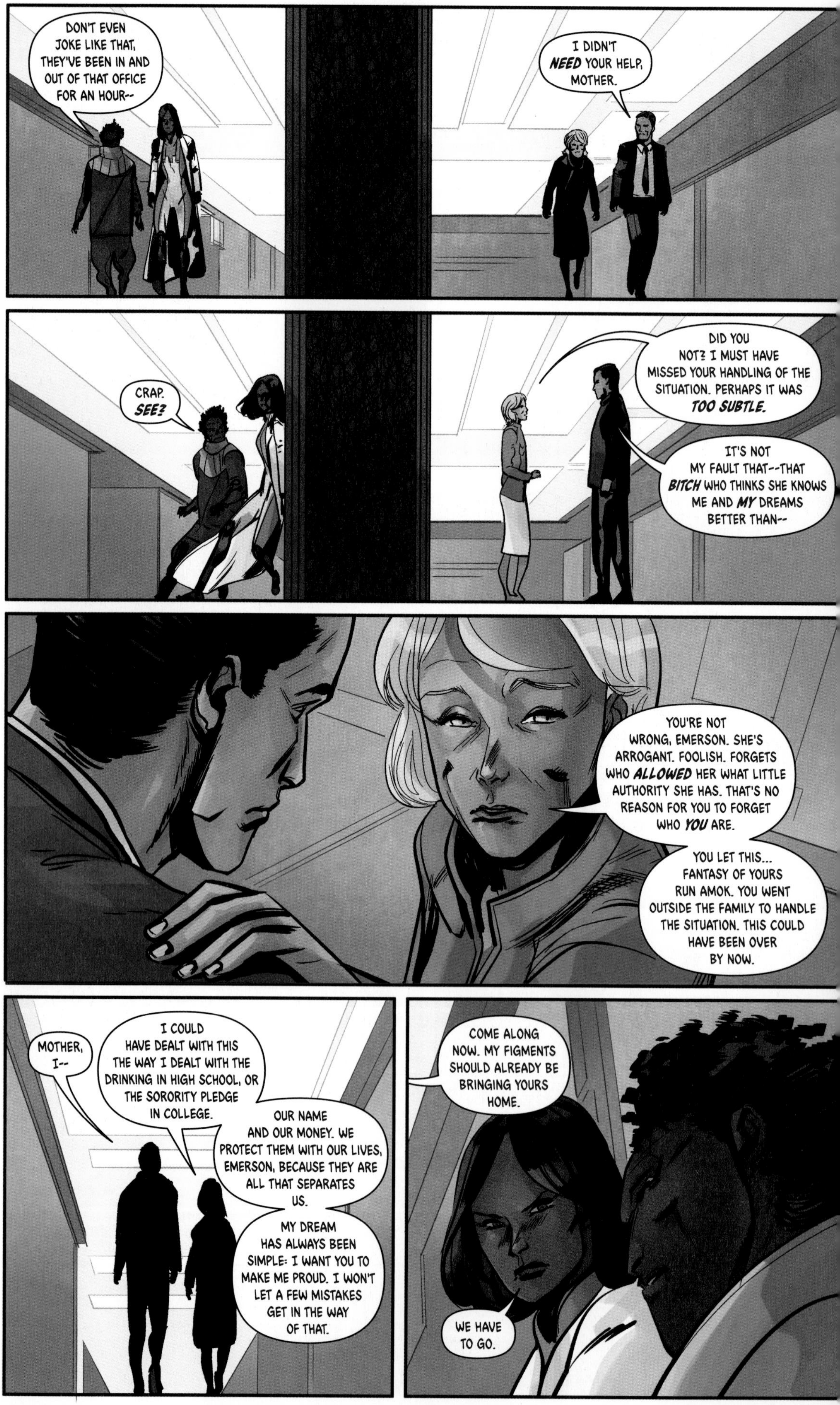
DON'T EVEN JOKE LIKE THAT, THEY'VE BEEN IN AND OUT OF THAT OFFICE FOR AN HOUR--
I DIDN'T NEED YOUR HELP, MOTHER.
CRAP. SEE?
DID YOU NOT? I MUST HAVE MISSED YOUR HANDLING OF THE SITUATION. PERHAPS IT WAS TOO SUBTLE.
IT'S NOT MY FAULT THAT--THAT BITCH WHO THINKS SHE KNOWS ME AND MY DREAMS BETTER THAN--
YOU'RE NOT WRONG, EMERSON. SHE'S ARROGANT. FOOLISH. FORGETS WHO ALLOWED HER WHAT LITTLE AUTHORITY SHE HAS. THAT'S NO REASON FOR YOU TO FORGET WHO YOU ARE.
YOU LET THIS... FANTASY OF YOURS RUN AMOK. YOU WENT OUTSIDE THE FAMILY TO HANDLE THE SITUATION. THIS COULD HAVE BEEN OVER BY NOW.
MOTHER, I--
I COULD HAVE DEALT WITH THIS THE WAY I DEALT WITH THE DRINKING IN HIGH SCHOOL, OR THE SORORITY PLEDGE IN COLLEGE.
OUR NAME AND OUR MONEY. WE PROTECT THEM WITH OUR LIVES, EMERSON, BECAUSE THEY ARE ALL THAT SEPARATES US.
MY DREAM HAS ALWAYS BEEN SIMPLE: I WANT YOU TO MAKE ME PROUD. I WON'T LET A FEW MISTAKES GET IN THE WAY OF THAT.
COME ALONG NOW. MY FIGMENTS SHOULD ALREADY BE BRINGING YOURS HOME.
WE HAVE TO GO.

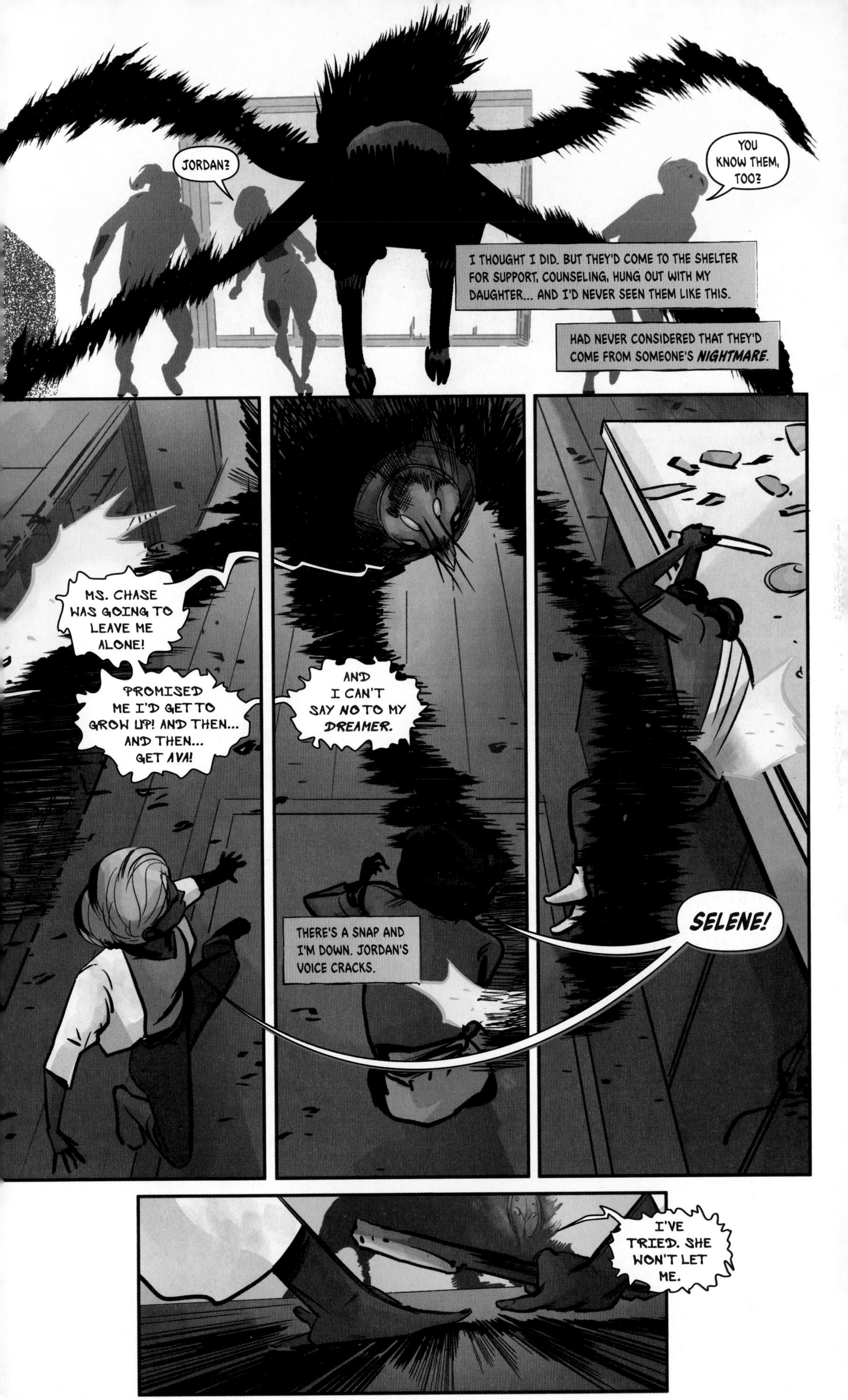
JORDAN?
YOU KNOW THEM, TOO?
I THOUGHT I DID. BUT THEY'D COME TO THE SHELTER FOR SUPPORT, COUNSELING, HUNG OUT WITH MY DAUGHTER... AND I'D NEVER SEEN THEM LIKE THIS.
HAD NEVER CONSIDERED THAT THEY'D COME FROM SOMEONE'S NIGHTMARE.
MS. CHASE WAS GOING TO LEAVE ME ALONE!
PROMISED ME I'D GET TO GROW UP! AND THEN... AND THEN... GET AVA!
AND I CAN'T SAY NO TO MY DREAMER.
THERE'S A SNAP AND I'M DOWN. JORDAN'S VOICE CRACKS.
SELENE!
I'VE TRIED. SHE WON'T LET ME.

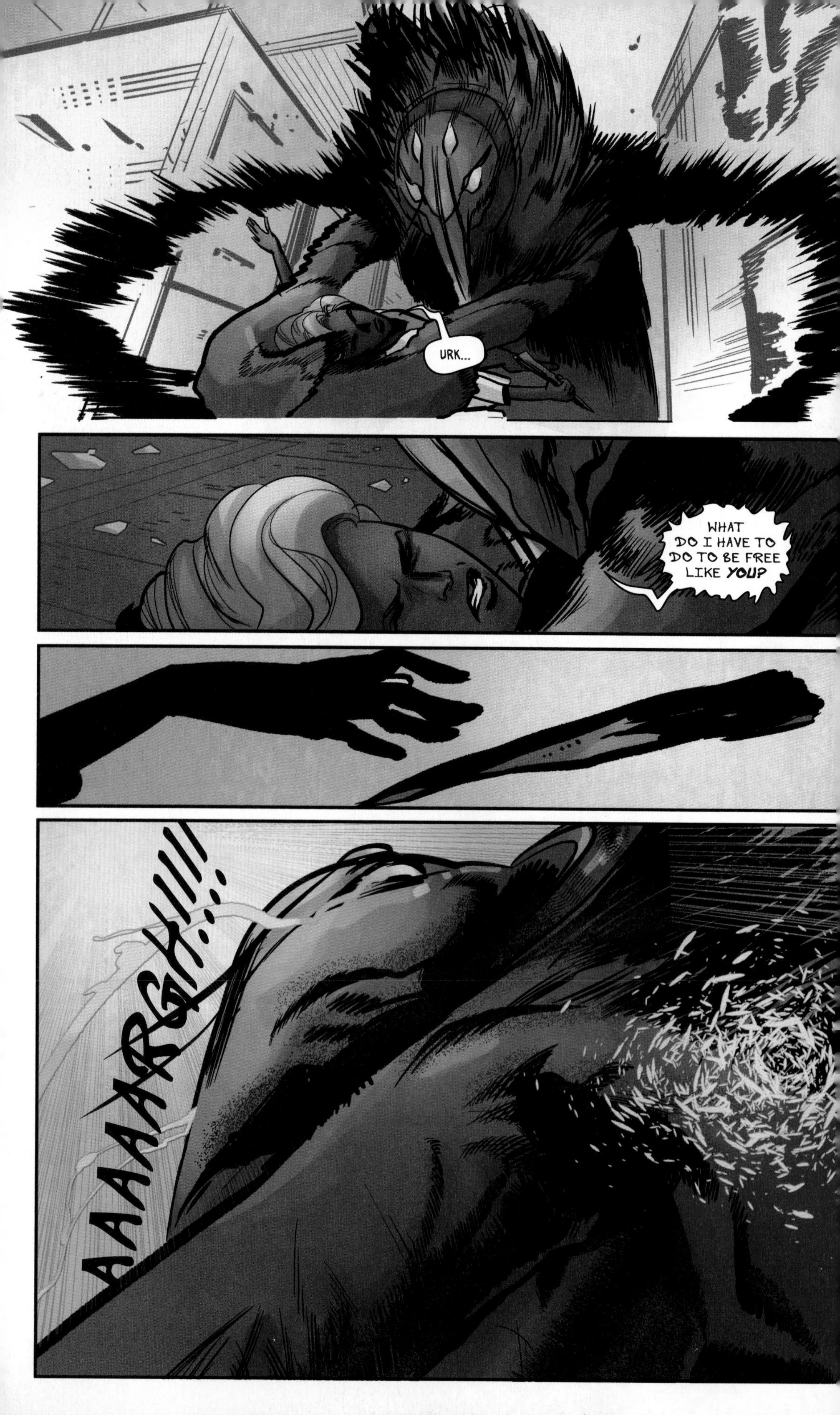
URK...
WHAT DO I HAVE TO DO TO BE FREE LIKE YOU?
AAAARGH!!!!

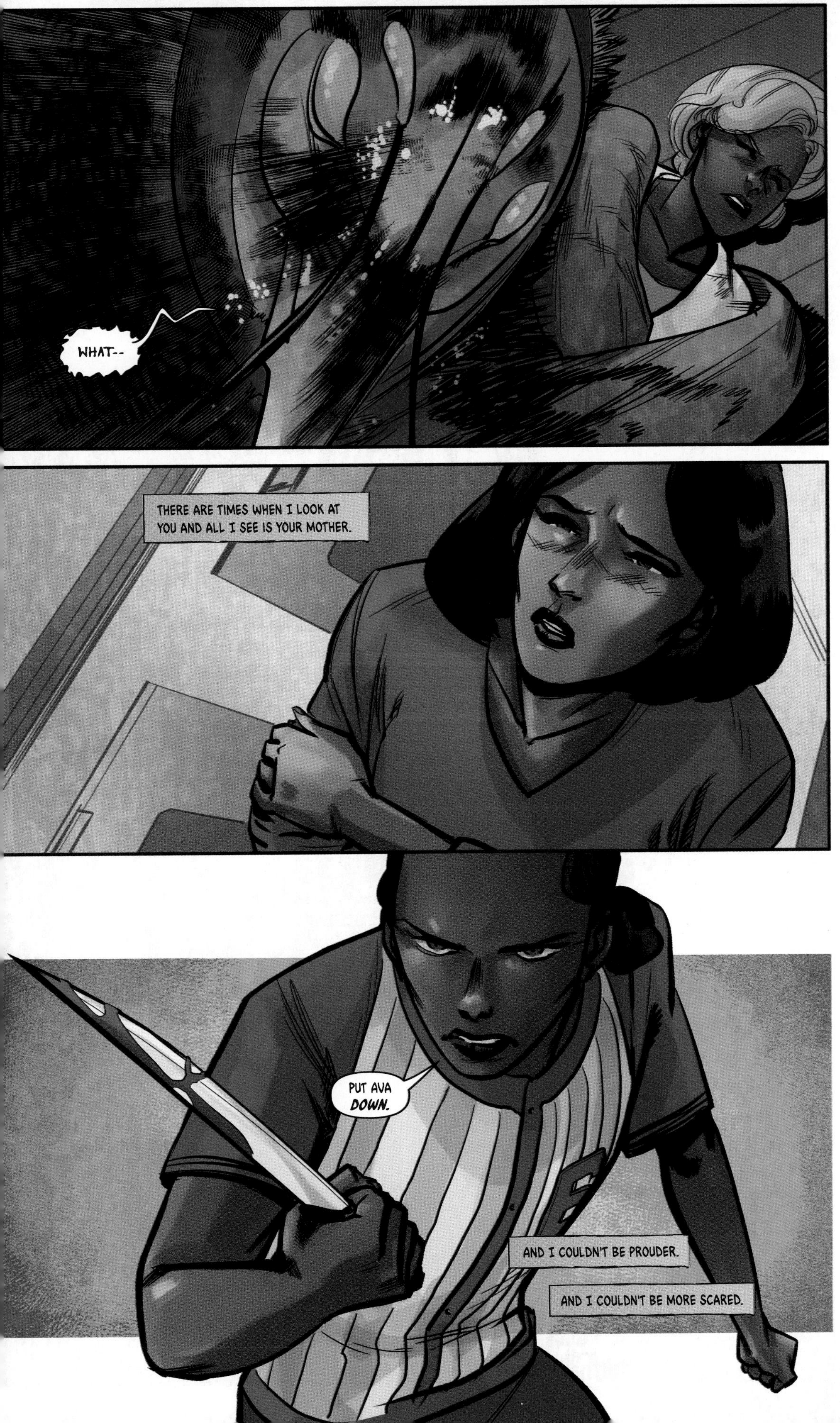
WHAT--
THERE ARE TIMES WHEN I LOOK AT YOU AND ALL I SEE IS YOUR MOTHER.
PUT AVA DOWN.
AND I COULDN'T BE PROUDER.
AND I COULDN'T BE MORE SCARED.

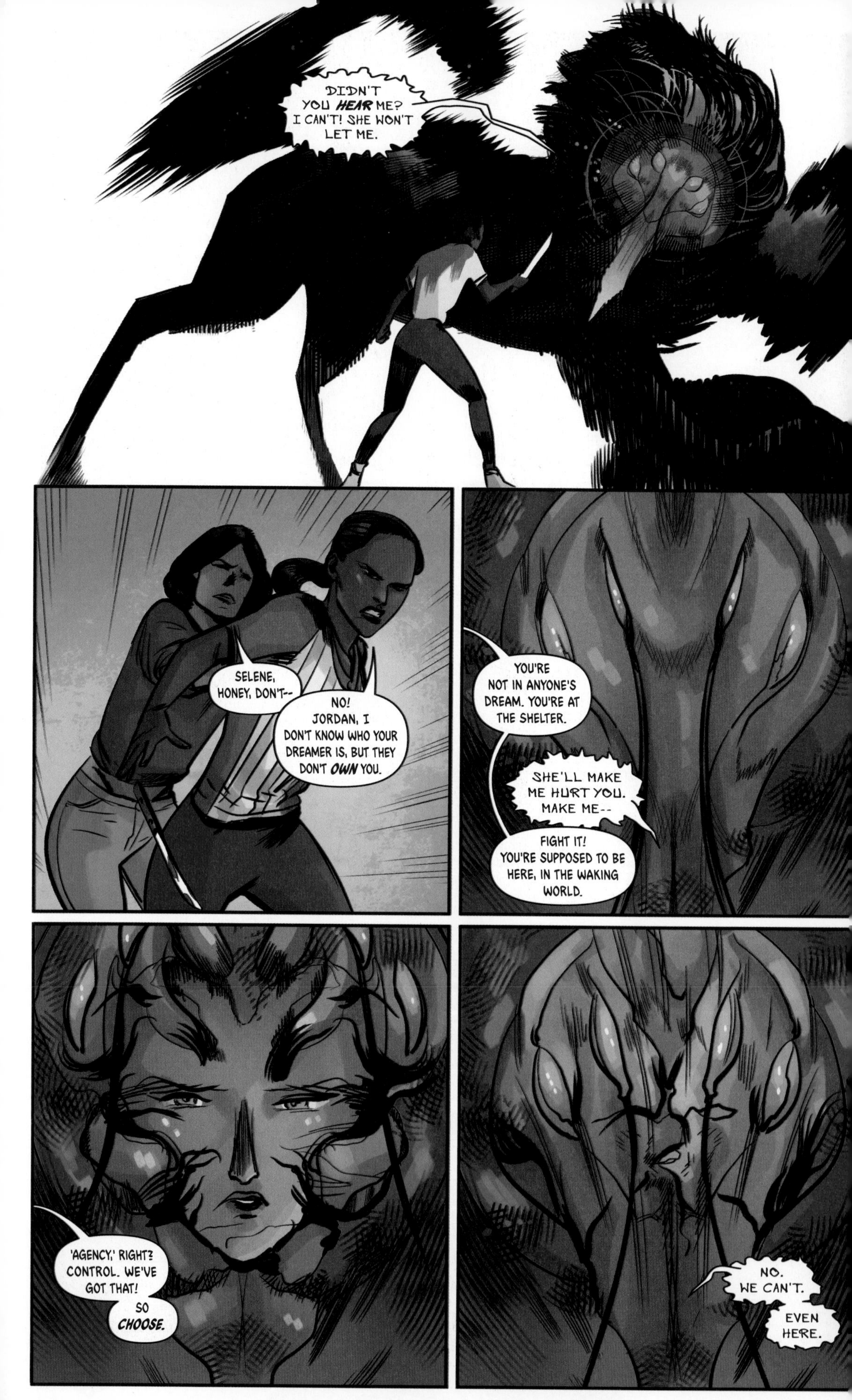
DIDN'T YOU *HEAR* ME? I CAN'T! SHE WON'T LET ME.
SELENE, HONEY, DON'T--
NO! JORDAN, I DON'T KNOW WHO YOUR DREAMER IS, BUT THEY DON'T *OWN* YOU.
YOU'RE NOT IN ANYONE'S DREAM. YOU'RE AT THE SHELTER.
SHE'LL MAKE ME HURT YOU. MAKE ME--
FIGHT IT! YOU'RE SUPPOSED TO BE HERE, IN THE WAKING WORLD.
'AGENCY,' RIGHT? CONTROL. WE'VE GOT THAT!
SO *CHOOSE.*
NO. WE CAN'T.
EVEN HERE.

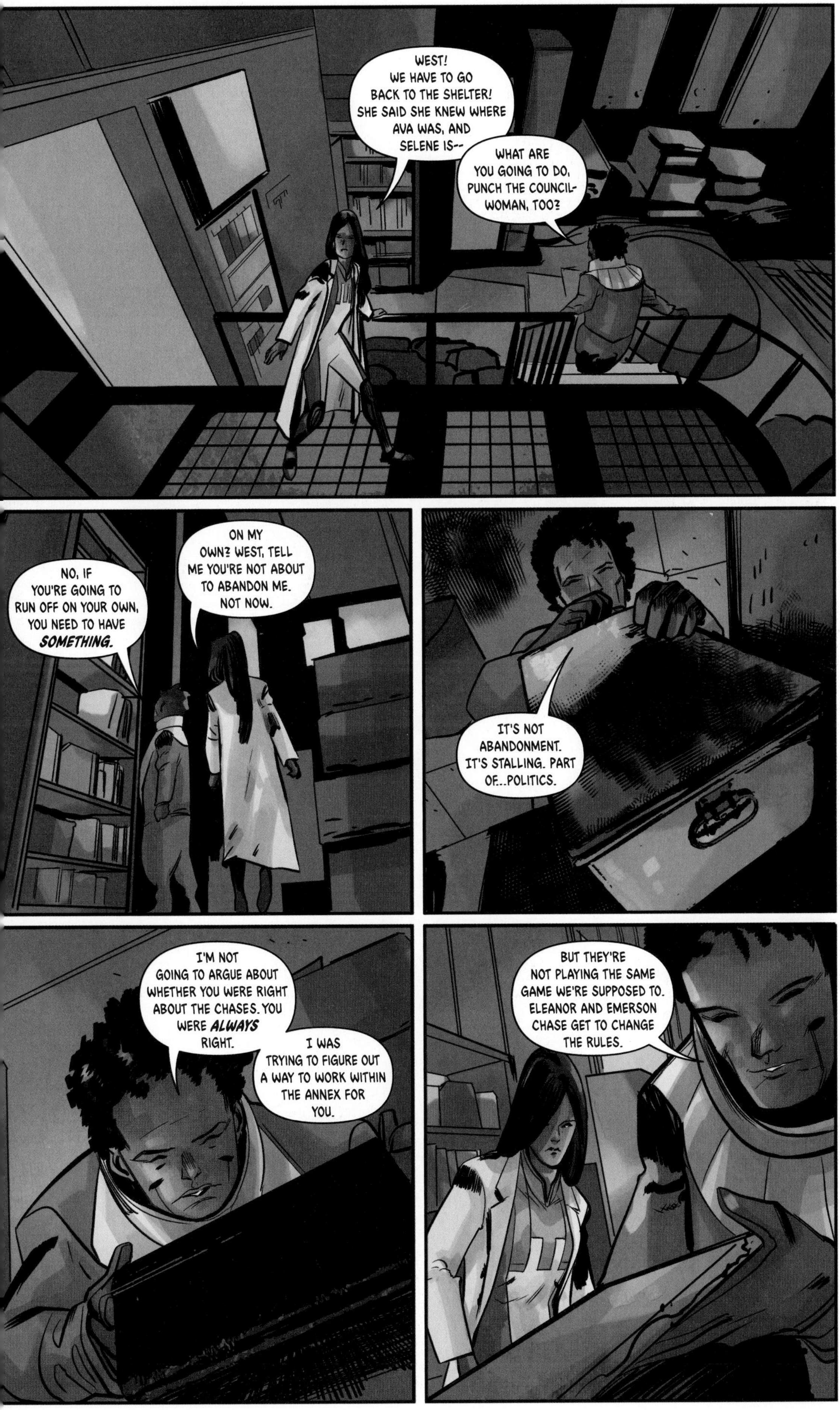
WEST! WE HAVE TO GO BACK TO THE SHELTER! SHE SAID SHE KNEW WHERE AVA WAS, AND SELENE IS--
WHAT ARE YOU GOING TO DO, PUNCH THE COUNCIL-WOMAN, TOO?
NO, IF YOU'RE GOING TO RUN OFF ON YOUR OWN, YOU NEED TO HAVE *SOMETHING.*
ON MY OWN? WEST, TELL ME YOU'RE NOT ABOUT TO ABANDON ME. NOT NOW.
IT'S NOT ABANDONMENT. IT'S STALLING. PART OF...POLITICS.
I'M NOT GOING TO ARGUE ABOUT WHETHER YOU WERE RIGHT ABOUT THE CHASES. YOU WERE *ALWAYS* RIGHT.
I WAS TRYING TO FIGURE OUT A WAY TO WORK WITHIN THE ANNEX FOR YOU.
BUT THEY'RE NOT PLAYING THE SAME GAME WE'RE SUPPOSED TO. ELEANOR AND EMERSON CHASE GET TO CHANGE THE RULES.

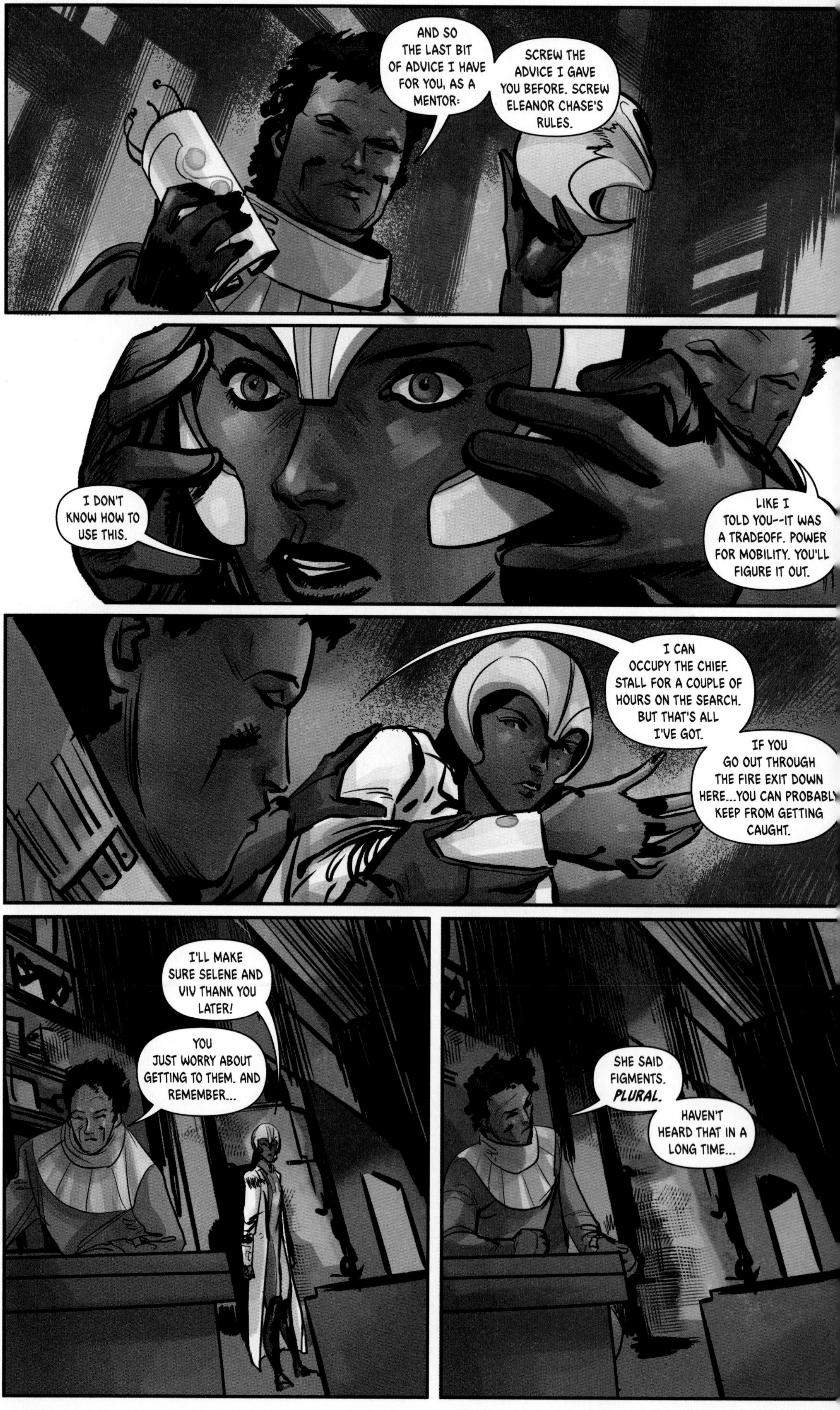
AND SO THE LAST BIT OF ADVICE I HAVE FOR YOU, AS A MENTOR:
SCREW THE ADVICE I GAVE YOU BEFORE. SCREW ELEANOR CHASE'S RULES.
I DON'T KNOW HOW TO USE THIS.
LIKE I TOLD YOU--IT WAS A TRADEOFF. POWER FOR MOBILITY. YOU'LL FIGURE IT OUT.
I CAN OCCUPY THE CHIEF. STALL FOR A COUPLE OF HOURS ON THE SEARCH. BUT THAT'S ALL I'VE GOT.
IF YOU GO OUT THROUGH THE FIRE EXIT DOWN HERE...YOU CAN PROBABLY KEEP FROM GETTING CAUGHT.
I'LL MAKE SURE SELENE AND VIV THANK YOU LATER!
YOU JUST WORRY ABOUT GETTING TO THEM. AND REMEMBER...
SHE SAID FIGMENTS. *PLURAL.*
HAVEN'T HEARD THAT IN A LONG TIME...

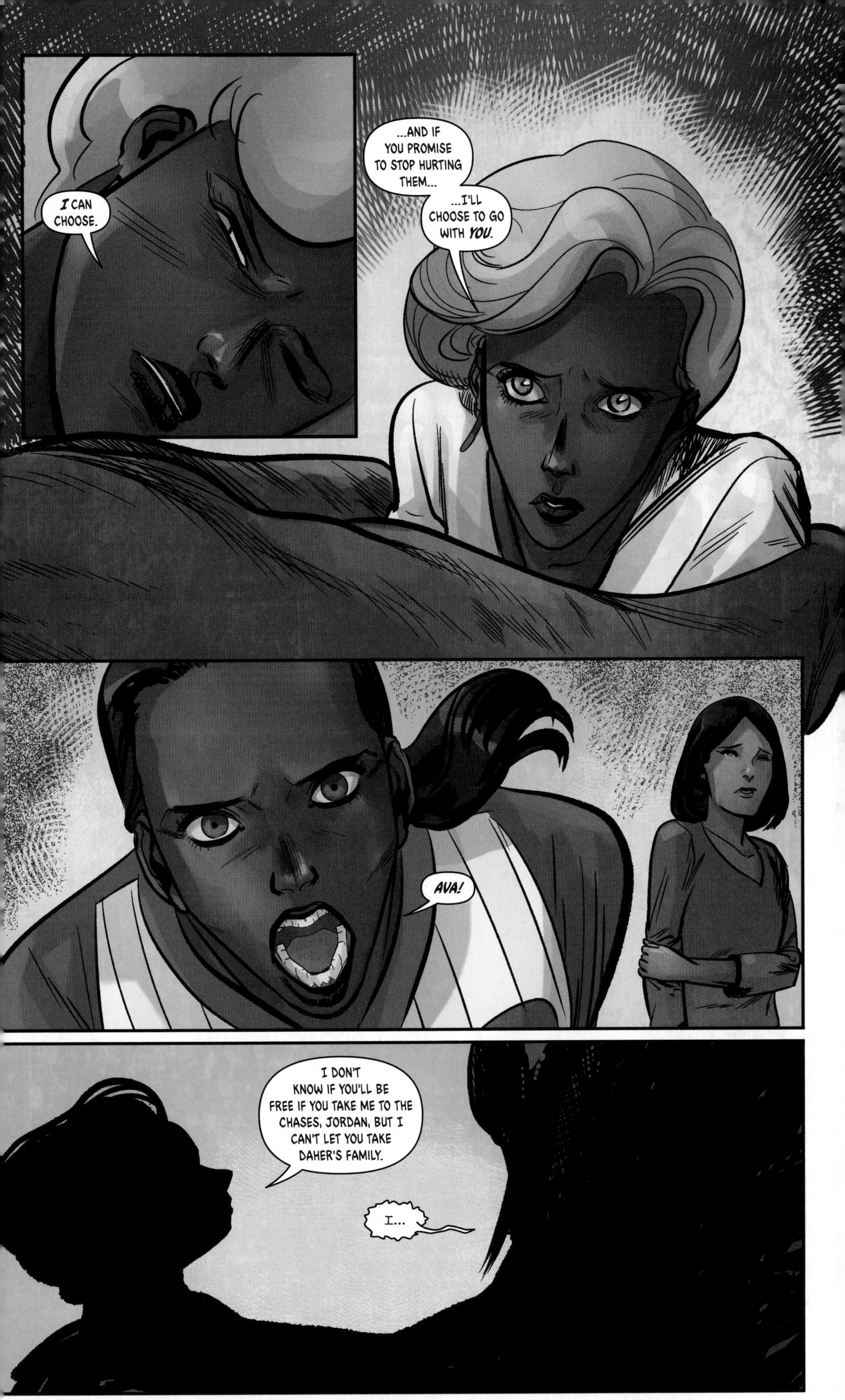
I CAN CHOOSE.
...AND IF YOU PROMISE TO STOP HURTING THEM...
...I'LL CHOOSE TO GO WITH YOU.
AVA!
I DON'T KNOW IF YOU'LL BE FREE IF YOU TAKE ME TO THE CHASES, JORDAN, BUT I CAN'T LET YOU TAKE DAHER'S FAMILY.
I...

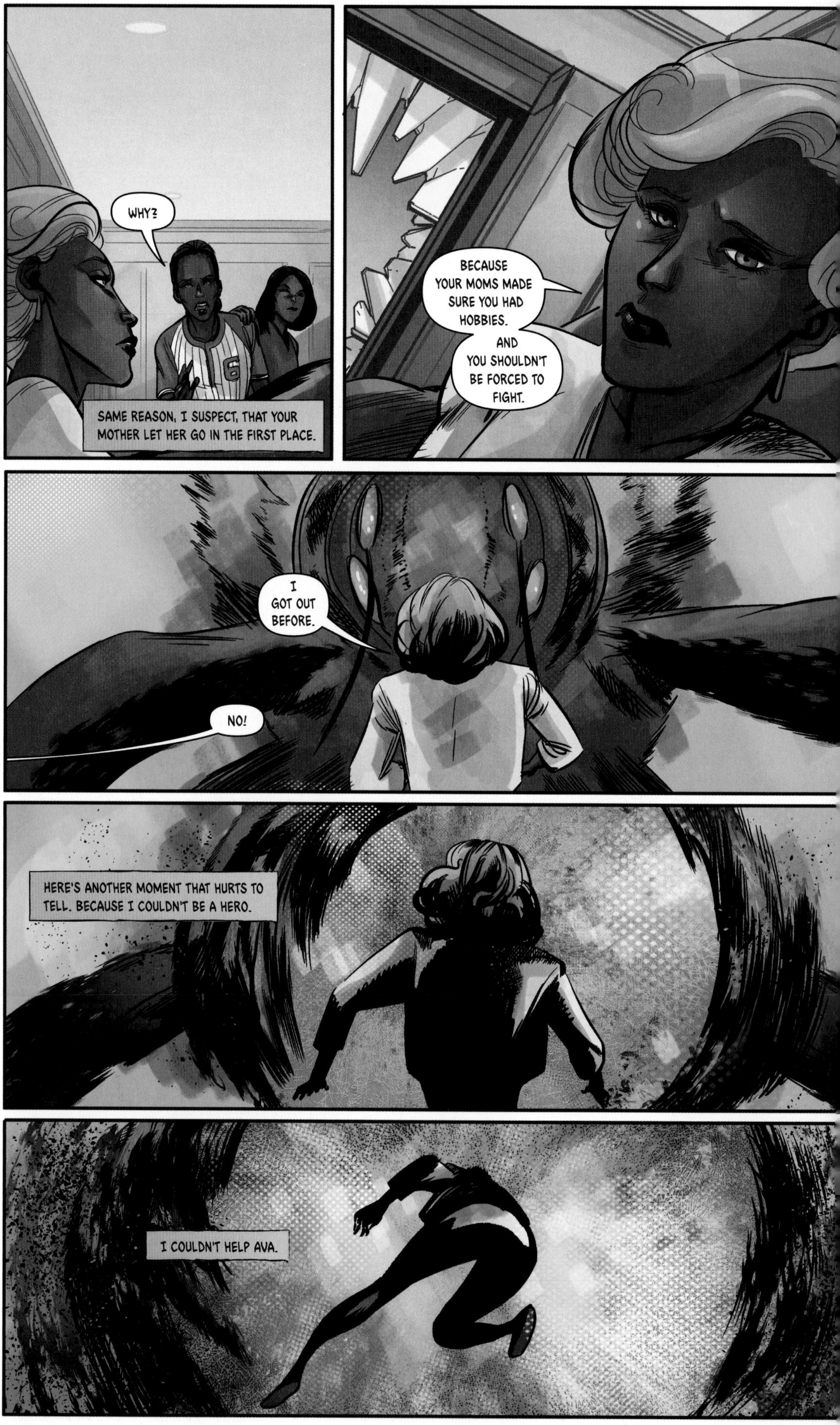
WHY?
SAME REASON, I SUSPECT, THAT YOUR MOTHER LET HER GO IN THE FIRST PLACE.
BECAUSE YOUR MOMS MADE SURE YOU HAD HOBBIES.
AND YOU SHOULDN'T BE FORCED TO FIGHT.
I GOT OUT BEFORE.
NO!
HERE'S ANOTHER MOMENT THAT HURTS TO TELL. BECAUSE I COULDN'T BE A HERO.
I COULDN'T HELP AVA.

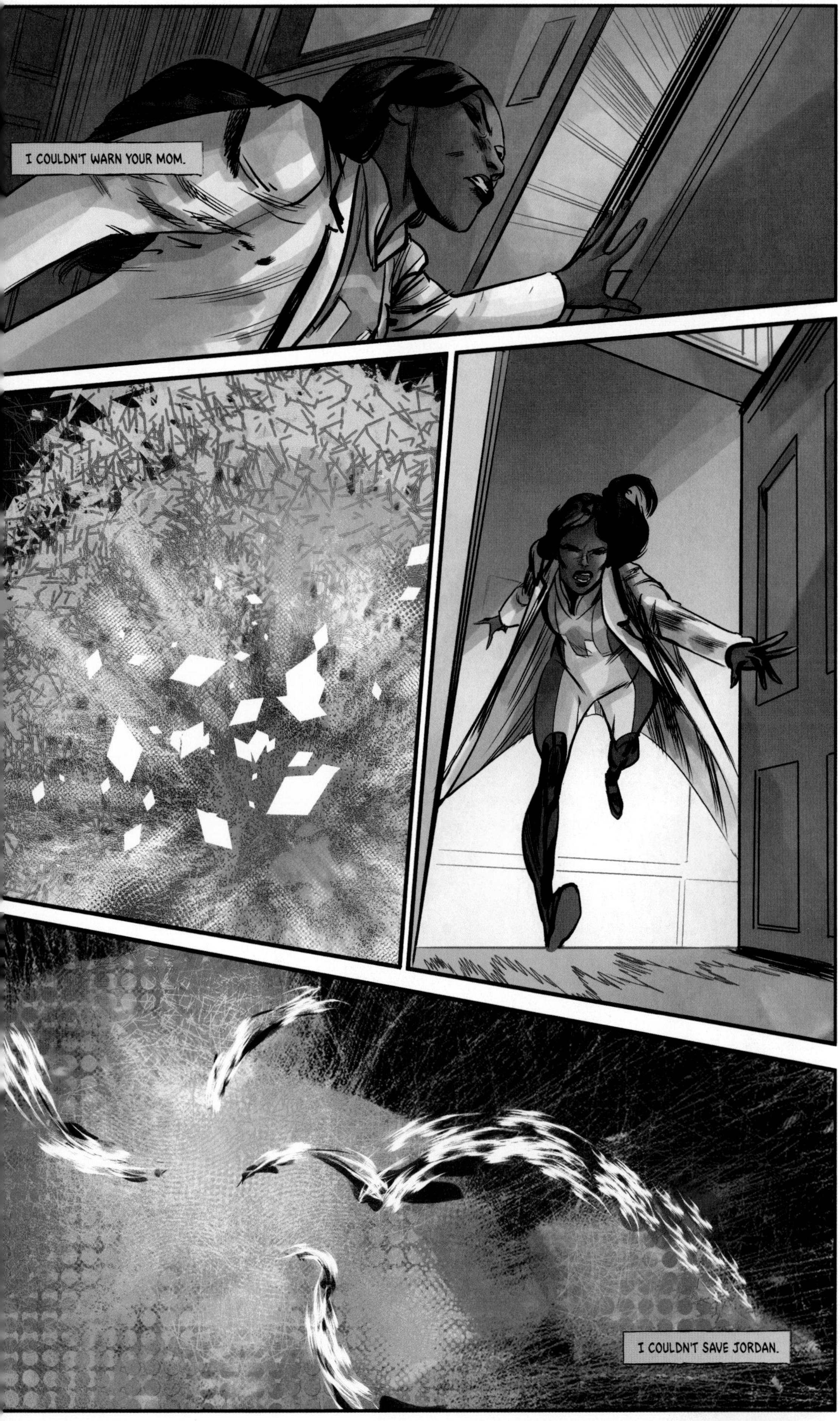
I COULDN'T WARN YOUR MOM.
I COULDN'T SAVE JORDAN.

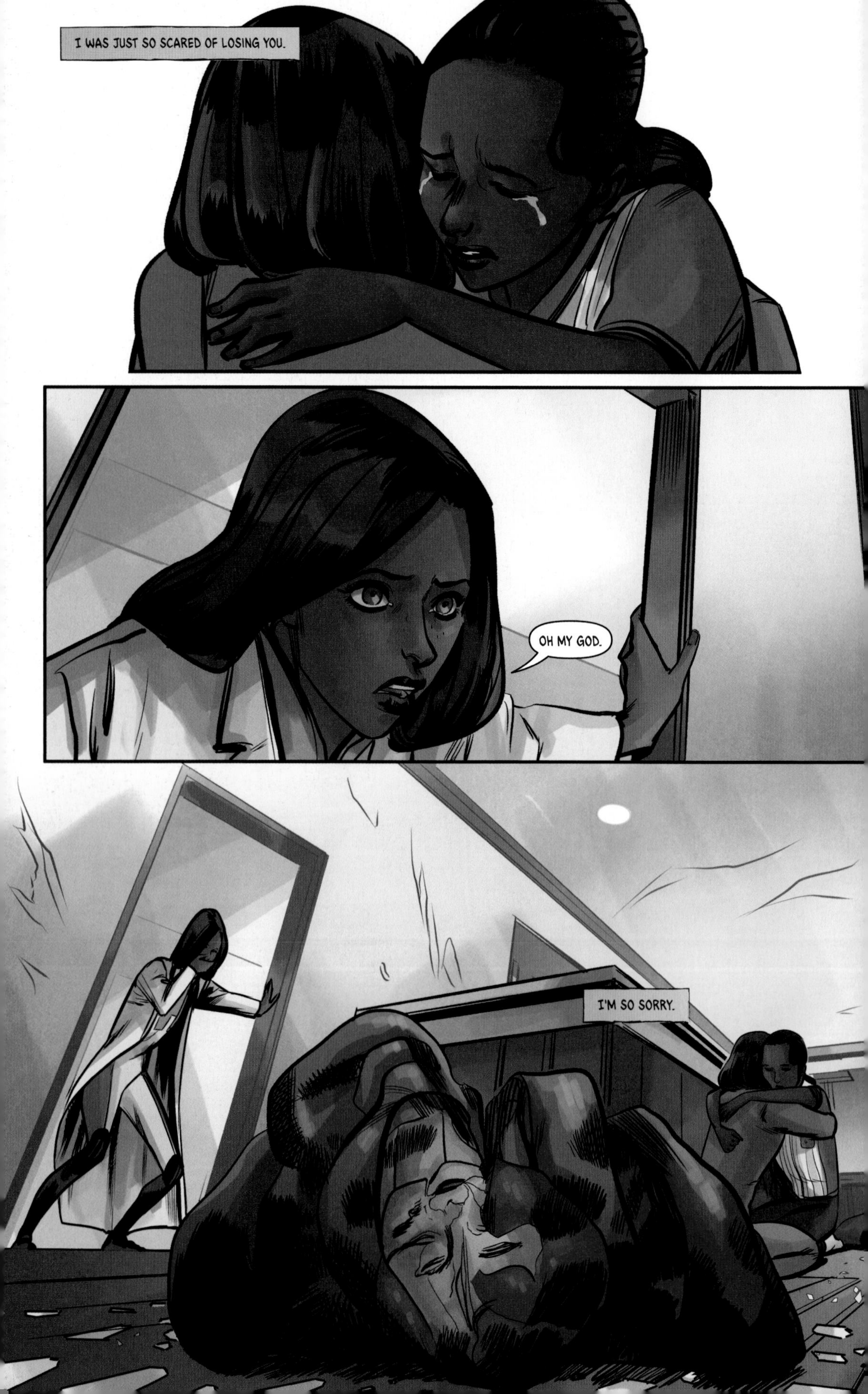
I WAS JUST SO SCARED OF LOSING YOU.
OH MY GOD.
I'M SO SORRY.

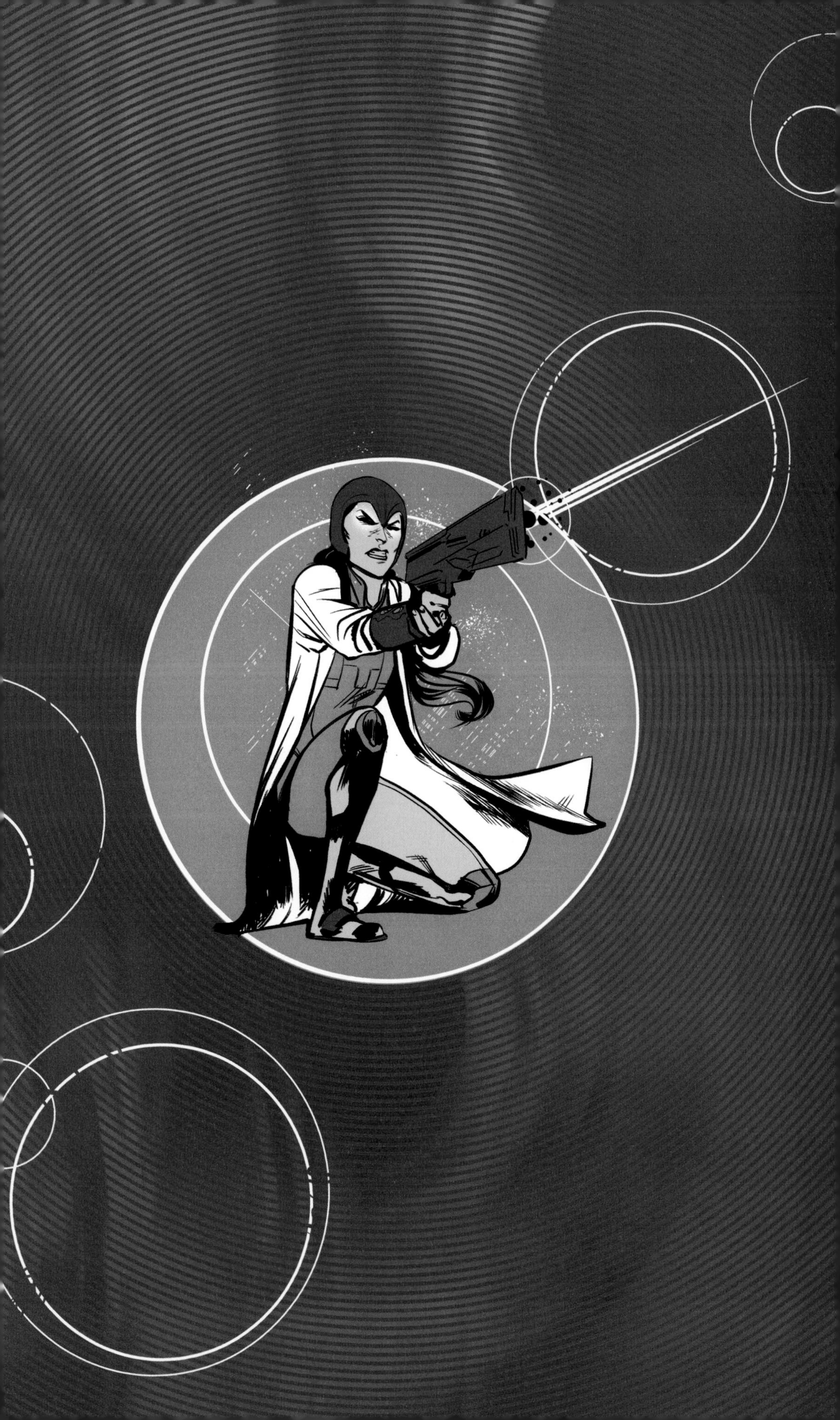

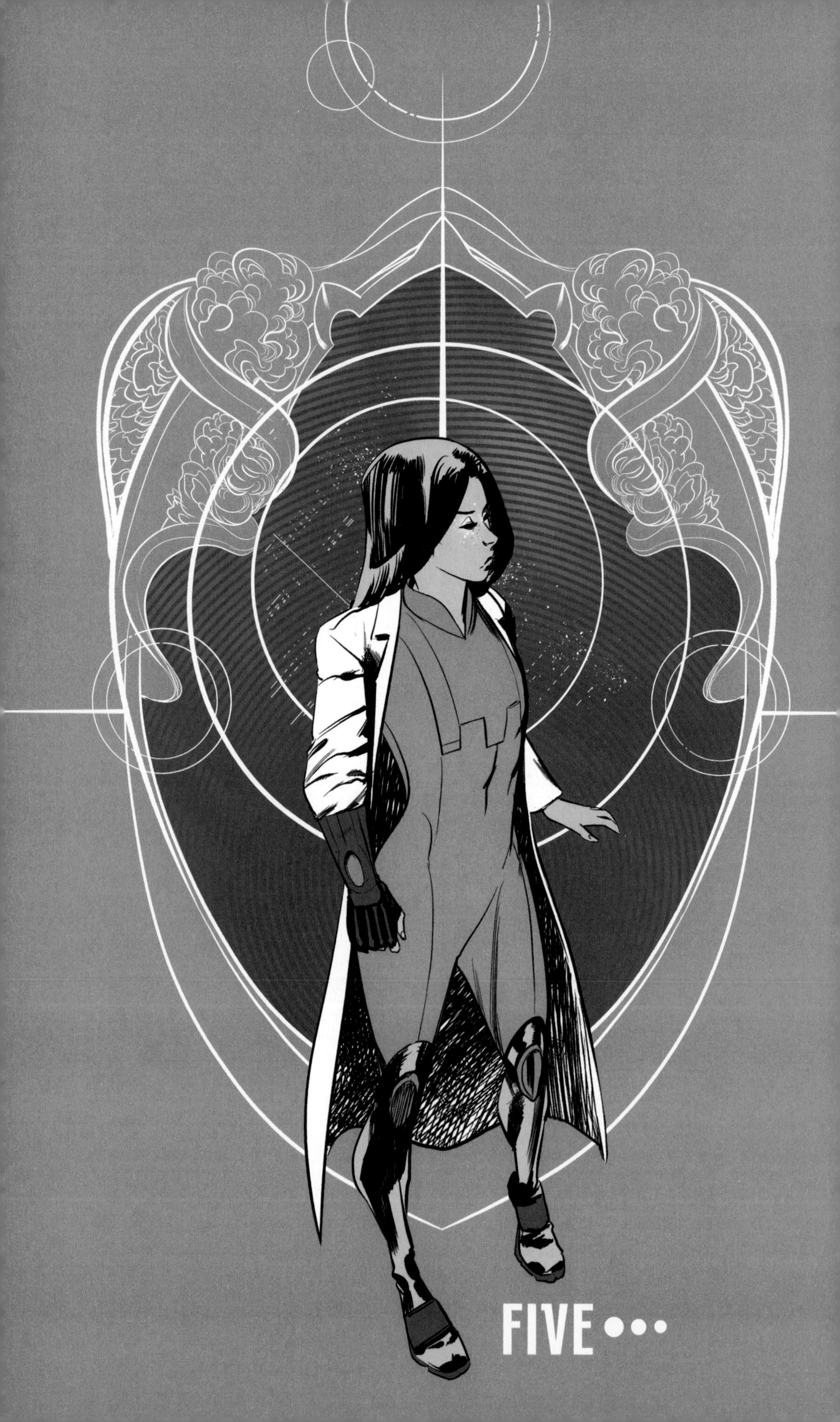

FIVE •••

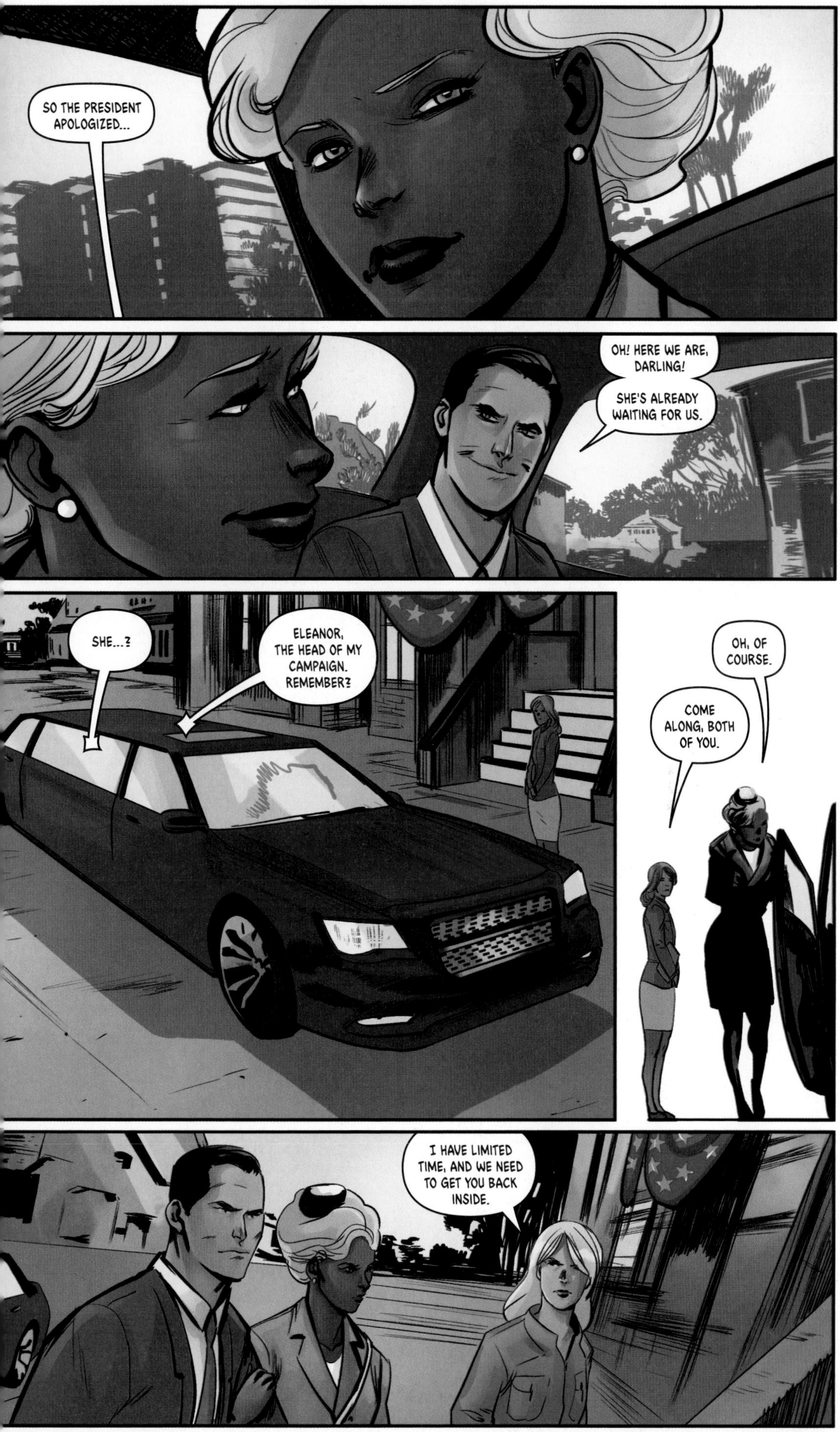
SO THE PRESIDENT APOLOGIZED...
OH! HERE WE ARE, DARLING!
SHE'S ALREADY WAITING FOR US.
SHE...?
ELEANOR, THE HEAD OF MY CAMPAIGN. REMEMBER?
OH, OF COURSE.
COME ALONG, BOTH OF YOU.
I HAVE LIMITED TIME, AND WE NEED TO GET YOU BACK INSIDE.

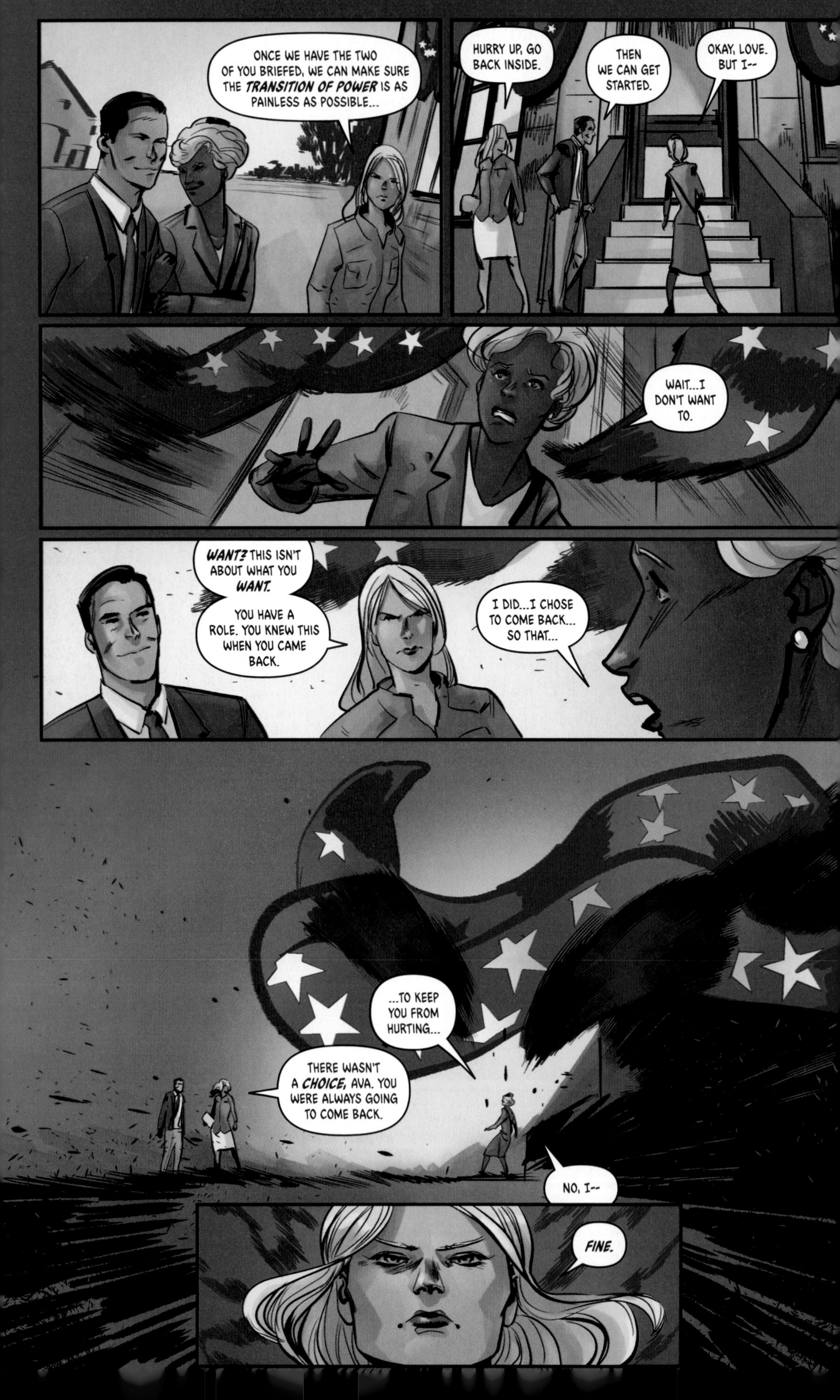
ONCE WE HAVE THE TWO OF YOU BRIEFED, WE CAN MAKE SURE THE ***TRANSITION OF POWER*** IS AS PAINLESS AS POSSIBLE...
HURRY UP, GO BACK INSIDE.
THEN WE CAN GET STARTED.
OKAY, LOVE. BUT I--
WAIT...I DON'T WANT TO.
WANT? THIS ISN'T ABOUT WHAT YOU ***WANT.***
YOU HAVE A ROLE. YOU KNEW THIS WHEN YOU CAME BACK.
I DID...I CHOSE TO COME BACK... SO THAT...
...TO KEEP YOU FROM HURTING...
THERE WASN'T A ***CHOICE,*** AVA. YOU WERE ALWAYS GOING TO COME BACK.
NO, I--
FINE.

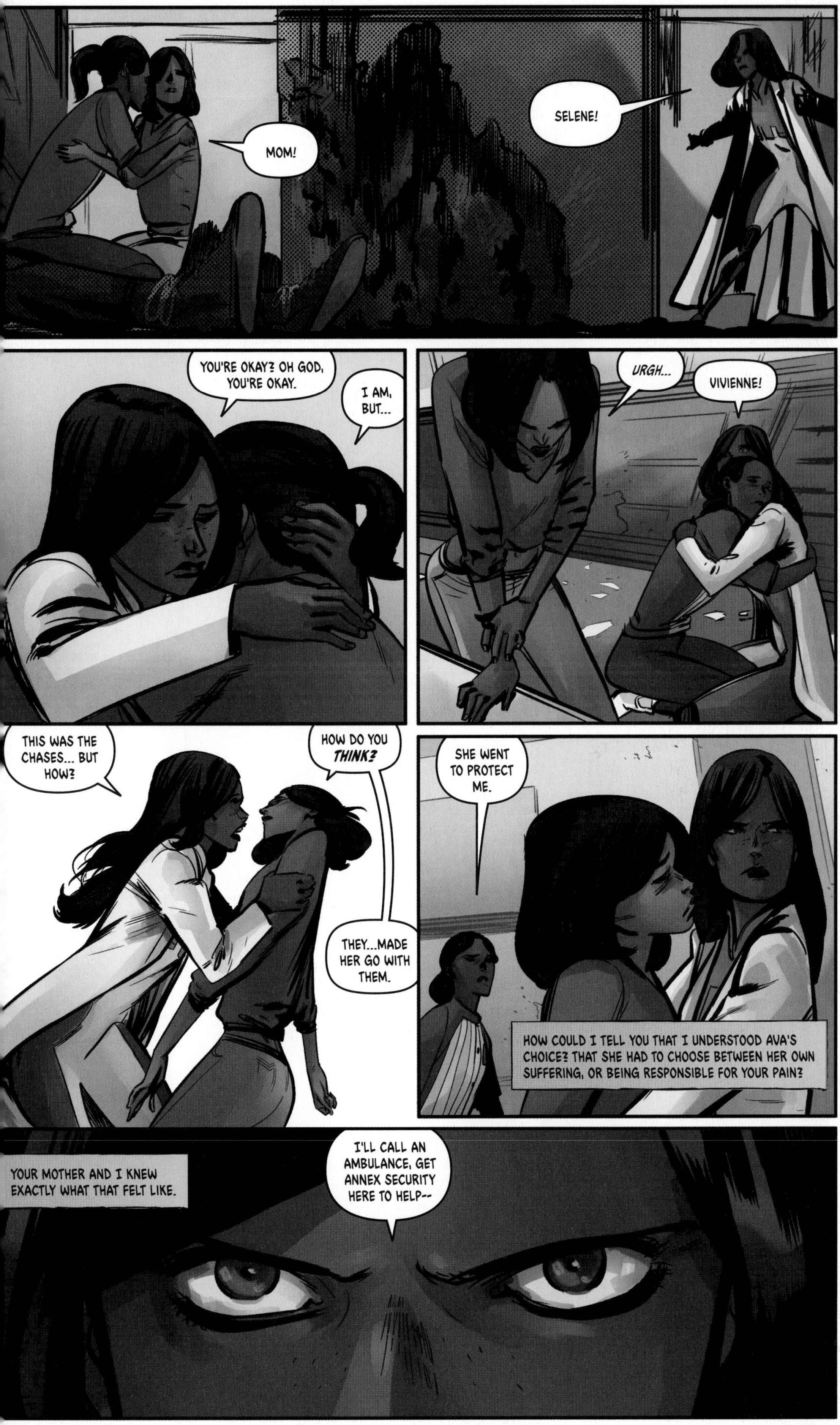
MOM!
SELENE!
YOU'RE OKAY? OH GOD, YOU'RE OKAY.
I AM, BUT...
URGH...
VIVIENNE!
THIS WAS THE CHASES... BUT HOW?
HOW DO YOU *THINK?*
THEY...MADE HER GO WITH THEM.
SHE WENT TO PROTECT ME.
HOW COULD I TELL YOU THAT I UNDERSTOOD AVA'S CHOICE? THAT SHE HAD TO CHOOSE BETWEEN HER OWN SUFFERING, OR BEING RESPONSIBLE FOR YOUR PAIN?
YOUR MOTHER AND I KNEW EXACTLY WHAT THAT FELT LIKE.
I'LL CALL AN AMBULANCE, GET ANNEX SECURITY HERE TO HELP--

I CAN STILL... USE A DAMN PHONE, DAHER. I MIGHT NOT BE A HERO, BUT I CAN DO THAT.

VIV, I'M SO SORRY, I'LL FIX THIS I'LL--

STOP.

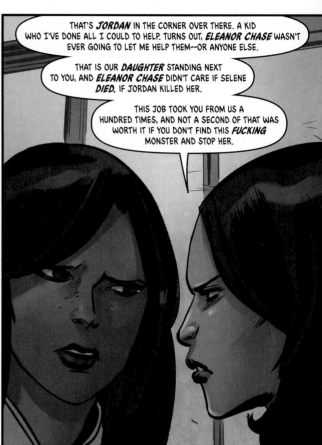

THAT'S *JORDAN* IN THE CORNER OVER THERE. A KID WHO I'VE DONE ALL I COULD TO HELP. TURNS OUT, *ELEANOR CHASE* WASN'T EVER GOING TO LET ME HELP THEM--OR ANYONE ELSE.

THAT IS OUR *DAUGHTER* STANDING NEXT TO YOU, AND *ELEANOR CHASE* DIDN'T CARE IF SELENE *DIED.* IF JORDAN KILLED HER.

THIS JOB TOOK YOU FROM US A HUNDRED TIMES, AND NOT A SECOND OF THAT WAS WORTH IT IF YOU DON'T FIND THIS *FUCKING* MONSTER AND STOP HER.

DON'T WASTE THAT CHOICE NOW. I WILL BE *FINE.*

SOMETIMES ADULTS LIE TO EACH OTHER. I DON'T KNOW IF I WAS LYING THEN. BUT I'M BEING HONEST *NOW* WHEN I TELL YOU THIS...

IN ALL THE TIME I'VE KNOWN YOUR MOTHER...

EVEN THROUGH OUR DIVORCE...

THAT WAS THE FIRST TIME I WAS AFRAID I'D NEVER SEE HER AGAIN.

I KNOW, MA. I WAS SCARED, TOO.

THEN WHY DID YOU FOLLOW HER INTO THAT NIGHTMARE?

BECAUSE I WAS SCARED.

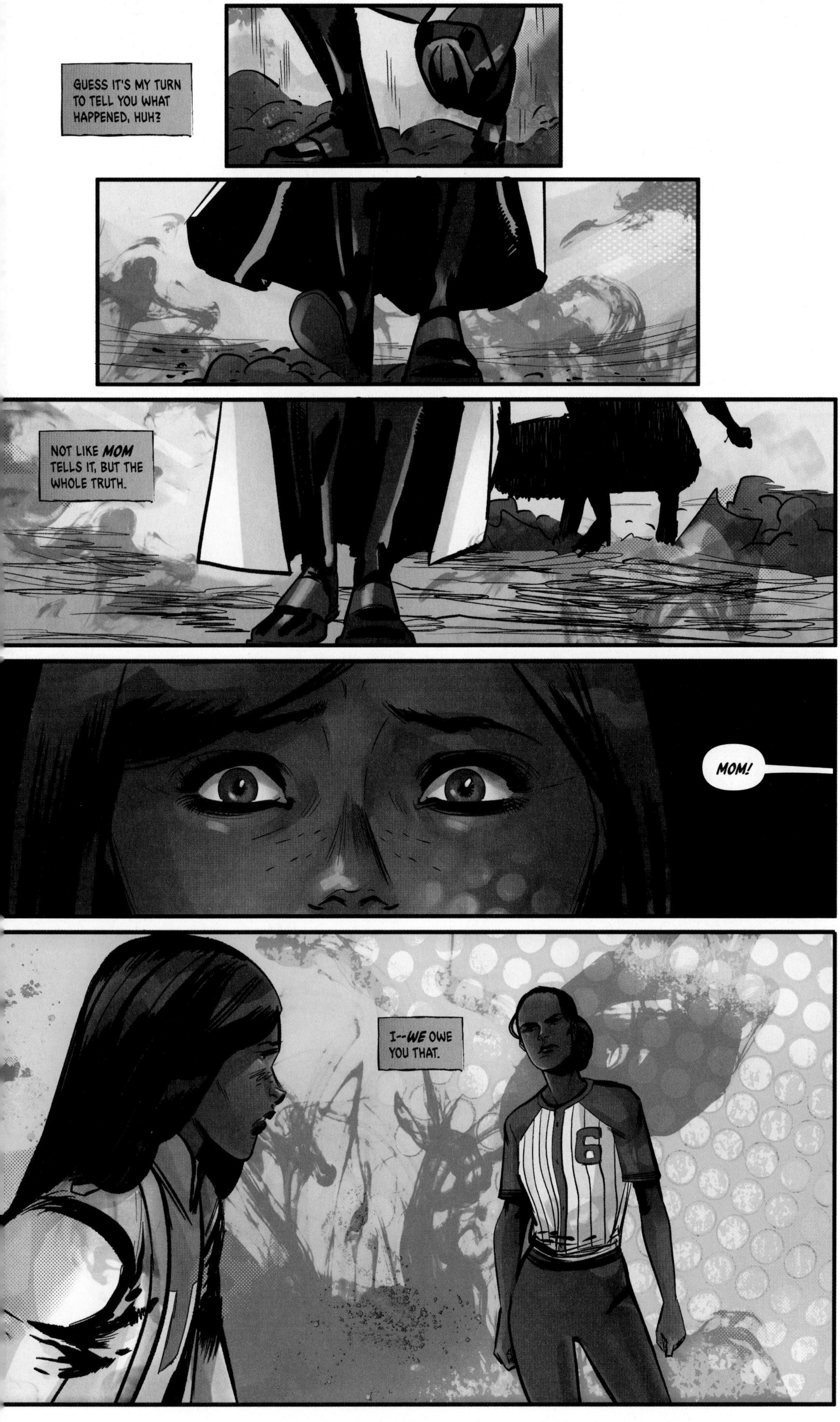
GUESS IT'S MY TURN TO TELL YOU WHAT HAPPENED, HUH?
NOT LIKE MOM TELLS IT, BUT THE WHOLE TRUTH.
MOM!
I--WE OWE YOU THAT.
6

FIRST THING YOU TAUGHT ME WAS I DON'T HAVE TO BE ALONE.

THAT WE DIDN'T HAVE TO GO THROUGH *ANYTHING* ALONE.

DIDN'T SEE WHY IT WAS ANY DIFFERENT WITH MOM.

WHATEVER FIGHT WAITED FOR HER IN THERE, I WANTED TO BE BESIDE HER.

DAMNIT!

STUPID *OLD* TECH--

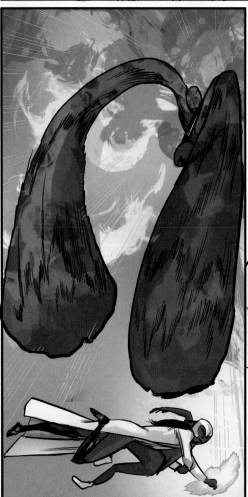

IT'S THE HELMET. WAY MORE POWERFUL THAN I'M USED TO, I CAN'T ADJUST--

AND THE THOUGHT OF MOM FIRING THAT THING WAS JUST AS SCARY AS EVERYTHING ELSE.

I REACTED. STUPID, I KNOW, ALREADY GOT CHEWED OUT FOR GRABBING THE GUN, BUT--

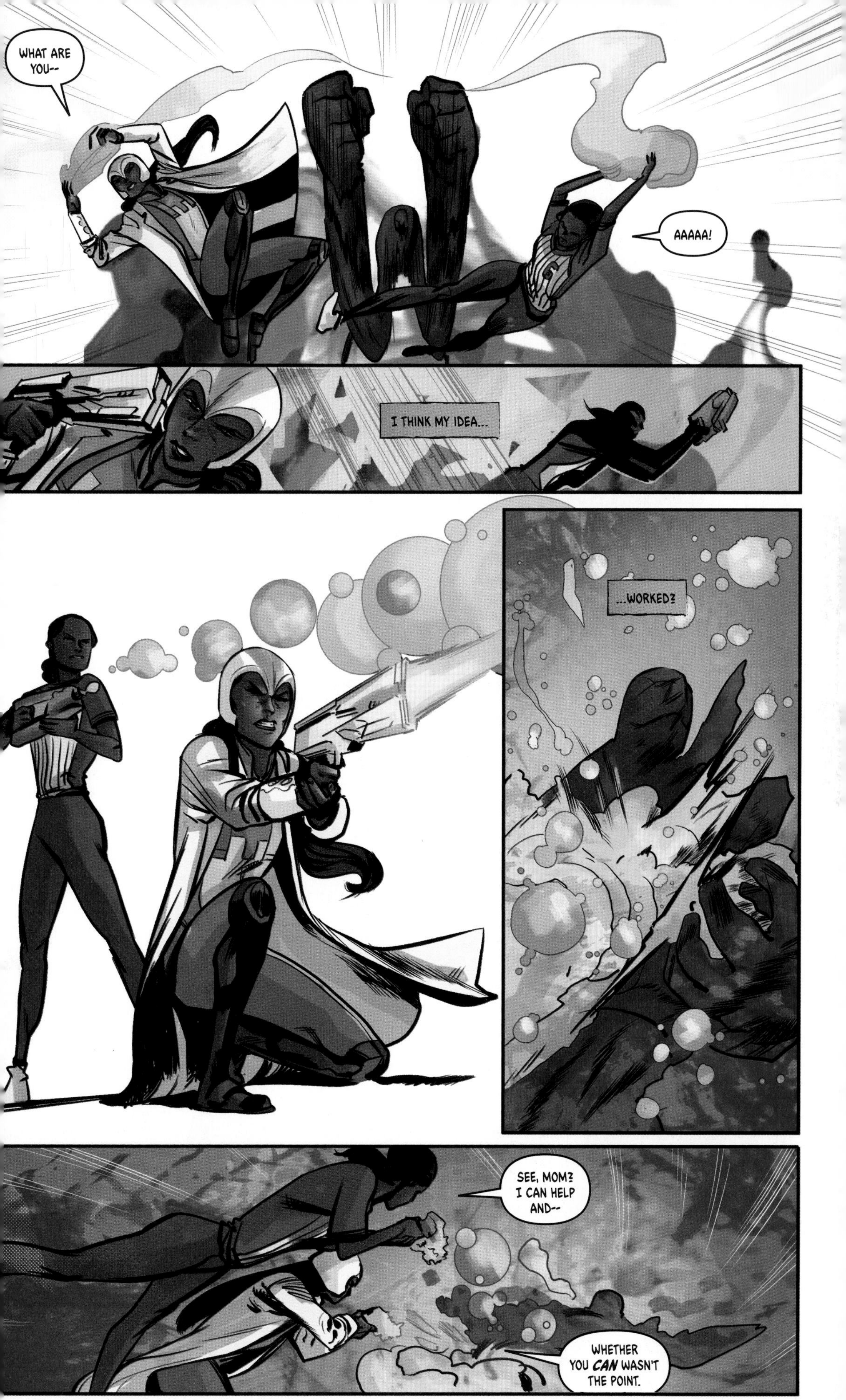
WHAT ARE YOU--
AAAAA!
I THINK MY IDEA...
...WORKED?
SEE, MOM? I CAN HELP AND--
WHETHER YOU CAN WASN'T THE POINT.

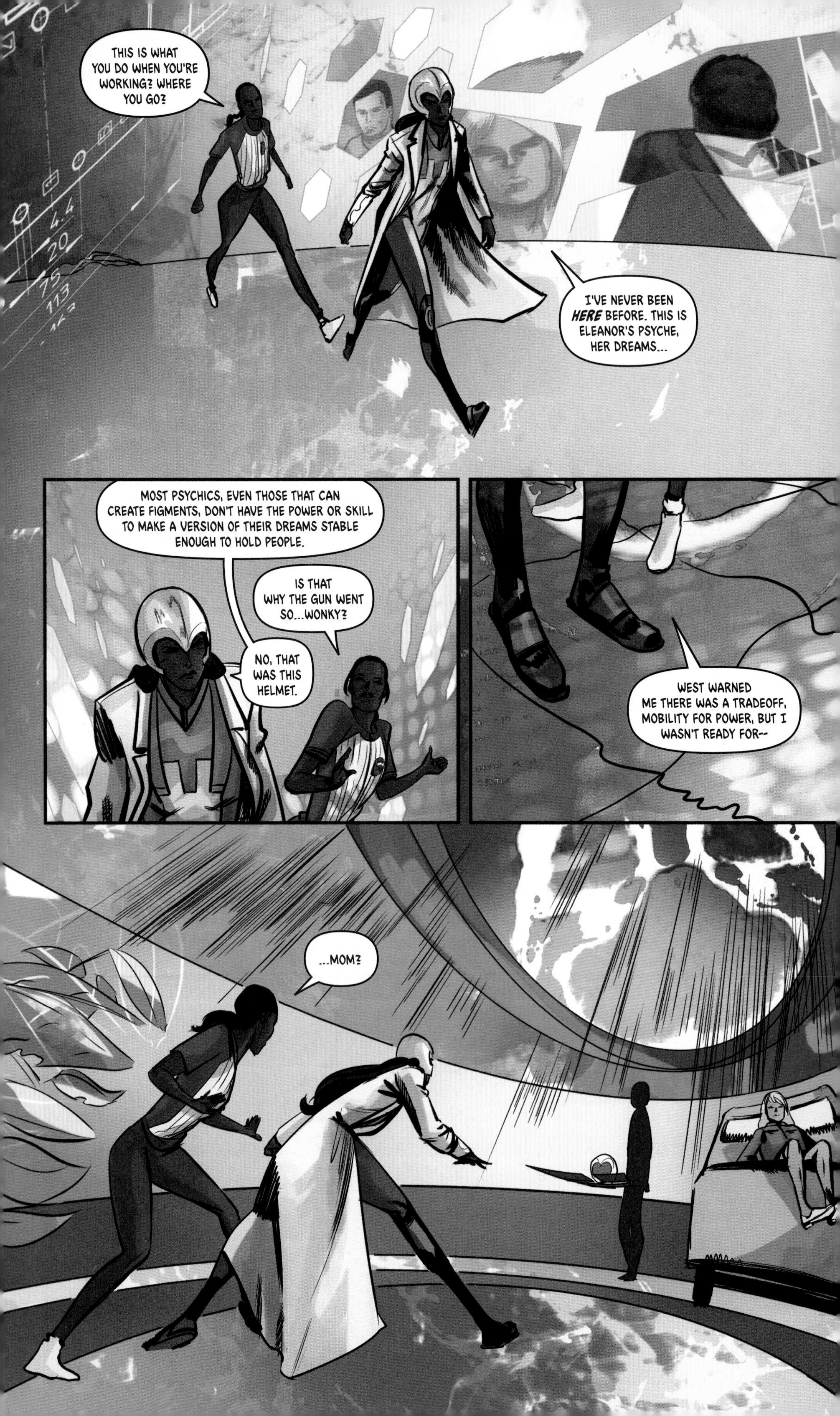
THIS IS WHAT YOU DO WHEN YOU'RE WORKING? WHERE YOU GO?
I'VE NEVER BEEN *HERE* BEFORE. THIS IS ELEANOR'S PSYCHE, HER DREAMS...
MOST PSYCHICS, EVEN THOSE THAT CAN CREATE FIGMENTS, DON'T HAVE THE POWER OR SKILL TO MAKE A VERSION OF THEIR DREAMS STABLE ENOUGH TO HOLD PEOPLE.
IS THAT WHY THE GUN WENT SO...WONKY?
NO, THAT WAS THIS HELMET.
WEST WARNED ME THERE WAS A TRADEOFF, MOBILITY FOR POWER, BUT I WASN'T READY FOR--
...MOM?

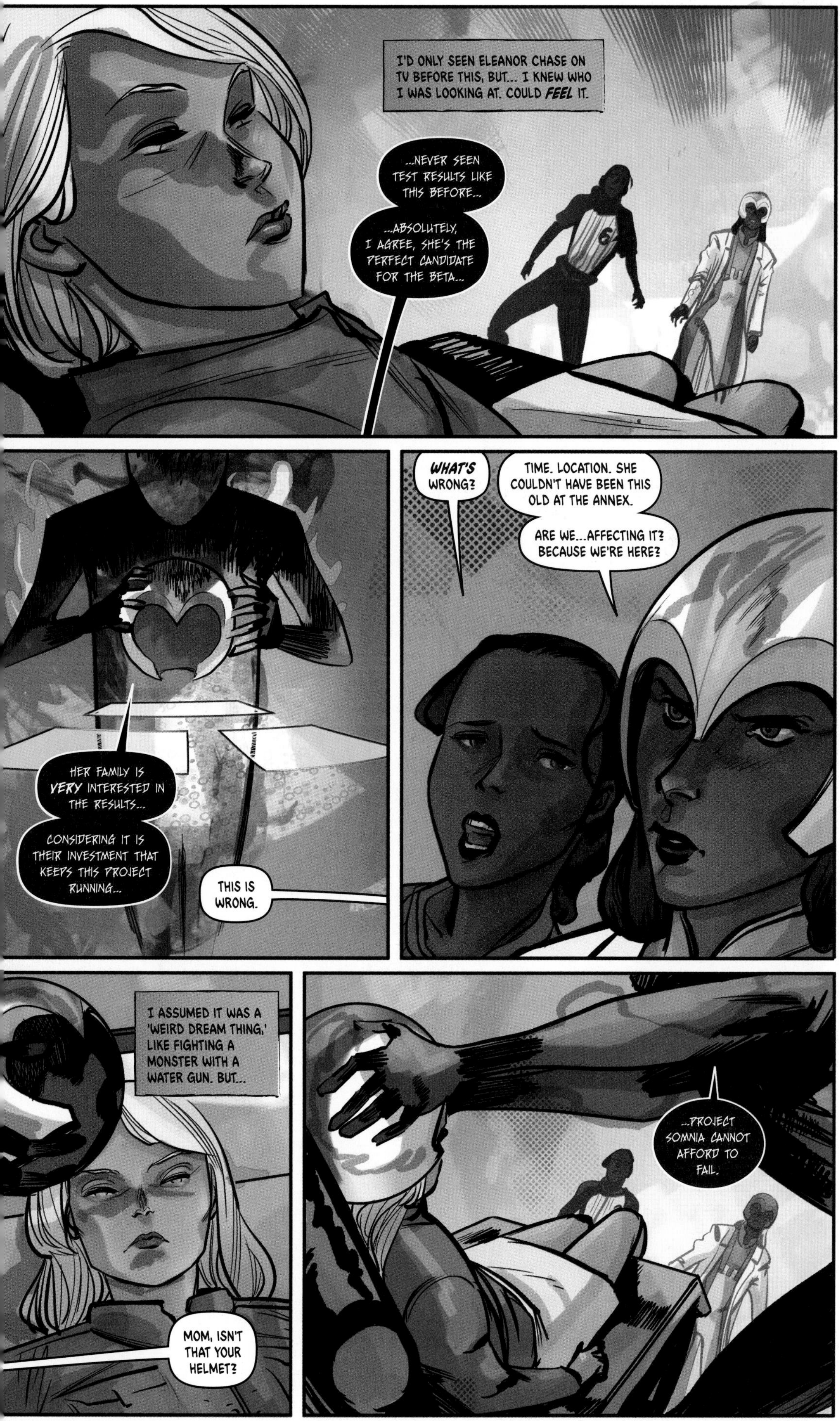
I'D ONLY SEEN ELEANOR CHASE ON TV BEFORE THIS, BUT... I KNEW WHO I WAS LOOKING AT. COULD *FEEL* IT.
...NEVER SEEN TEST RESULTS LIKE THIS BEFORE...
...ABSOLUTELY, I AGREE, SHE'S THE PERFECT CANDIDATE FOR THE BETA...
HER FAMILY IS *VERY* INTERESTED IN THE RESULTS...
CONSIDERING IT IS THEIR INVESTMENT THAT KEEPS THIS PROJECT RUNNING...
THIS IS WRONG.
WHAT'S WRONG?
TIME. LOCATION. SHE COULDN'T HAVE BEEN THIS OLD AT THE ANNEX.
ARE WE...AFFECTING IT? BECAUSE WE'RE HERE?
I ASSUMED IT WAS A 'WEIRD DREAM THING,' LIKE FIGHTING A MONSTER WITH A WATER GUN. BUT...
MOM, ISN'T THAT YOUR HELMET?
...PROJECT SOMNIA CANNOT AFFORD TO FAIL.

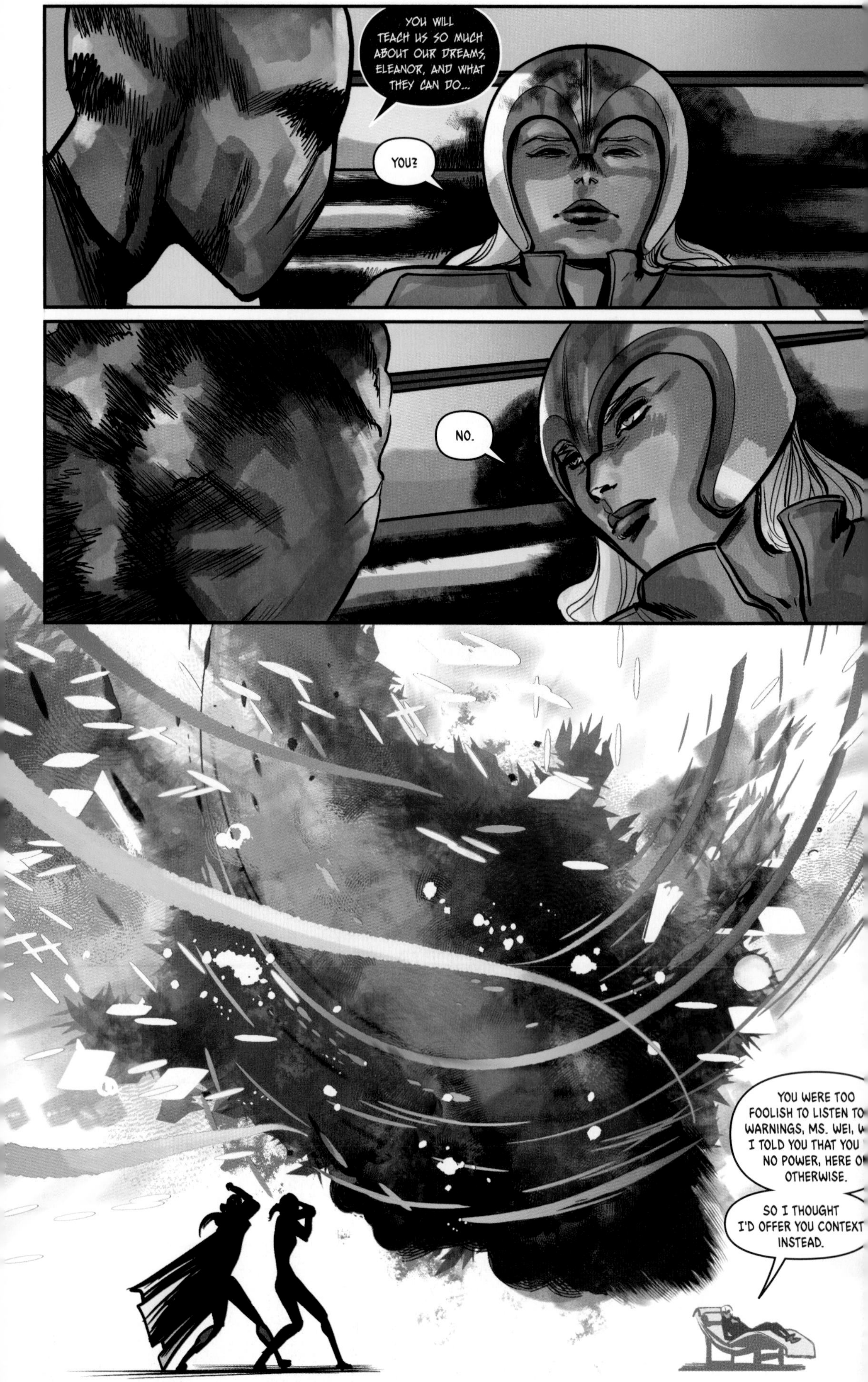

YOU WILL TEACH US SO MUCH ABOUT OUR DREAMS, ELEANOR, AND WHAT THEY CAN DO...
YOU?
NO.
YOU WERE TOO FOOLISH TO LISTEN TO WARNINGS, MS. WEI, I TOLD YOU THAT YOU NO POWER, HERE OTHERWISE.
SO I THOUGHT I'D OFFER YOU CONTEXT INSTEAD.

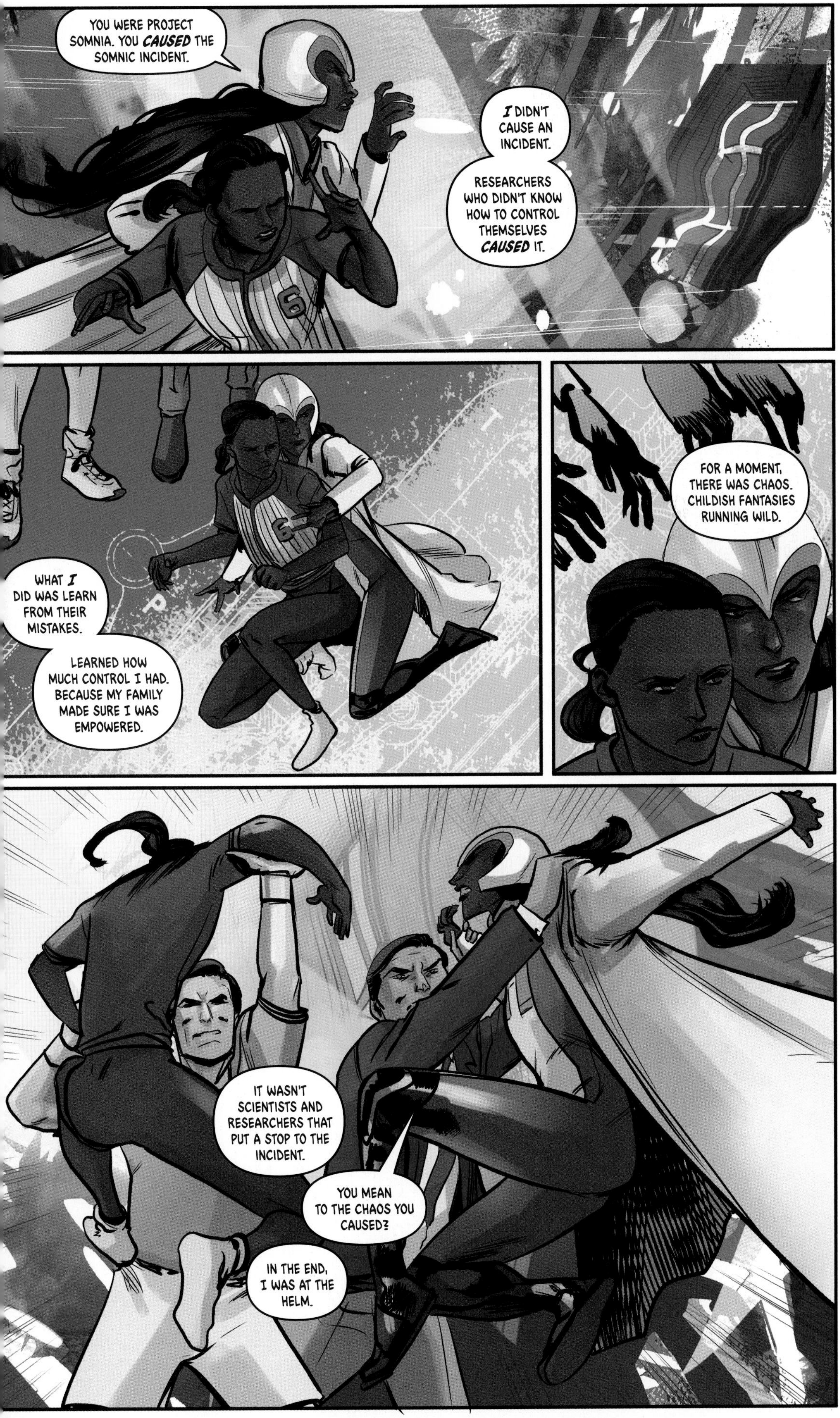
YOU WERE PROJECT SOMNIA. YOU **CAUSED** THE SOMNIC INCIDENT.
I DIDN'T CAUSE AN INCIDENT.
RESEARCHERS WHO DIDN'T KNOW HOW TO CONTROL THEMSELVES ***CAUSED*** IT.
WHAT ***I*** DID WAS LEARN FROM THEIR MISTAKES.
LEARNED HOW MUCH CONTROL I HAD. BECAUSE MY FAMILY MADE SURE I WAS EMPOWERED.
FOR A MOMENT, THERE WAS CHAOS. CHILDISH FANTASIES RUNNING WILD.
IT WASN'T SCIENTISTS AND RESEARCHERS THAT PUT A STOP TO THE INCIDENT.
YOU MEAN TO THE CHAOS YOU CAUSED?
IN THE END, I WAS AT THE HELM.

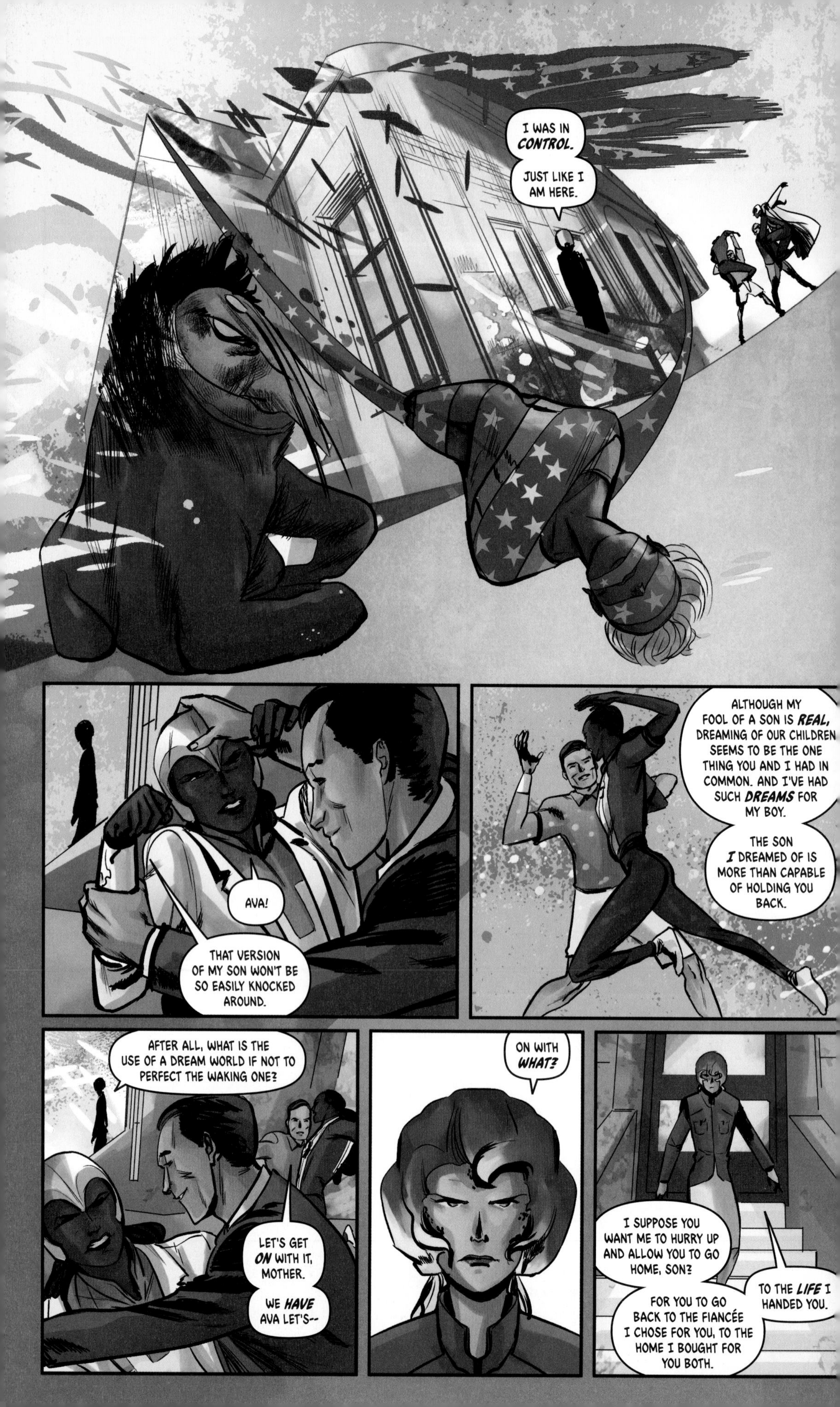
I WAS IN CONTROL.
JUST LIKE I AM HERE.
AVA!
THAT VERSION OF MY SON WON'T BE SO EASILY KNOCKED AROUND.
ALTHOUGH MY FOOL OF A SON IS REAL, DREAMING OF OUR CHILDREN SEEMS TO BE THE ONE THING YOU AND I HAD IN COMMON. AND I'VE HAD SUCH DREAMS FOR MY BOY.
THE SON I DREAMED OF IS MORE THAN CAPABLE OF HOLDING YOU BACK.
AFTER ALL, WHAT IS THE USE OF A DREAM WORLD IF NOT TO PERFECT THE WAKING ONE?
LET'S GET ON WITH IT, MOTHER.
WE HAVE AVA LET'S--
ON WITH WHAT?
I SUPPOSE YOU WANT ME TO HURRY UP AND ALLOW YOU TO GO HOME, SON?
FOR YOU TO GO BACK TO THE FIANCÉE I CHOSE FOR YOU, TO THE HOME I BOUGHT FOR YOU BOTH.
TO THE LIFE I HANDED YOU.

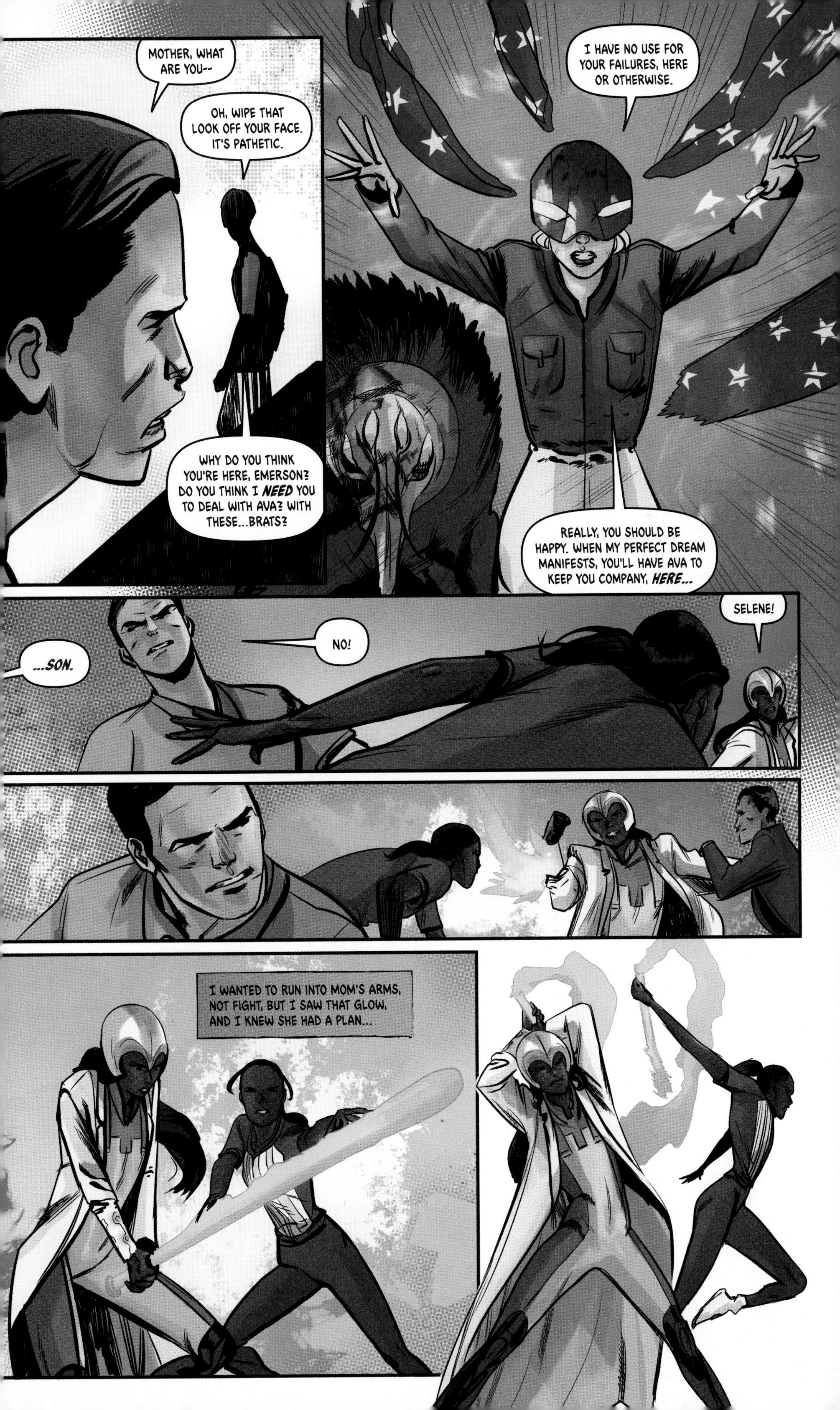
MOTHER, WHAT ARE YOU--
OH, WIPE THAT LOOK OFF YOUR FACE. IT'S PATHETIC.
WHY DO YOU THINK YOU'RE HERE, EMERSON? DO YOU THINK I NEED YOU TO DEAL WITH AVA? WITH THESE...BRATS?
I HAVE NO USE FOR YOUR FAILURES, HERE OR OTHERWISE.
REALLY, YOU SHOULD BE HAPPY. WHEN MY PERFECT DREAM MANIFESTS, YOU'LL HAVE AVA TO KEEP YOU COMPANY, HERE...
...SON.
NO!
SELENE!
I WANTED TO RUN INTO MOM'S ARMS, NOT FIGHT, BUT I SAW THAT GLOW, AND I KNEW SHE HAD A PLAN...

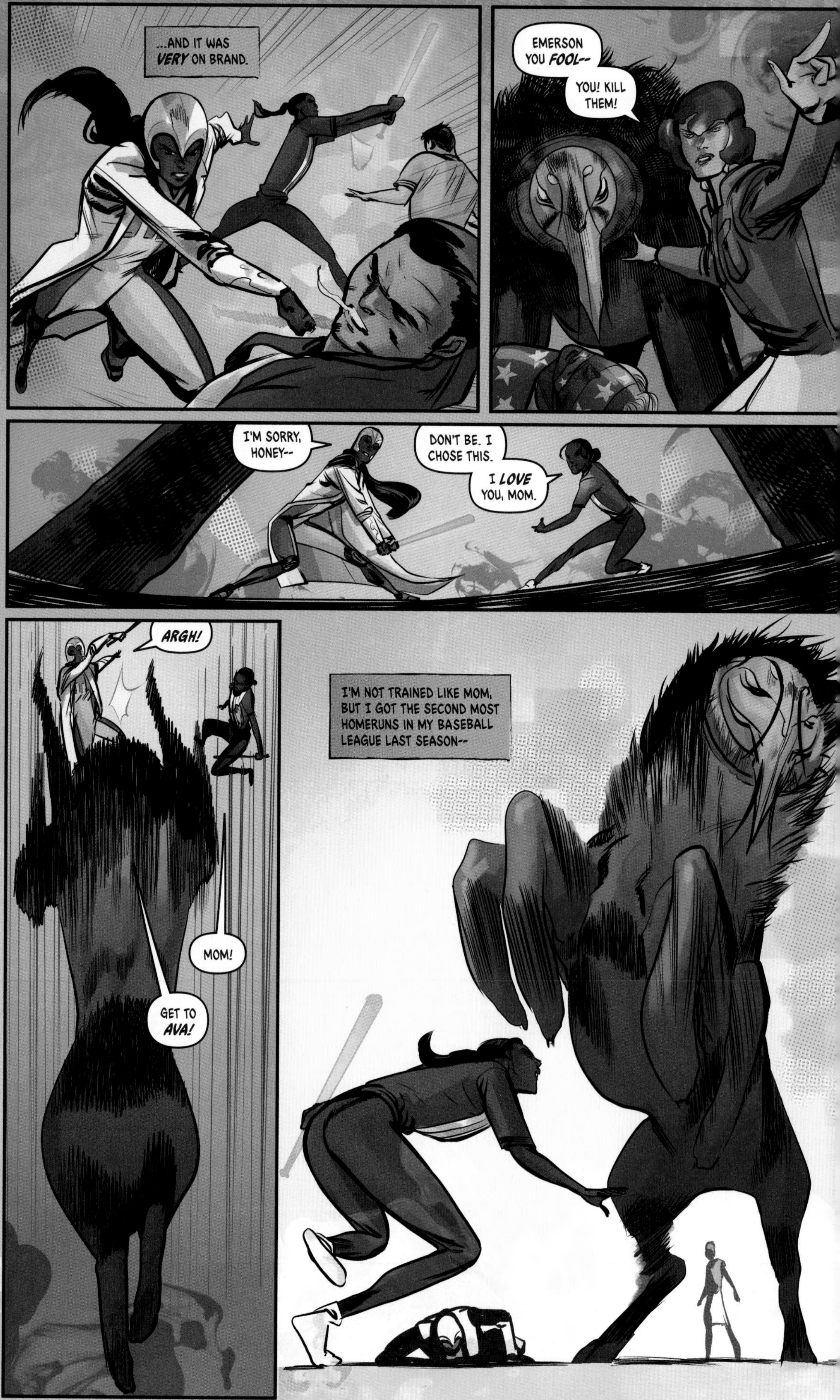

...AND IT WAS VERY ON BRAND.
EMERSON YOU FOOL--
YOU! KILL THEM!
I'M SORRY, HONEY--
DON'T BE. I CHOSE THIS.
I LOVE YOU, MOM.
ARGH!
MOM!
GET TO AVA!
I'M NOT TRAINED LIKE MOM, BUT I GOT THE SECOND MOST HOMERUNS IN MY BASEBALL LEAGUE LAST SEASON--

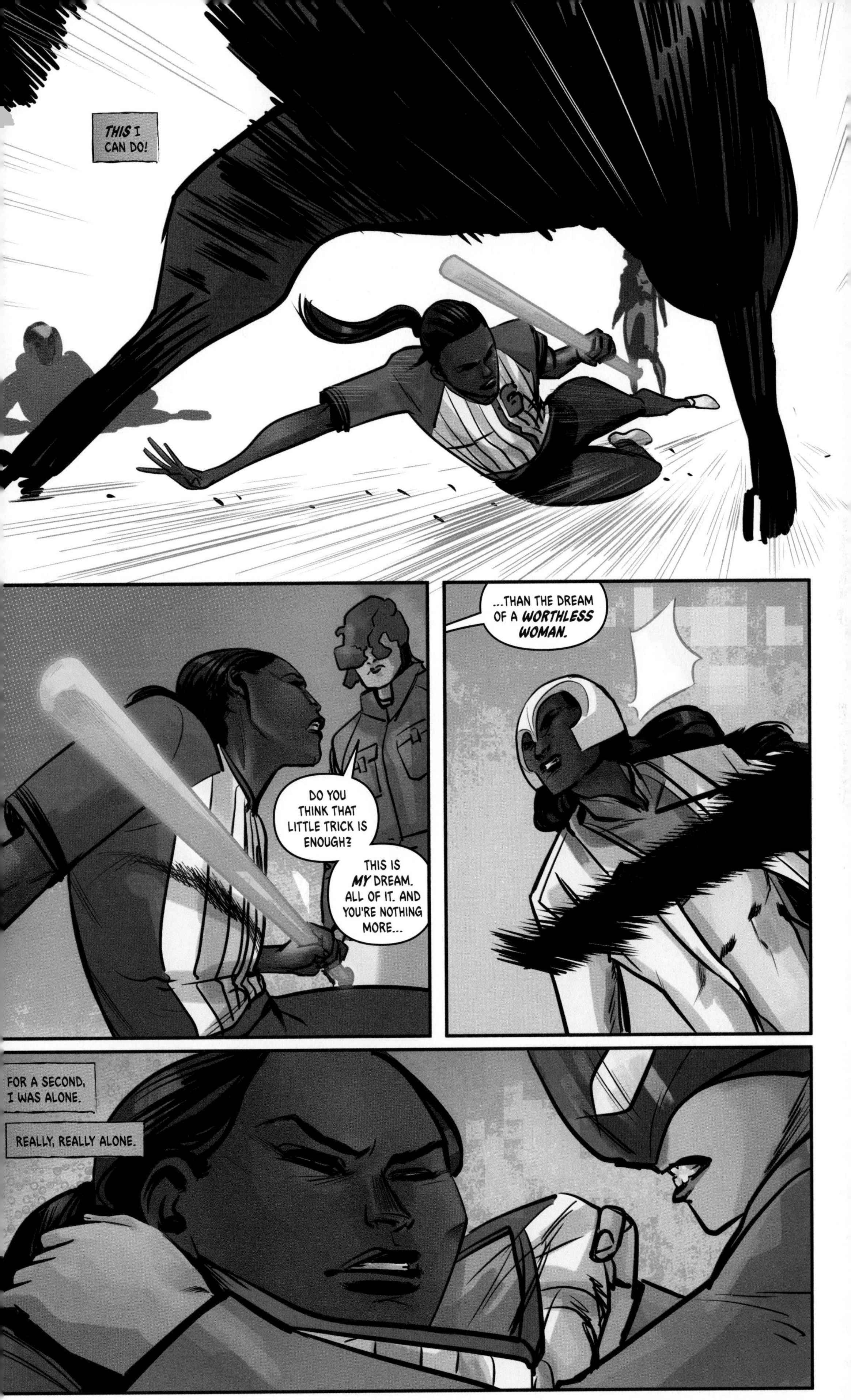
THIS I CAN DO!
DO YOU THINK THAT LITTLE TRICK IS ENOUGH?
THIS IS MY DREAM. ALL OF IT. AND YOU'RE NOTHING MORE...
...THAN THE DREAM OF A WORTHLESS WOMAN.
FOR A SECOND, I WAS ALONE.
REALLY, REALLY ALONE.

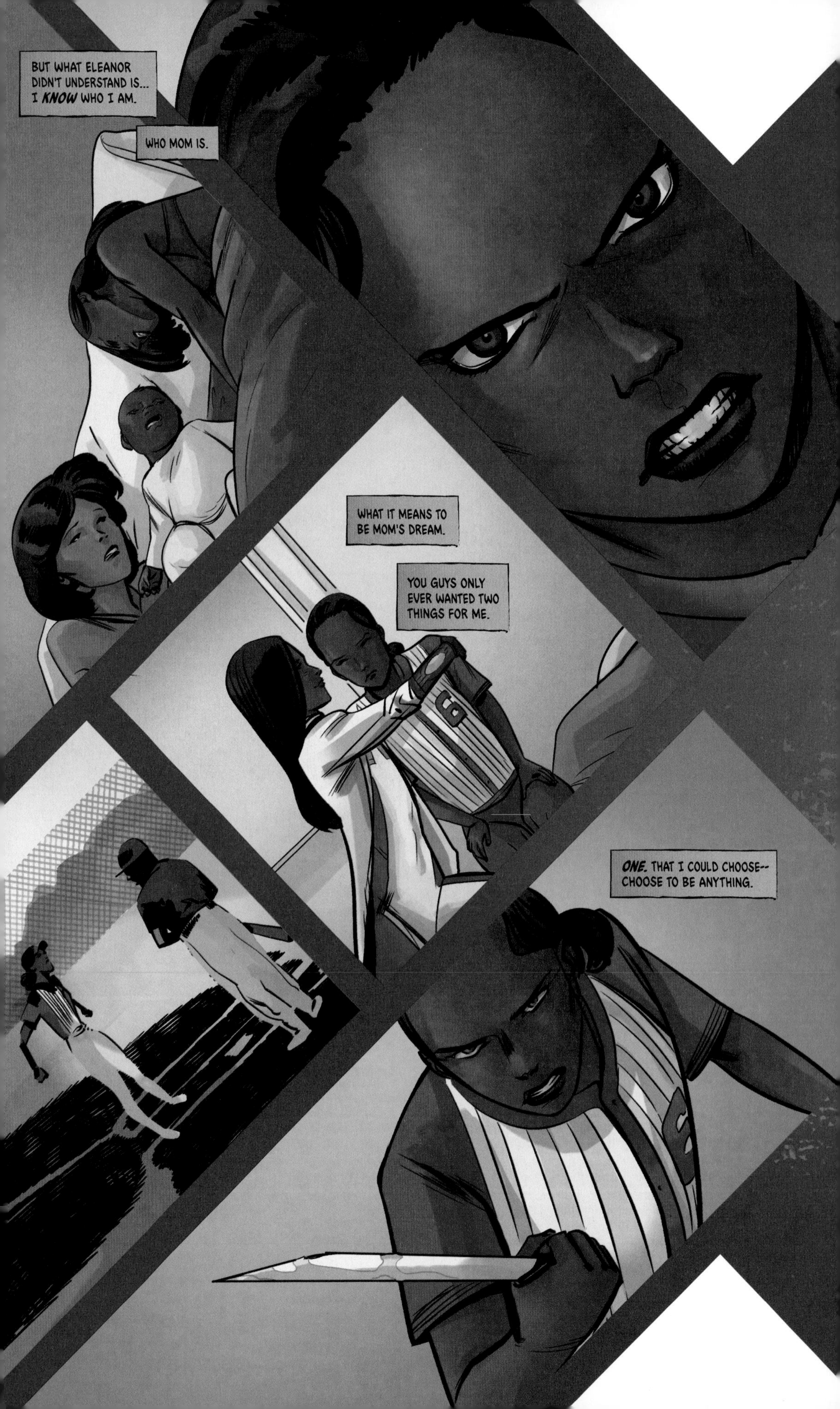
BUT WHAT ELEANOR DIDN'T UNDERSTAND IS... I *KNOW* WHO I AM.
WHO MOM IS.
WHAT IT MEANS TO BE MOM'S DREAM.
YOU GUYS ONLY EVER WANTED TWO THINGS FOR ME.
ONE. THAT I COULD CHOOSE-- CHOOSE TO BE ANYTHING.

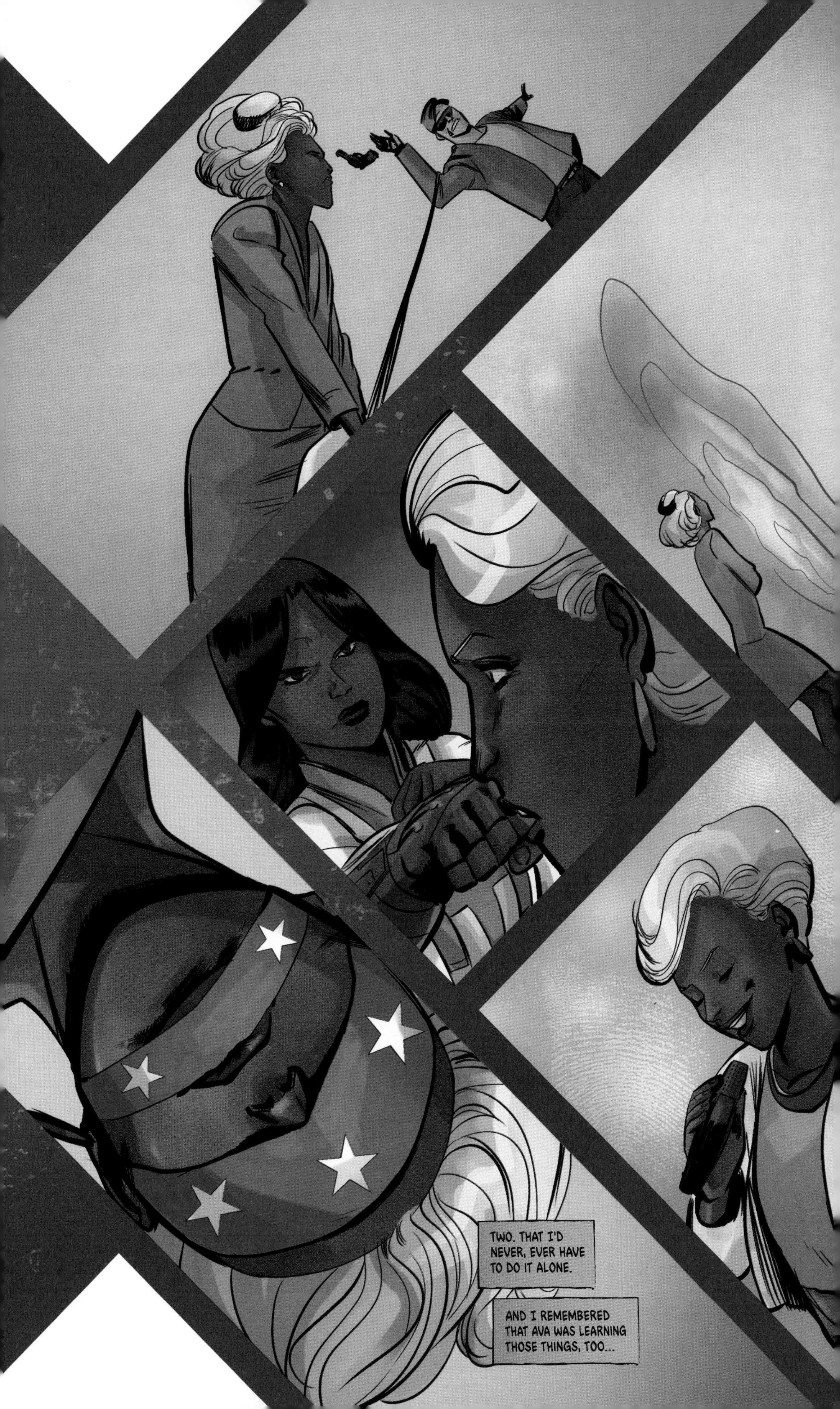

TWO. THAT I'D NEVER, EVER HAVE TO DO IT ALONE.
AND I REMEMBERED THAT AVA WAS LEARNING THOSE THINGS, TOO...

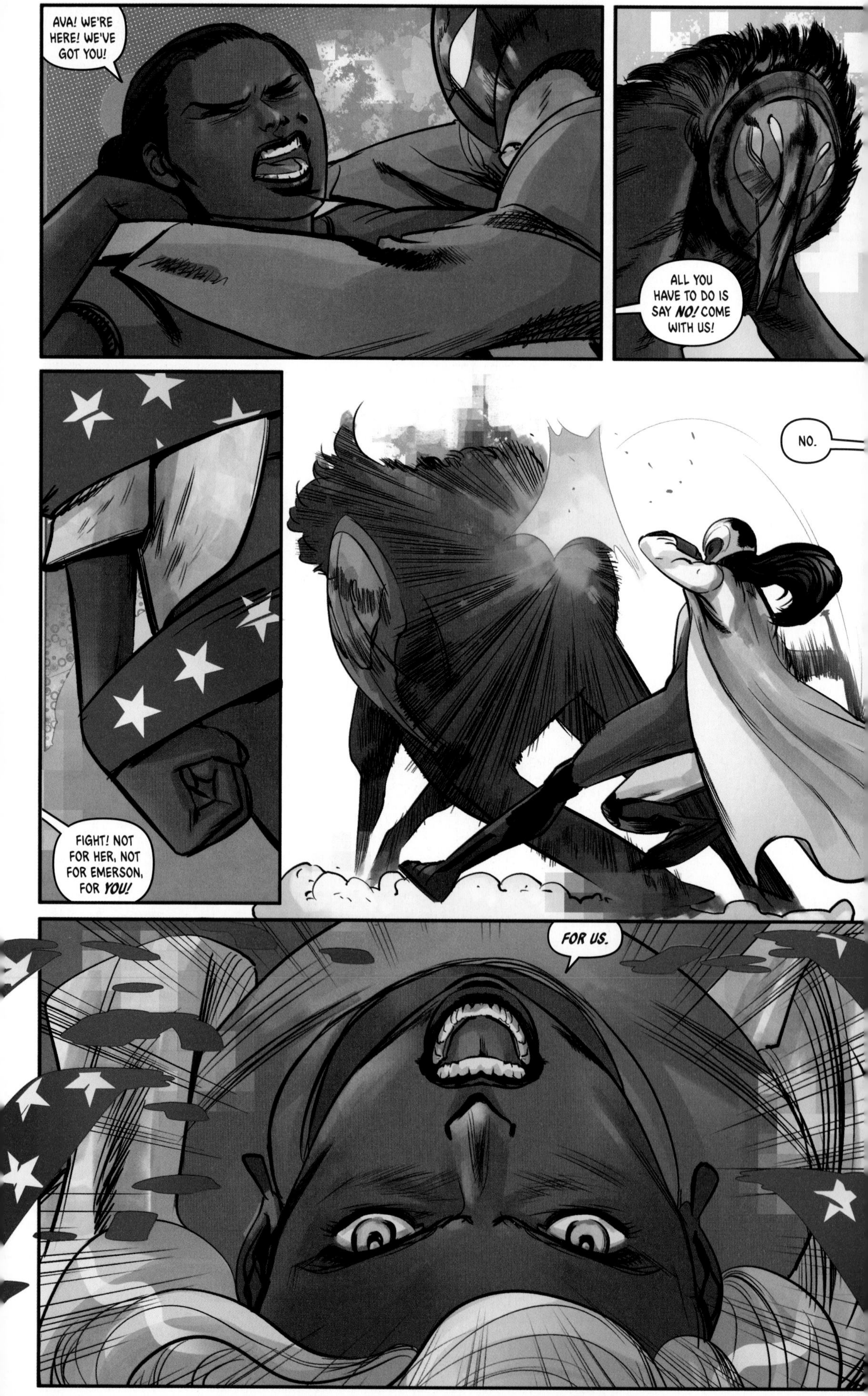
AVA! WE'RE HERE! WE'VE GOT YOU!
ALL YOU HAVE TO DO IS SAY NO! COME WITH US!
FIGHT! NOT FOR HER, NOT FOR EMERSON, FOR YOU!
NO.
FOR US.

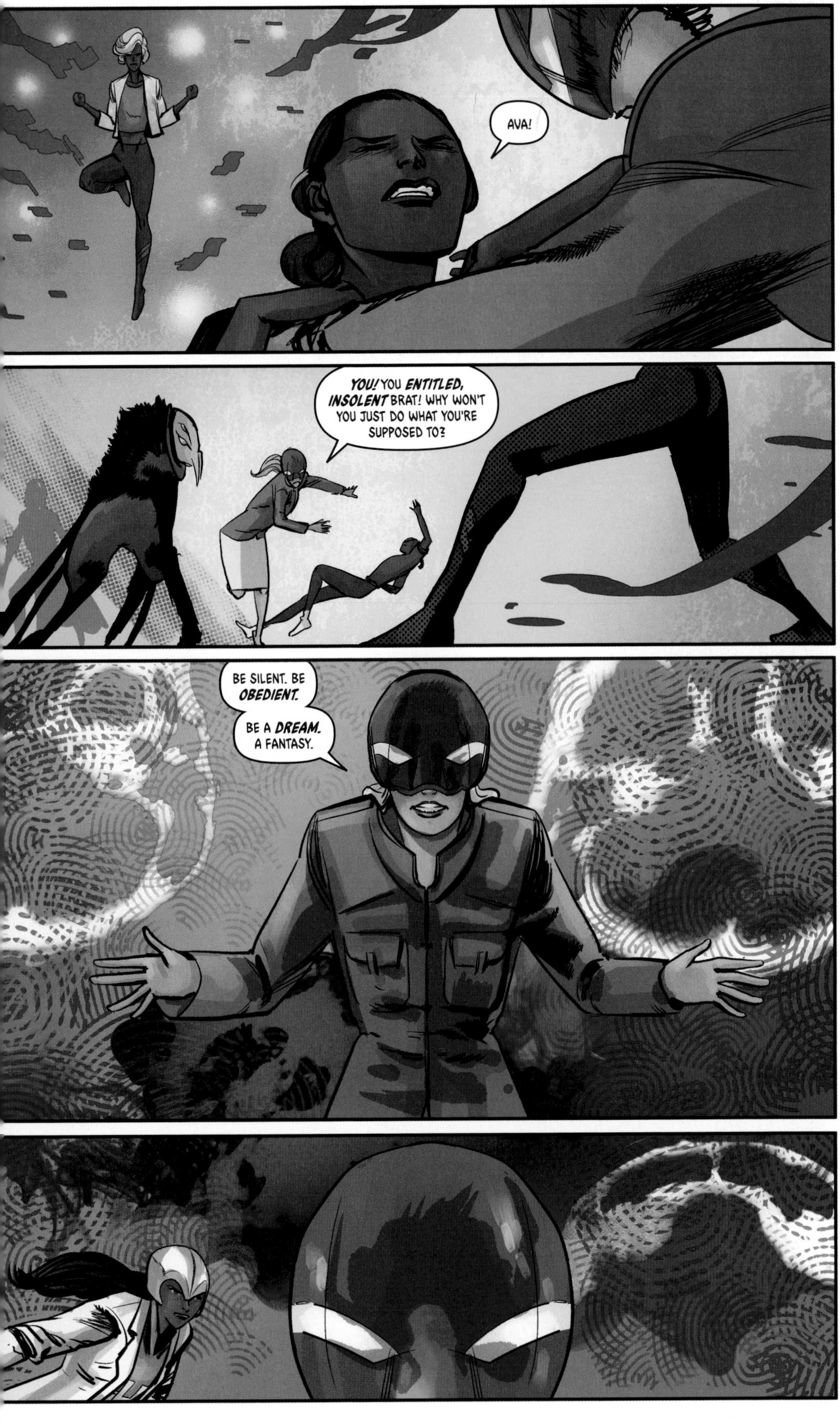
AVA!
YOU! YOU ENTITLED, INSOLENT BRAT! WHY WON'T YOU JUST DO WHAT YOU'RE SUPPOSED TO?
BE SILENT. BE OBEDIENT.
BE A DREAM. A FANTASY.

AAAAAH!

THIS IS THE PART THAT I HAD TO TALK ABOUT IN THERAPY. BECAUSE IT STICKS WITH ME A LOT.

MAKES ME ALMOST FEEL BAD FOR HER.

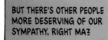

BUT THERE'S OTHER PEOPLE MORE DESERVING OF OUR SYMPATHY, RIGHT MA?

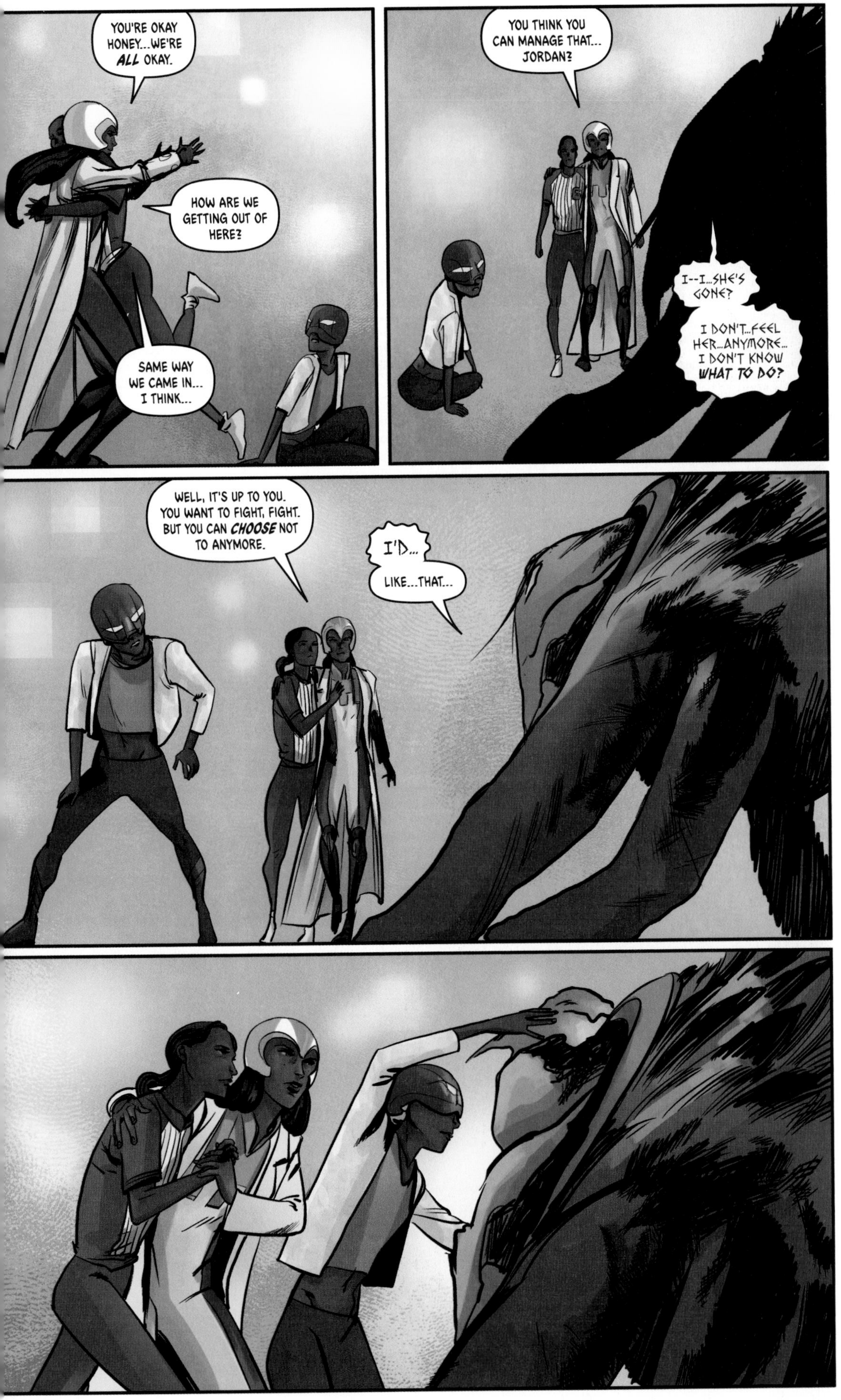

YOU'RE OKAY HONEY...WE'RE *ALL* OKAY.
HOW ARE WE GETTING OUT OF HERE?
SAME WAY WE CAME IN... I THINK...
YOU THINK YOU CAN MANAGE THAT... JORDAN?
I--I...SHE'S GONE?
I DON'T...FEEL HER...ANYMORE... I DON'T KNOW *WHAT TO DO?*
WELL, IT'S UP TO YOU. YOU WANT TO FIGHT, FIGHT. BUT YOU CAN *CHOOSE* NOT TO ANYMORE.
I'D...
LIKE...THAT...

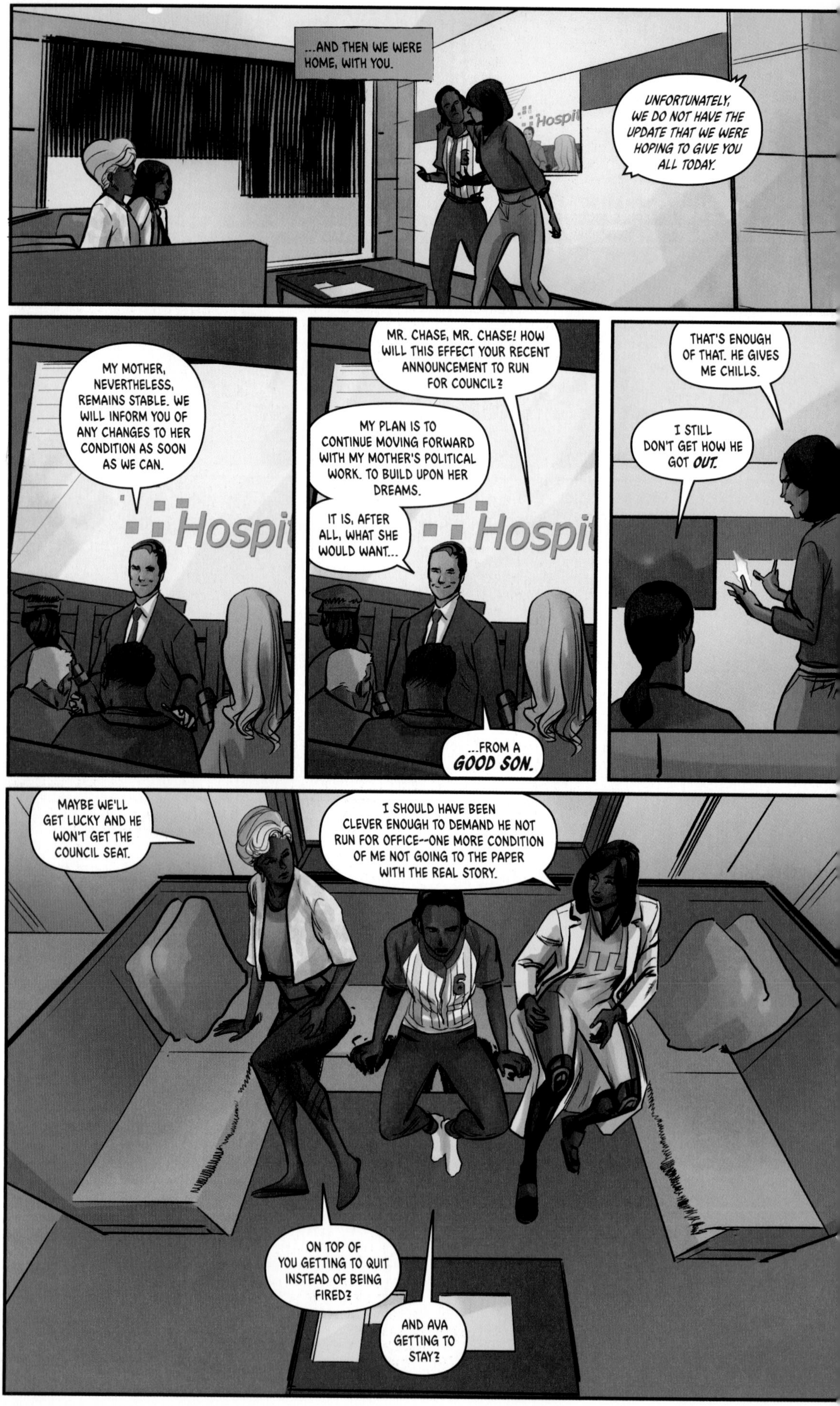
...AND THEN WE WERE HOME, WITH YOU.
UNFORTUNATELY, WE DO NOT HAVE THE UPDATE THAT WE WERE HOPING TO GIVE YOU ALL TODAY.
Hospit
MY MOTHER, NEVERTHELESS, REMAINS STABLE. WE WILL INFORM YOU OF ANY CHANGES TO HER CONDITION AS SOON AS WE CAN.
Hospit
MR. CHASE, MR. CHASE! HOW WILL THIS EFFECT YOUR RECENT ANNOUNCEMENT TO RUN FOR COUNCIL?
MY PLAN IS TO CONTINUE MOVING FORWARD WITH MY MOTHER'S POLITICAL WORK. TO BUILD UPON HER DREAMS.
IT IS, AFTER ALL, WHAT SHE WOULD WANT...
...FROM A GOOD SON.
Hospit
THAT'S ENOUGH OF THAT. HE GIVES ME CHILLS.
I STILL DON'T GET HOW HE GOT OUT.
MAYBE WE'LL GET LUCKY AND HE WON'T GET THE COUNCIL SEAT.
I SHOULD HAVE BEEN CLEVER ENOUGH TO DEMAND HE NOT RUN FOR OFFICE--ONE MORE CONDITION OF ME NOT GOING TO THE PAPER WITH THE REAL STORY.
ON TOP OF YOU GETTING TO QUIT INSTEAD OF BEING FIRED?
AND AVA GETTING TO STAY?

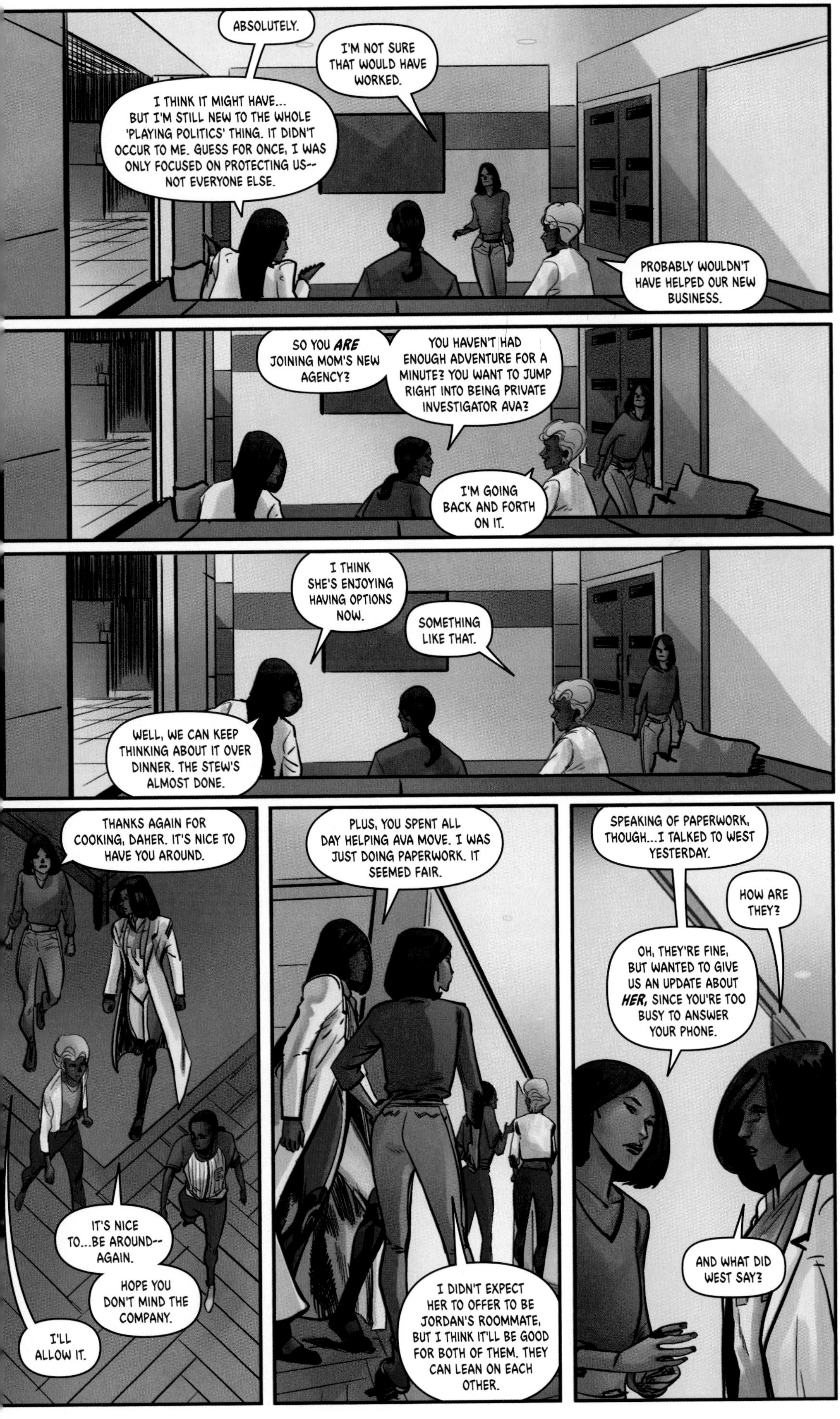
ABSOLUTELY.
I'M NOT SURE THAT WOULD HAVE WORKED.
I THINK IT MIGHT HAVE... BUT I'M STILL NEW TO THE WHOLE 'PLAYING POLITICS' THING. IT DIDN'T OCCUR TO ME. GUESS FOR ONCE, I WAS ONLY FOCUSED ON PROTECTING US-- NOT EVERYONE ELSE.
PROBABLY WOULDN'T HAVE HELPED OUR NEW BUSINESS.
SO YOU ARE JOINING MOM'S NEW AGENCY?
YOU HAVEN'T HAD ENOUGH ADVENTURE FOR A MINUTE? YOU WANT TO JUMP RIGHT INTO BEING PRIVATE INVESTIGATOR AVA?
I'M GOING BACK AND FORTH ON IT.
I THINK SHE'S ENJOYING HAVING OPTIONS NOW.
SOMETHING LIKE THAT.
WELL, WE CAN KEEP THINKING ABOUT IT OVER DINNER. THE STEW'S ALMOST DONE.
THANKS AGAIN FOR COOKING, DAHER. IT'S NICE TO HAVE YOU AROUND.
IT'S NICE TO...BE AROUND-- AGAIN.
HOPE YOU DON'T MIND THE COMPANY.
I'LL ALLOW IT.
PLUS, YOU SPENT ALL DAY HELPING AVA MOVE. I WAS JUST DOING PAPERWORK. IT SEEMED FAIR.
I DIDN'T EXPECT HER TO OFFER TO BE JORDAN'S ROOMMATE, BUT I THINK IT'LL BE GOOD FOR BOTH OF THEM. THEY CAN LEAN ON EACH OTHER.
SPEAKING OF PAPERWORK, THOUGH...I TALKED TO WEST YESTERDAY.
HOW ARE THEY?
OH, THEY'RE FINE, BUT WANTED TO GIVE US AN UPDATE ABOUT HER, SINCE YOU'RE TOO BUSY TO ANSWER YOUR PHONE.
AND WHAT DID WEST SAY?

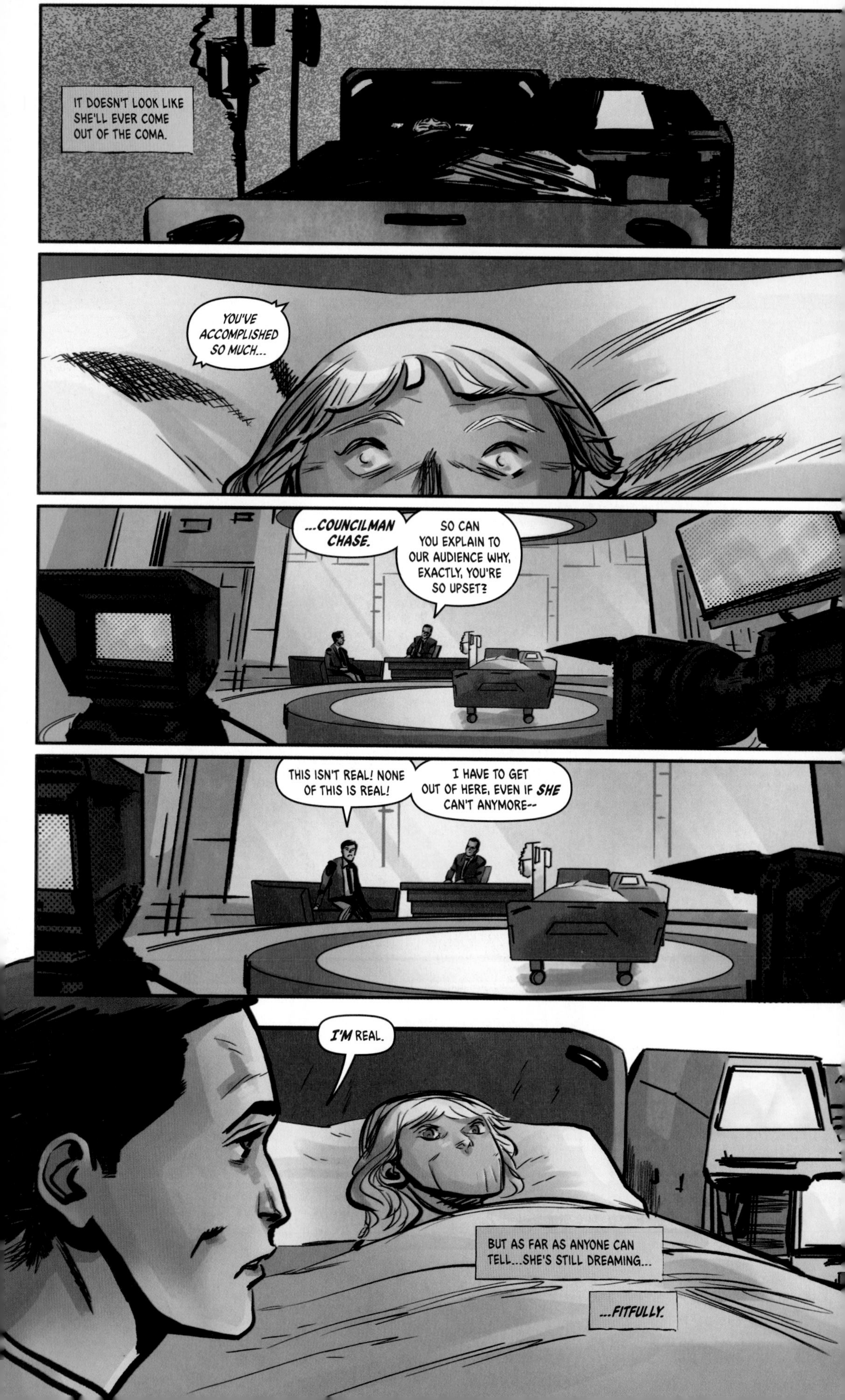
IT DOESN'T LOOK LIKE SHE'LL EVER COME OUT OF THE COMA.
YOU'VE ACCOMPLISHED SO MUCH...
...COUNCILMAN CHASE.
SO CAN YOU EXPLAIN TO OUR AUDIENCE WHY, EXACTLY, YOU'RE SO UPSET?
THIS ISN'T REAL! NONE OF THIS IS REAL!
I HAVE TO GET OUT OF HERE, EVEN IF SHE CAN'T ANYMORE--
I'M REAL.
BUT AS FAR AS ANYONE CAN TELL...SHE'S STILL DREAMING...
...FITFULLY.

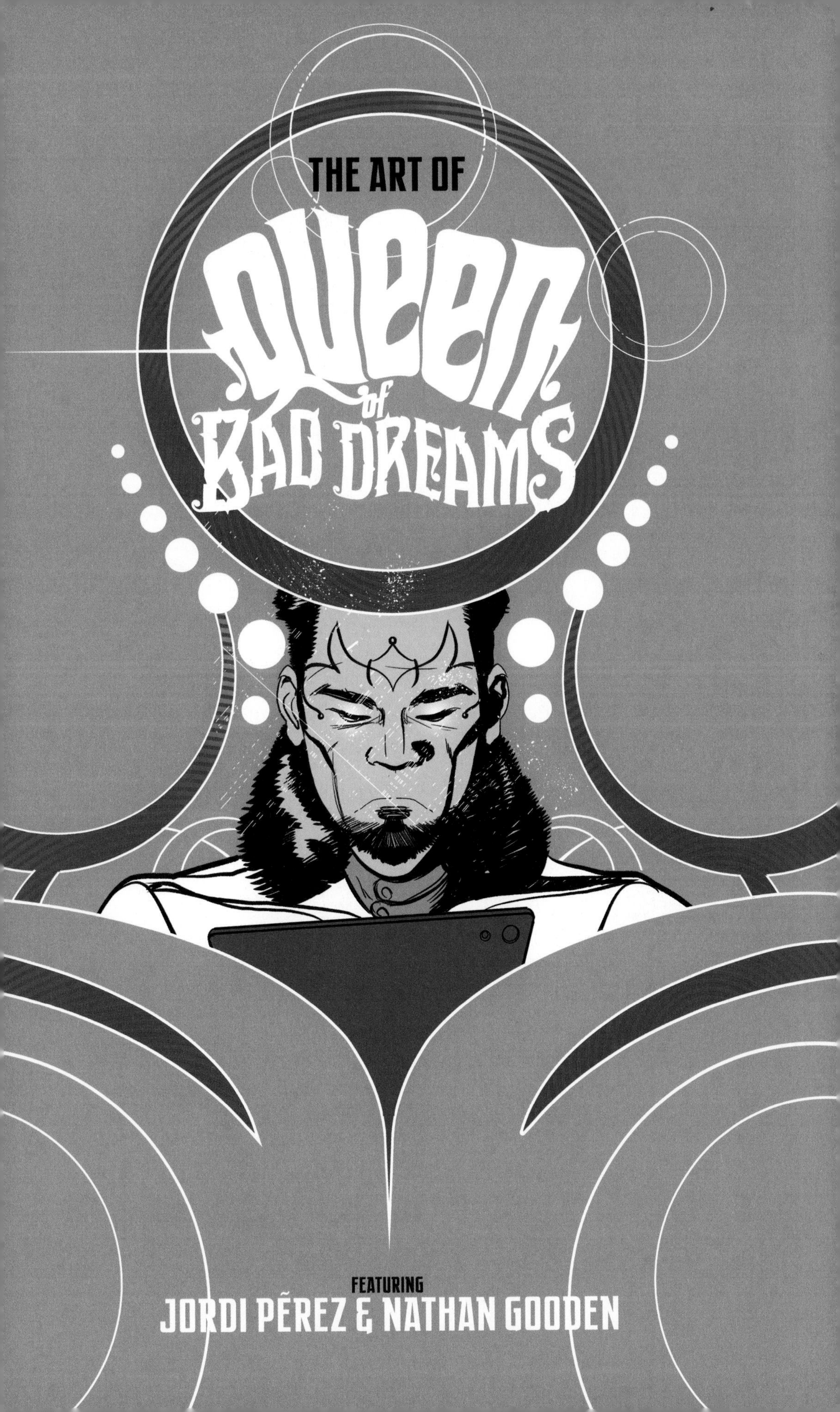
THE ART OF
QUEEN of BAD DREAMS
FEATURING
JORDI PÉREZ & NATHAN GOODEN

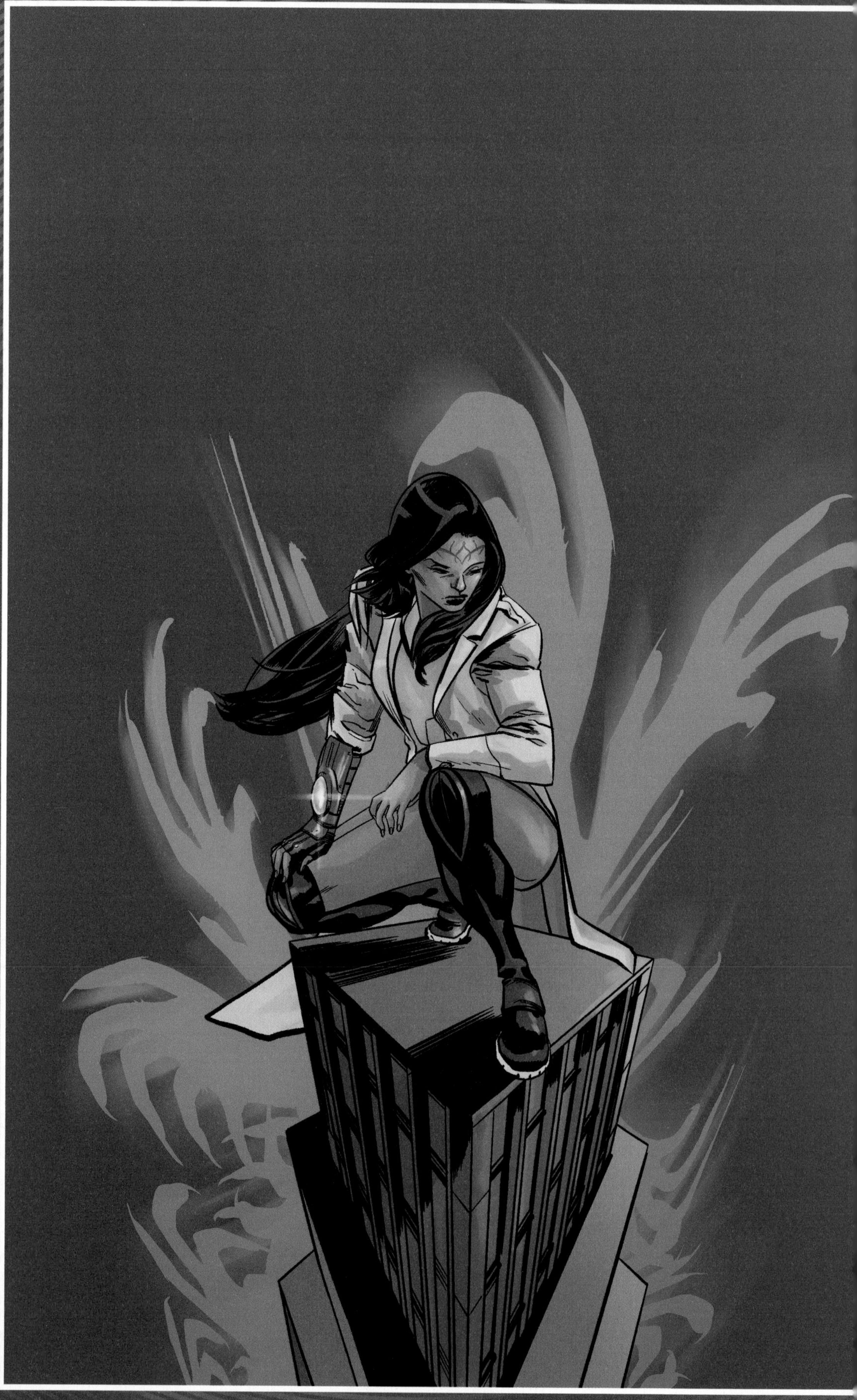

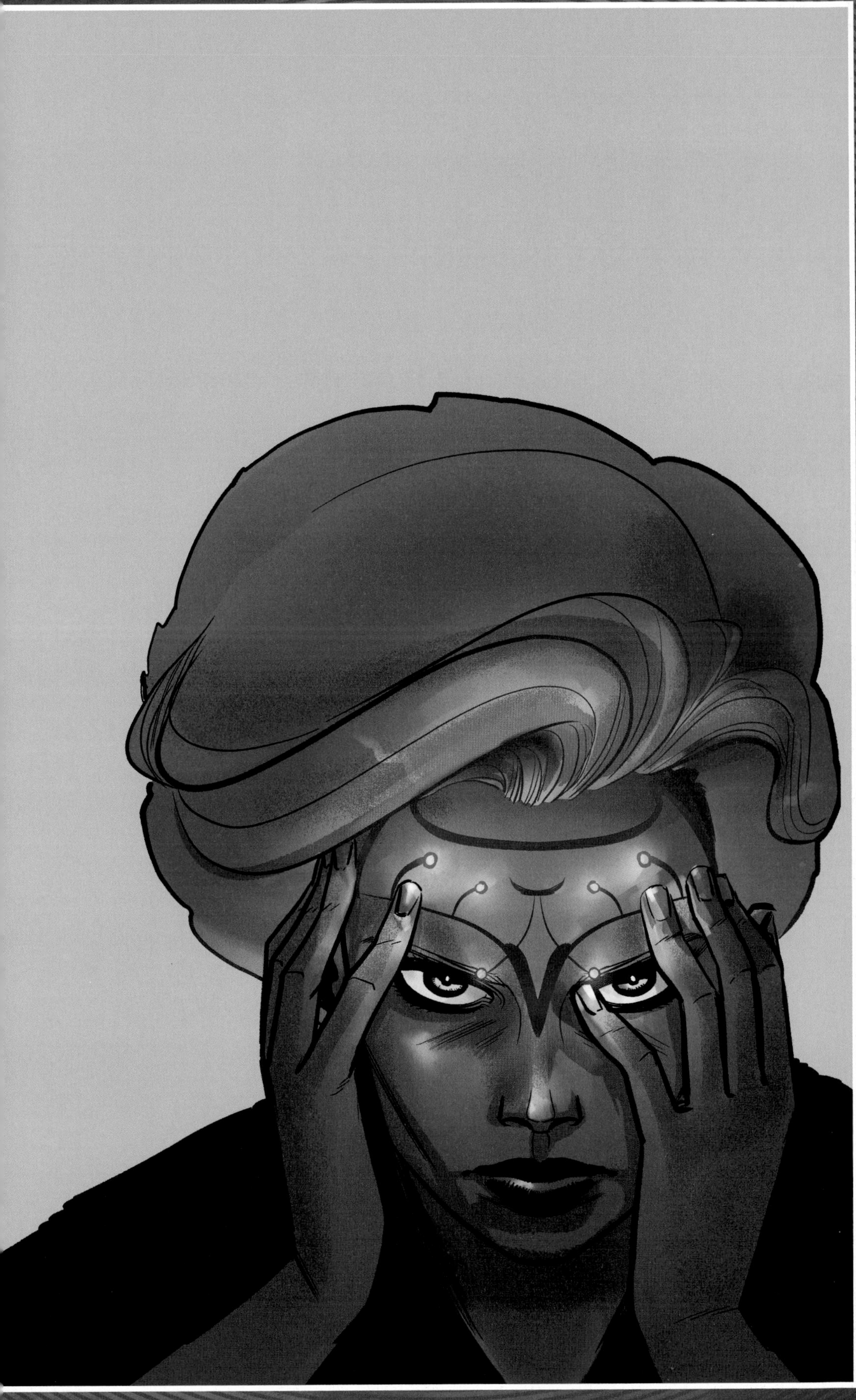

ISSUE 3: JORDI PÉREZ

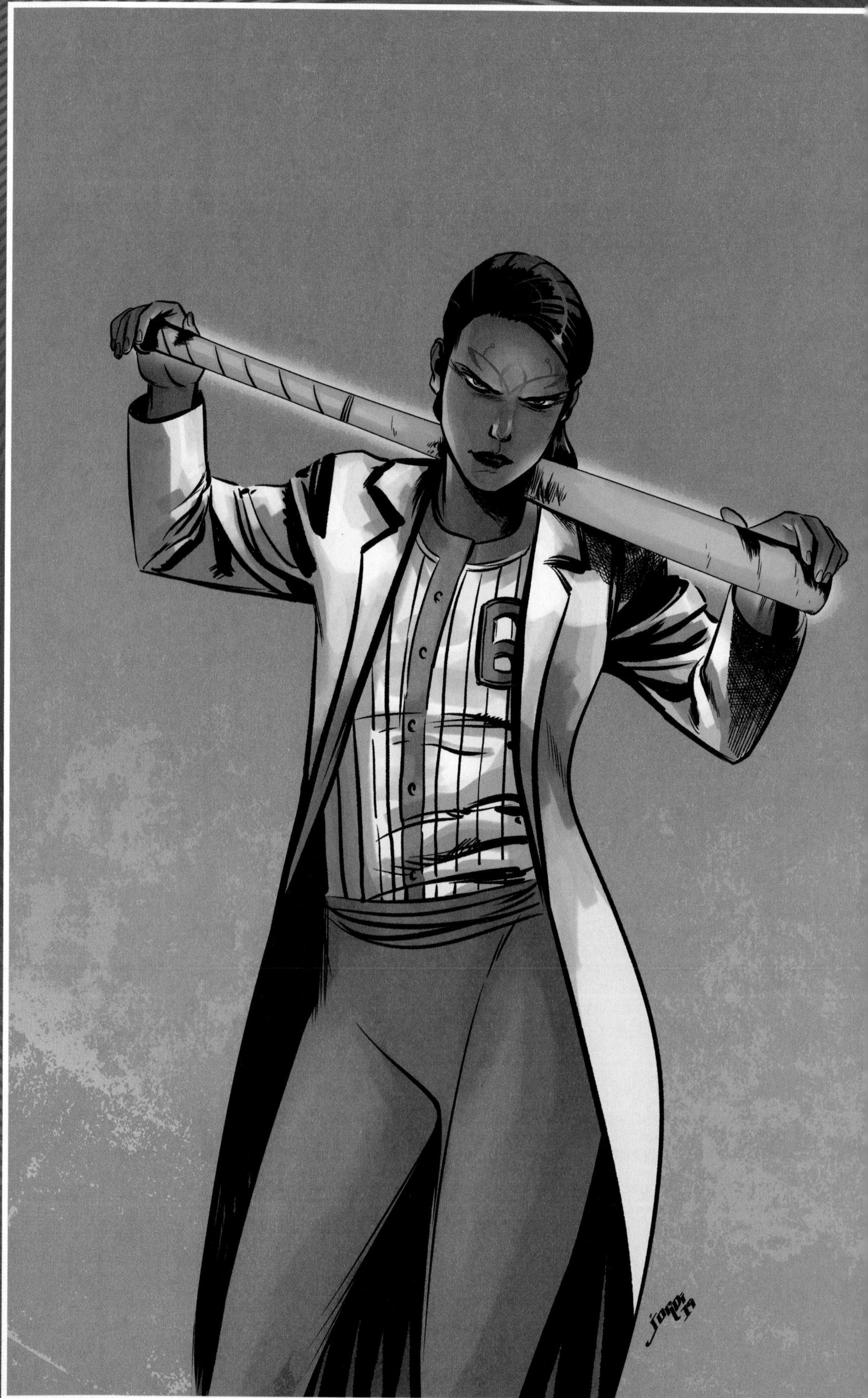

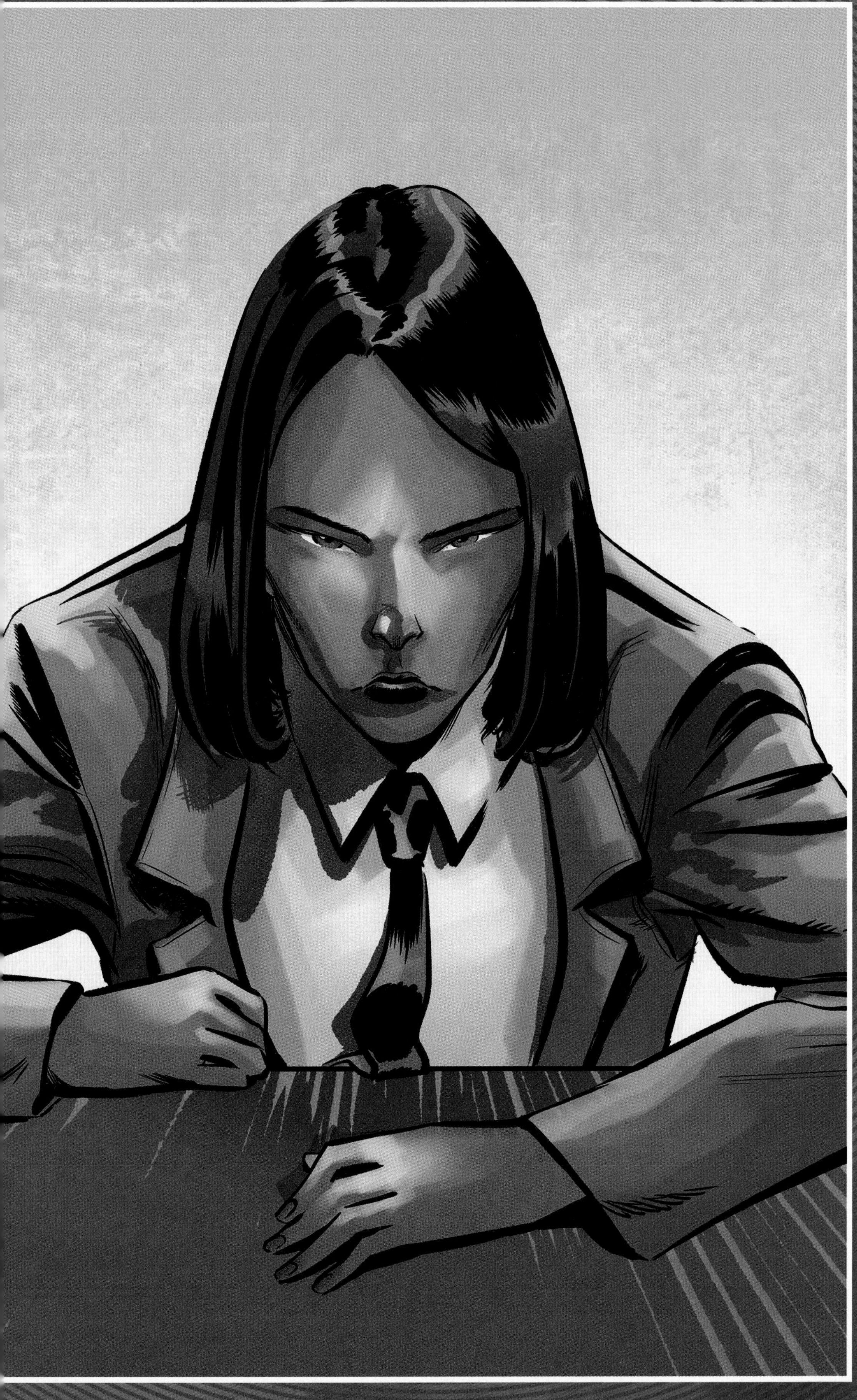

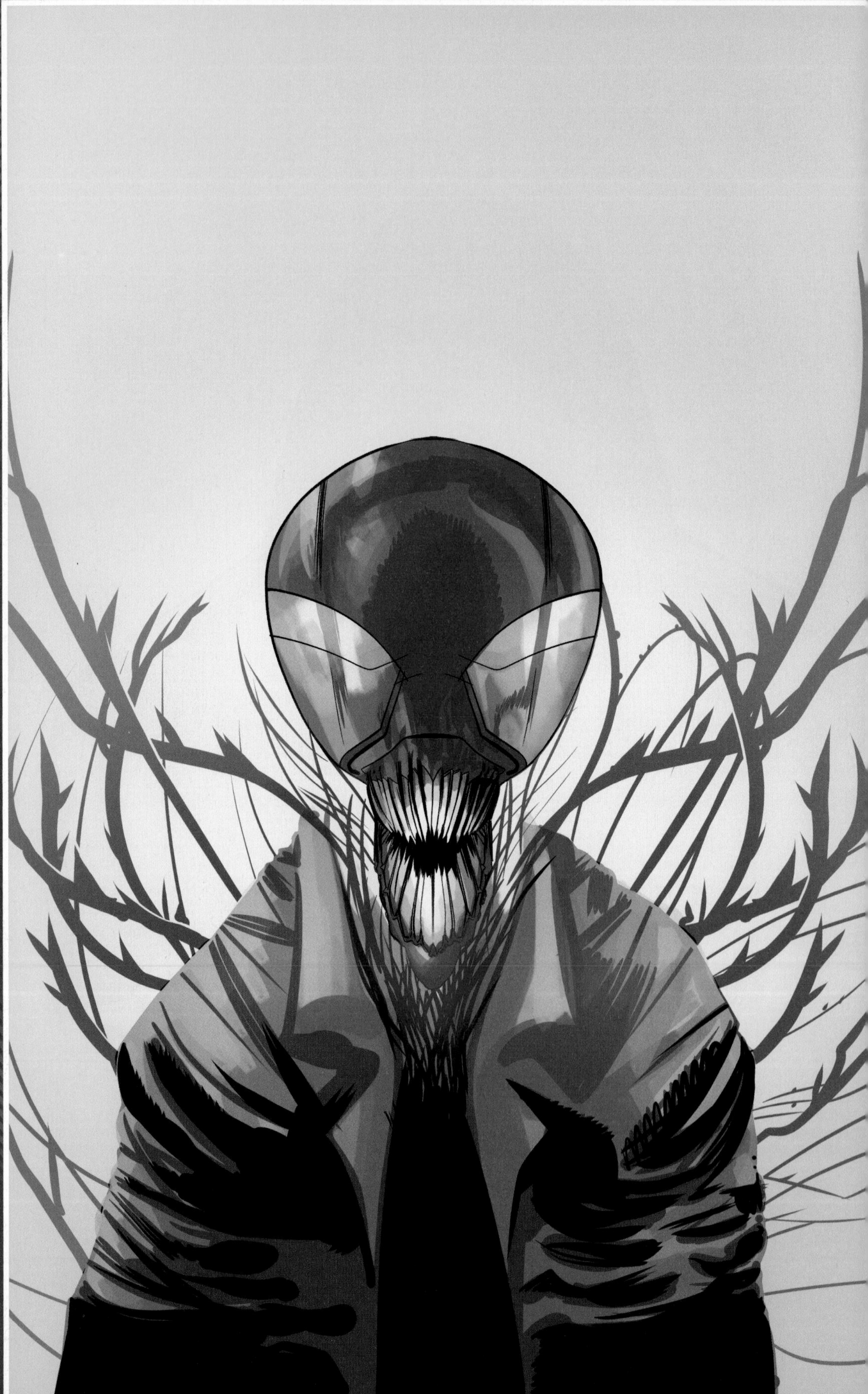

UE 1: VAULT VINTAGE/NATHAN GOODEN

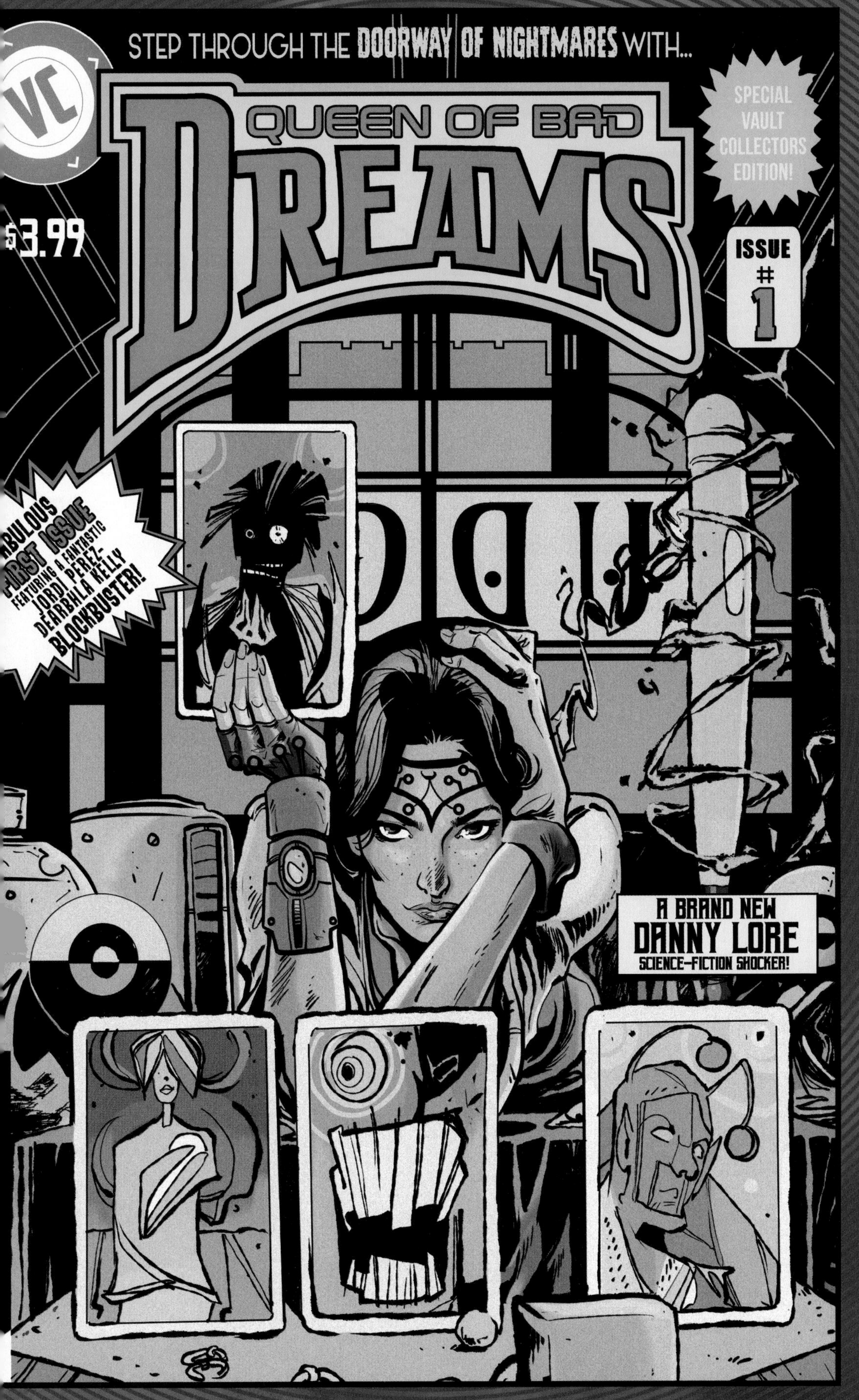
STEP THROUGH THE DOORWAY OF NIGHTMARES WITH...
VC
QUEEN OF BAD
DREAMS
SPECIAL VAULT COLLECTORS EDITION!
$3.99
ISSUE # 1
BULOUS
RST ISSUE
FEATURING A FANTASTIC
JORDI PEREZ-
DEARBHLA KELLY
BLOCKBUSTER!
A BRAND NEW
DANNY LORE
SCIENCE-FICTION SHOCKER!

ISSUE 1: RETAILER VINTAGE/NATHAN GOODEN

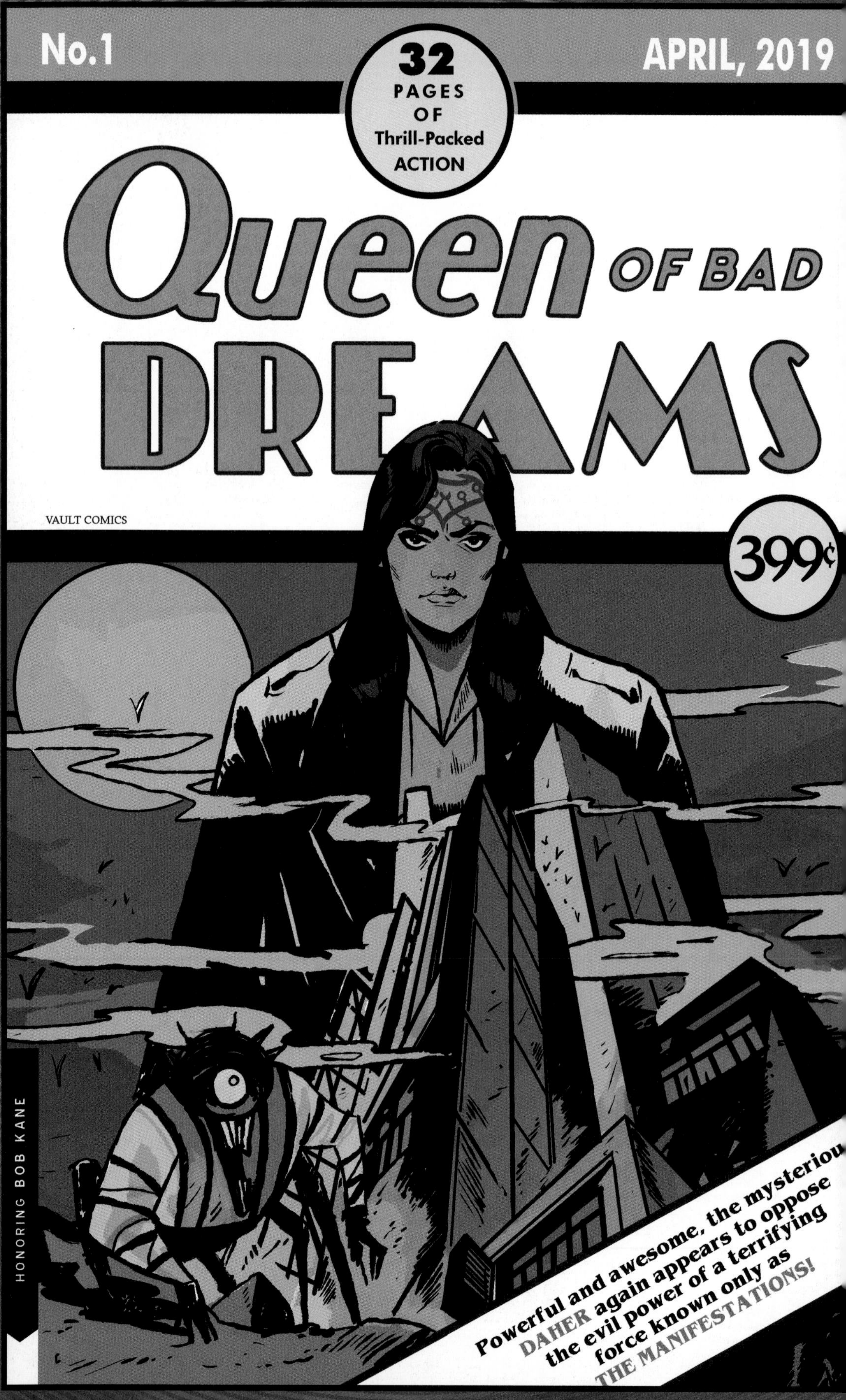

SUE 1: RETAILER VINTAGE/NATHAN GOODEN

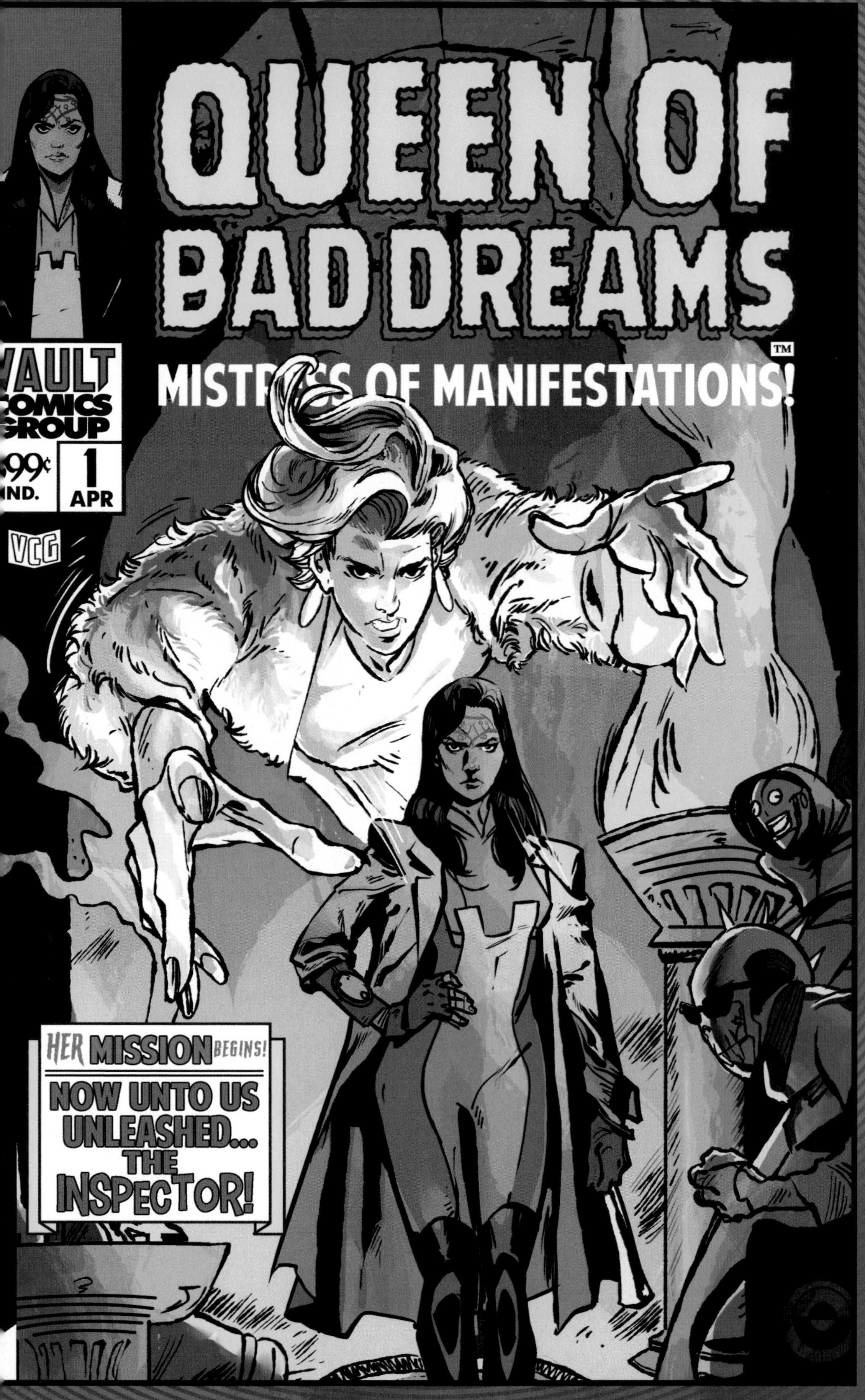
QUEEN OF BAD DREAMS
™
MISTRESS OF MANIFESTATIONS!
VAULT COMICS GROUP
99¢ IND.
1 APR
VCG
HER MISSION BEGINS!
NOW UNTO US UNLEASHED... THE INSPECTOR!

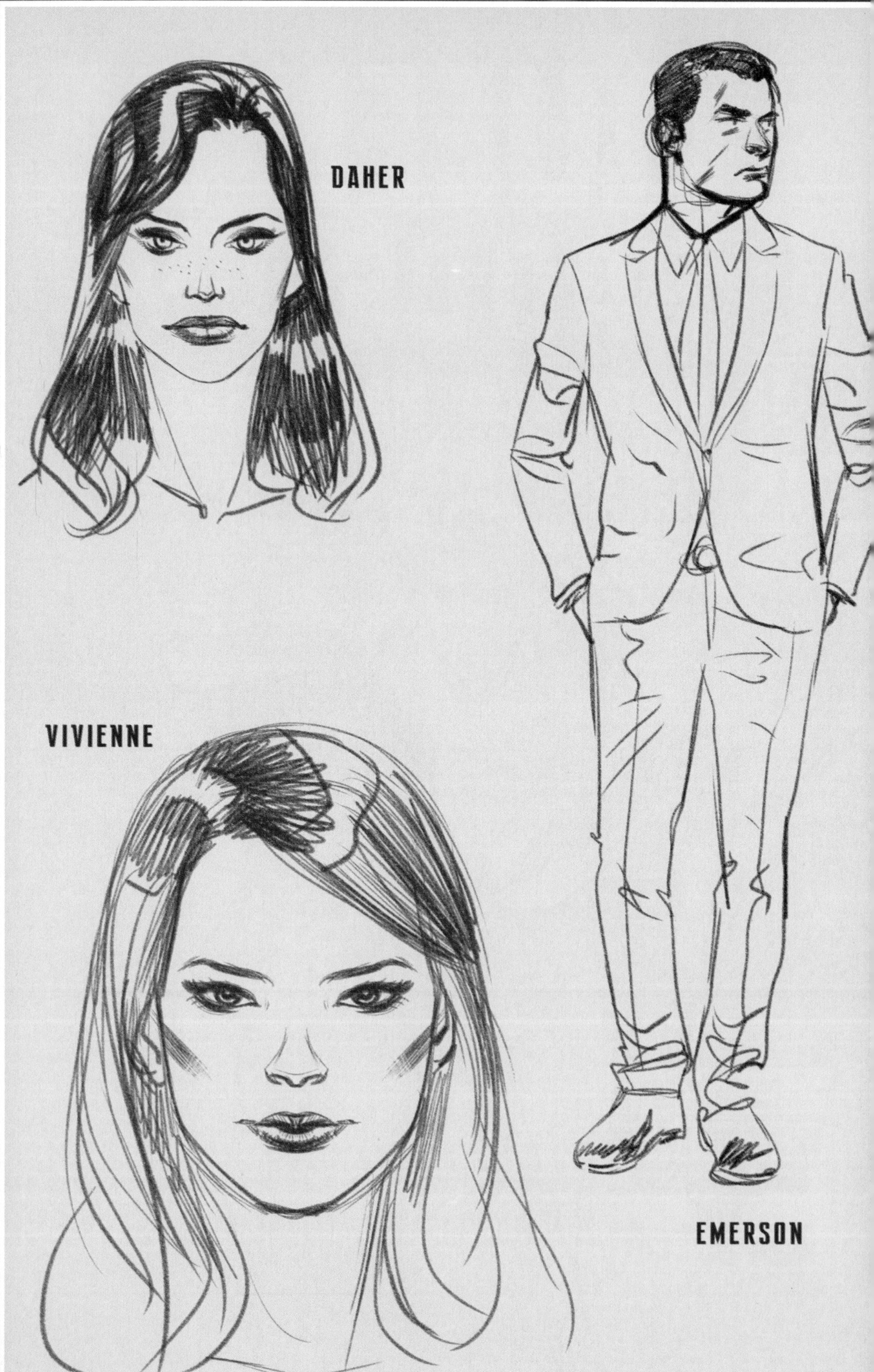
DAHER
VIVIENNE
EMERSON

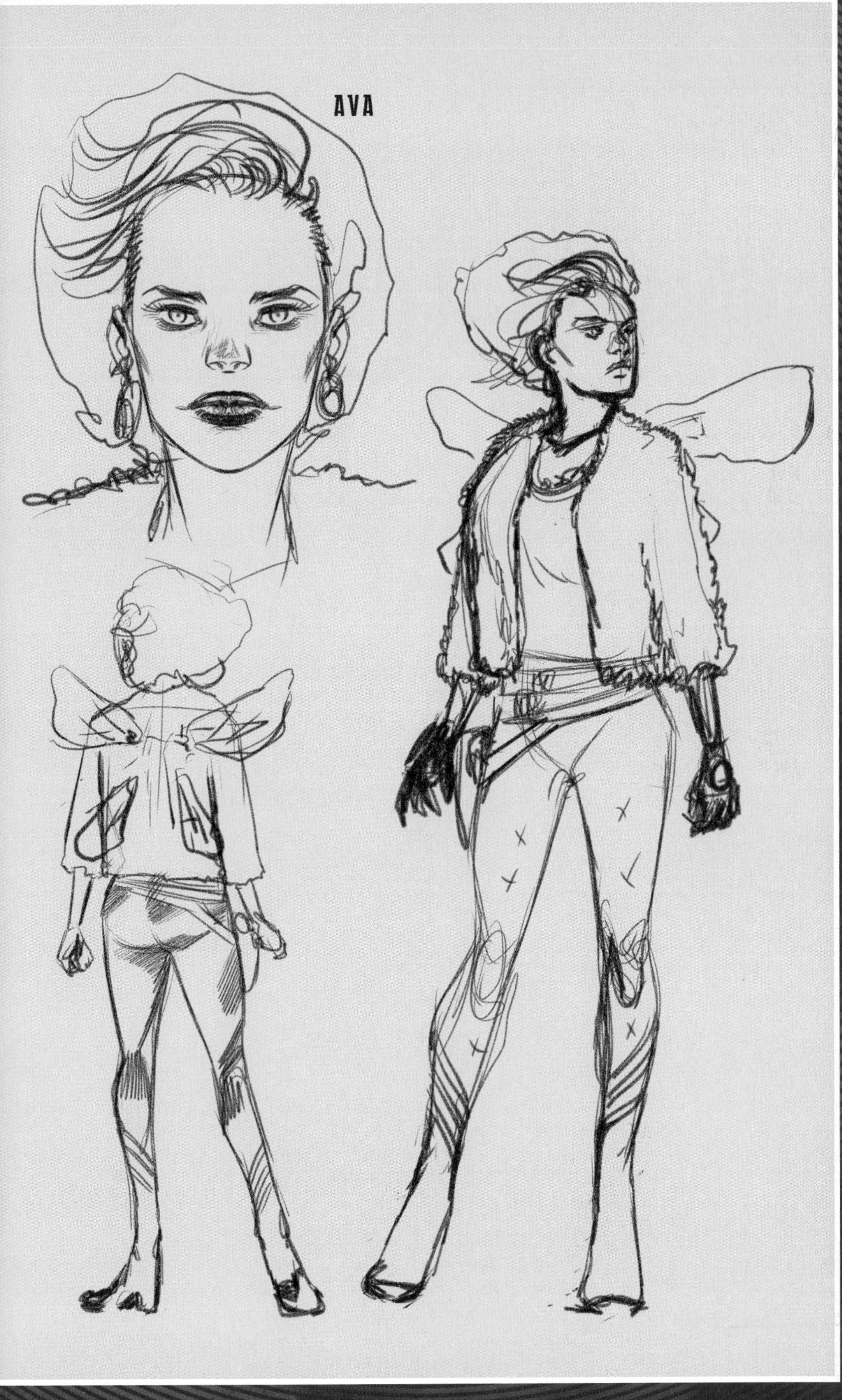
AVA

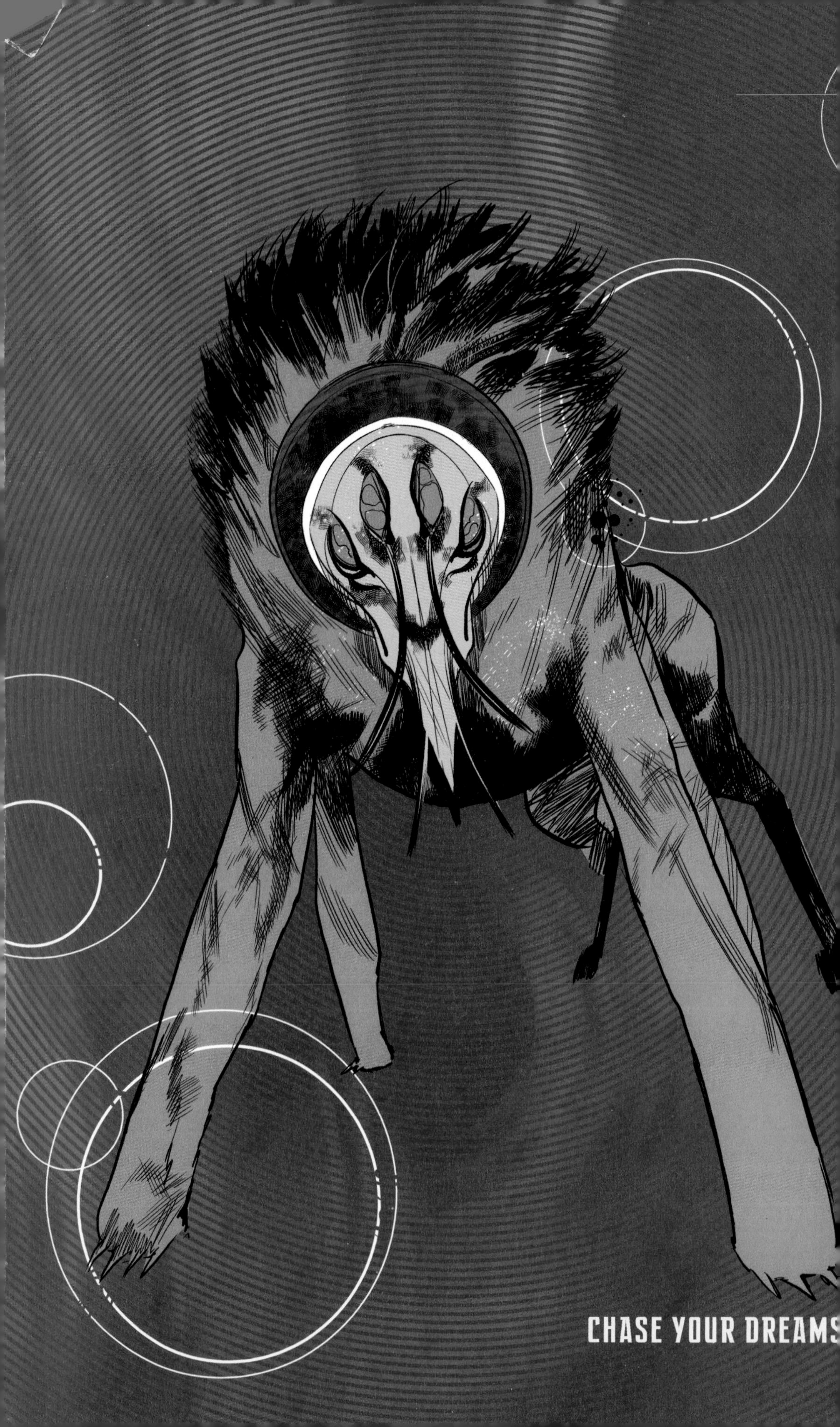
CHASE YOUR DREAMS